The FIRE That Is ETERNAL

Exploring
The

Nature of Man
And The
Reality of Hell

The Fire That Is Eternal

Exploring the Nature of Man
and the Reality of Hell
and Exposing the "Conditional" Error

By Jack W. Langford

xulon
PRESS

The Fire That Is Eternal
Exploring the Nature of Man and the Reality of Hell
and Exposing the "Conditional" Error
by Jack W. Langford

Printed in the United States of America

ISBN 9781628712216

Unless otherwise indicated, Bible quotations are taken from The NEW KING JAMES VERSION. Copyright © 1979, 1980, 1982 by Thomas Nelson, Inc.; and The NEW AMERICAN STANDARD BIBLE. Copyright © 1960, 1962, 1963, 1968, 1971, 1972, 1973, 1975, 1977 by the Lockman Foundation.

www.xulonpress.com

TRANSLATIONS USED

I n this study I have purposely quoted from several different translations. That may be frustrating to anyone who is trying to follow the references when one is accustomed to using only one translation in the study of the Scriptures. Please forgive me for this inconvenience. I normally use the New King James Version. However, in my studies I also compare with other translations and with the Greek and Hebrew Interlinears to check on the accuracy of the translation. In this case, on the subject before us, I am making an effort to be as careful as possible on critical passages and with important words. I want to make sure that we can understand with a degree of clarity, within my ability and resources, what the Hebrew and Greek texts actually say. Therefore, for accuracy's sake, I have also used some of the various interlinears which are excellent and are available to the layman. In addition, you will note that I often research further clarification from the popular Hebrew and Greek Lexical works.

Here are the translations and interlinears that I have used in this study —

The New King James Version (especially from the Greek Scriptures)
The New American Standard Bible (especially from the Hebrew Scriptures)
The Interlinear Hebrew-English Old Testament, by Kohlenberger
The Interlinear Greek-English New Testament, by Marshall (The Nestle Greek Text)
The Interlinear Greek-English New Testament, by Berry (The Textus Receptus Greek Text)

CONTENTS

❧

Author's Note xvii
Introduction xix

SECTION ONE—THE NATURE OF MAN
Spiritual Physiology

Chapter One—DEFINITIONS 27

IMMORTALITY..27
Two Aspects to IMMORTALITY 29
A Third Aspect to IMMORTALITY 31
DEATH 32
Death, A Cardinal Doctrine 34
Various Kinds of Death 35
   Six Kinds of Death for the Unregenerated Family 36
   Six Kinds of Death for the Regenerated Family 38
Conclusion about Life, Death and Immortality 41

Chapter Two—WHAT IS THE REAL NATURE
OF MAN? 44

Spiritual Physiology 44
The Body a "House" 45
The "INSIDE" and "OUTSIDE" Parts of Man 48
The "INWARD MAN" and The "OUTWARD MAN"..........49
The Total Separation of the Two 51
   1. 2 Corinthians 5:1–9 52
   2. Philippians 1:21–25 54

3. *2 Corinthians 12:2–5* 55
4. *2 Peter 1:13, 14 and 2 Timothy 4:6* 56

Chapter Three—"SOUL" and "SPIRIT" 58
The Words "SOUL" or "SPIRIT" used
of the "Inward Man" 58
The Sadducees 60
Further Scriptures—1 Corinthians 5:4, 5 61
1 Corinthians 6:19–20 and 7:34 62
2 Corinthians 7:1 and Galatians 6:18 63
Matthew 10:28 63
Revelation 6:9–11 65
Acts 2:25–27 and 31 66
Distinction Between Soul and Spirit 67

Chapter Four—FURTHER VITAL PROOFS 70
The Dual Nature of Jesus Christ 70
The Origin of Man's Spiritual Nature 73

Chapter Five—THE NATURE OF
THE NEW NATURE 79
The NATURE of the NEW CREATION in Christ 79
In Summary 89
"Living" Witnesses 89

SECTION TWO—THE BIBLICAL DOCTRINE
OF ETERNAL JUDGMENT, Hebrews 6:2

Chapter Six—INTRODUCTION 97
THERE IS A HELL! 97
THE BASIC WORDS 101
THE GOSPEL OF CHRIST 106
Why Then, Will People Today Go To Hell? 108
Some People Need Convincing! 108
"But There Has To Be A Hell!" 110

PART ONE: THE HEBREW SCRIPTURES

Chapter Seven—WELCOME TO SHEOL 115

TRANSLATIONS 115
Etymology of the word "Sheol" 118
SHEOL OF THE BOOK OF JOB 119
  1. The Setting For Job 120
  2. Job's Understanding of the Nature of Man 122
  3. Truly, God Opens the Doors on Death 124
  4. Job Foresees Ultimate Liberation 125
  5. God Alone Knows All About Sheol 126
  6. Additional Revelations in Job About Sheol 127
  7. "Sheol" and "Abaddon" 129
IN SUMMARY FROM JOB 132

Chapter Eight—SHEOL OF THE TORAH
(The Five Books of Moses) 135

GENESIS 135
  "Gathered to his people" 135
  "Sheol" 137
  "Fire" 138
LEVITICUS—The Burnt Sacrifices 139
  "Into A Land of Separation" 140
    1. Explanation 141
    2. Procedure—The Two Goats 142
    3. Procedure—The Two Lots 143
    4. Procedure—The One Sacrifice 144
    5. Procedure—The Awful Trek 145
    6. Conclusion and Revelation 147
NUMBERS and DEUTERONOMY 148

Chapter Nine—SHEOL OF THE PROPHETS 150

The "Bringing Back" of Samuel 150
King David and his son 155
The Book of ISAIAH 156
Continuing in the PROPHETS 161

Chapter Ten—SHEOL OF THE WRITINGS And OTHER DESIGNATIONS 163

The Book of PSALMS..163
The Book of PROVERBS and SONG of SOLOMON 165
Other Important Designations.....................................167
    "The PIT" and "The Lower Parts of the Earth" 169
    EZEKIEL 31 and 32, under the word "Pit"....................172
    Other Related References 175
        Daniel 7:11 175
        Daniel 12:2 176
        Isaiah 33:14..177
        Isaiah 66:24..177
    Solomon on Ultimate Judgment 178

Chapter Eleven—SUMMARY AND CONCLUSION 180

INTRODUCTION 180
SUMMARY OF FACTS ABOUT SHEOL—
Derived from The Hebrew Scriptures 182
  I   *Sheol Should Never be Confused*
        with the Grave 182
  II   *The Greek Septuagint* 183
  III   *The Location of Sheol*.....................................184
  IV   *Descriptive Terms of A Residence*.....................185
  V   *The Occupancy, All that Die—* 186
  VI   *Living People Went Down to Sheol* 189
  VII   *Classification of Souls—A. The Righteous* 189
  VIII *The Righteous Expected*
        Ultimate Deliverance.....................................190
  IX   *Classification of Souls—*
        B. The Unrighteous 190
  X   *Condition of Sheol—*Suffering for the
        Unrighteous 191
  XI   *The Occupants Stirred up and Speak*.................193
  XII   *SUMMARY DEFINITION OF SHEOL* 195

PART TWO: THE GREEK SCRIPTURES

Chapter Twelve—HADES 197

   "HADES" 197
   The "Fiery" Ministry of John the Baptist 198
   "Hades" under the Ministry of Jesus Christ 201
   The Rich Man and Lazarus 206
   Objections to this Account Answered 212
   Remaining References to Hades 217
   Other References Applicable to Hades 218
   References by the Apostle Paul to Final Punishment 220

Chapter Thirteen—GEHENNA 224

   Origin of the Word "GEHENNA" 224
   Christ Speaks of "Gehenna" 226
   Other references to the Final Judgment 230
   "TARTARUS" 234

Chapter Fourteen—The Book of REVELATION 235

   "In The Spirit On The Lord's Day" 236
   Revelation 5:13 "Under The Earth" 238
   The Souls of Those In Heaven 238
   "The Bottomless Pit" (Abyss) 241
   The Meaning of the Word "Abyss" 242
   Other Uses of Abussos 243
   The Final Use of Abussos 244
   Revelation 14:9-11 246
   "THE LAKE OF FIRE" 247
   "THE SECOND DEATH" 249

*Chapter Fifteen—SUMMARY and CONCLUDING
OBSERVATIONS* 252

   SUMMARY From The Greek Scriptures 252

   OBJECTIONS ANSWERED! 255
      "Is not God a God of love and compassion?" 255

"Does not the Bible say
'The Dead know not anything'?" 263
"Eternal punishment is not Eternal punishing!" 267
"'Eternal', 'Everlasting' and 'Forever' do not
mean 'Endless Duration'" 271
DEGREES OF PUNISHMENT IN HELL 275

SECTION THREE—THE SUFFERINGS
OF JESUS CHRIST EVEN TO THE DEPTH OF HELL

Chapter Sixteen—INTRODUCTION And PRELIMINARY
THOUGHTS ON THE CROSS WORK OF CHRIST 281

INTRODUCTION 281
The Apostles' Creed 283
A Fundamental Diversion 284
    1. The Spectacle Of The Cross 287
    2. The Irony Of The Cross 288
    3. The Confusion Of The Cross 292
    4. The Idolatry Of The Cross 295
    5. The Bronze Serpent on the Pole 298
        "Nehustan" 300

Chapter Seventeen—THE SUFFERINGS OF JESUS
CHRIST EVEN TO THE DEPTH OF HELL 301

The Sufferings of Christ Prior to the Cross 301
The Sufferings of Christ in Preparation for the Cross 303
The Real Sufferings of Christ are not Understood
by the Natural Man 304
The Sinners' Death 305
Jonah as a Type of Christ 307
The Shadow of Christ in the Psalms 312
    Psalm 69 313
    Psalm 88 314
    Psalm 18 316
Acts 2:23, 24 and Acts 17:3 317
The Baptism of Death 318
"My Father! Behold, Here is the Fire, . . ." 320

Contents

The Type of the Sacrifices 322
The Day of Atonement 325
The Type of Joseph 332
The Type of Jeremiah 334
SUMMARY — The Total Story 335

Chapter Eighteen — OBJECTIONS ANSWERED 338

IN CONCLUSION 351

AUTHOR'S NOTE

The following Bible studies contain a reservoir of information concerning the nature of man and different facets of the subject which we commonly call "Hell." In exploring the true nature of man we shall first sit at the feet of the Lord Jesus Christ. Then we will search the epistles of the apostle Paul and other New Testament writers. Finally, we will compare this with the revelation in the Hebrew Scriptures. On the subject of Hell this material is organized in such a way, from the beginning of the Hebrew Scriptures through to the end of the book of Revelation, so as to give a sequential and orderly revelation. No doubt this may be a most distasteful subject to some as it pertains to the eternal destiny of the lost and of our archenemy, Satan; nevertheless, the subject matter, contrary to the assumptions of many false teachers, is abundantly spoken on in the Scriptures. Every child of God needs to know and understand its ramifications as an important reality in the conflict between good and evil. The apostle Paul, as did the Lord Jesus Christ before him, actually includes it as a crucial point in his ministry in this age of grace—". . . in the day when God will judge the secrets of men by Jesus Christ, according to my gospel" (Rom. 2:16). In Hebrews 6:1 and 2 the "doctrine of Eternal Judgment" is listed as a "foundational" subject.

This will NOT be a study of what various theologians (whether Protestant or Catholic), philosophers, sociologists, historians, so-called "church fathers," various schools of thought, certain ancient cultures or pseudo-scriptures have said about Hell or the nature of man. If you are looking for that information, it is not here!

This is strictly a Biblical study. It concerns itself with a careful examination of the Scriptural revelations on the subjects. In other words, this study will go directly to the only source which gives us the actual, factual and original information on the issues. If you are a careful Bible student, and have a real desire for the information, you can read for yourself what God has revealed to us from His Word. I would even hope that you also come to agree with my understanding and explanation of that revelation, even though most of the Scriptures will speak for themselves. For this reason I have gathered and organized a great deal of information from the Bible on the various aspects of the subjects. This should enable anyone to make a comprehensive conclusion on the issues. I have tried to ensure the translations of the Scriptures are as accurate as possible. Of foremost importance is to observe the relationship of the gospel of Christ to the subject of Hell. In conclusion, we are encouraged to ask for God's Holy Spirit to guide our hearts in understanding that information—"Open my eyes, that I may behold wonderful things from Thy Law" (Psalm 119:18). Amazing as it may seem, the revelation is comprehensible because God has promised to help us make such a discernment—"There is a spirit in man, and the inspiration of the Almighty gives them under-standing" (Job 32:8).

This is my prayer and purpose.
Jack W. Langford, September, 2013

INTRODUCTION

T he most subtle and dangerous thoughts to be entertained in
human consciousness about life's most important issues come
in the form of doubt or disbelief in what God has clearly revealed.
Such doubt or disbelief causes one to turn and be guided by his own
self-induced emotional impulses rather than having explicit faith in
God's Word.

This was exactly the path followed at the very beginning of
the human family tree. Eve focused her attention upon the striking
beauty, nourishment and desirable wisdom to be attained by eating
of "the tree of the knowledge of good and evil" instead of soberly
considering God's command (Gen. 3:1–7). In musing upon the tree's
appealing attributes of beauty, health and—above all—wisdom, the
idea of "death" seemed totally remote and out of balance. In fact,
the tempter's words, "*You will not surely die*," sounded rational to
her emotions. "After all," she might have thought, "how can 'death'
come as a reprisal for attaining such desirable qualities as beauty,
health and wisdom?" And as an extra sales pitch the tempter had
added that this "wisdom" would make her "*like God*, to know
good and evil." With this prospect she, no doubt, concluded in her
thinking, "Surely one would not be rewarded with 'death' simply for
having such splendid fruit."

Had Eve given the subject of disobedience to God and of consequent "*death*" more serious consideration, she may have postponed
or put off entirely the tragedy which followed. Having cast doubt in
Eve's mind about the consequence of disobedience—"death"—the
subtle tempter had diverted her attention and her emotions to the

qualities of the tree with its beauty, health and wisdom. Any reminder of the fact of "death" was met by the words "You will not surely die." In a sense this became Satan's "gospel" which moved Eve to rely upon her emotions rather than God's explicit instructions. Having removed "*death*" from the dread and fear in Eve's heart meant she would be free to partake of the tree. Of course, we all know the end of the story. What Eve thought was "good news" was actually "*not good news*" at all (Gal. 1:6–7). Whatever "death" meant in Adam and Eve's understanding, it seemed to be unrealistic as a harsh measure to come in response to merely eating of the forbidden fruit. Adam and Eve trusted in a false message which denied the fear of "death," and as a result the awful reality of "death" entered into the human family.

Throughout the ages of human history—like some visionary dream—this shadowy messenger, the fact and reality of "death," has repeatedly stalked the conscious mind, bringing thoughts of fear, doubt and even in some cases out and out distrust in God's revelation. Many seem to reject any evidence of the existence of consciousness after physical death. As a consequence, men have been left to their own speculations about the reality and definition of the human soul. And most of all, certain ones even mock the very idea of whether or not there is conscious punishment after death.

To be sure, in the original Biblical account, Adam and Eve immediately experienced death. God's word literally translated was "dying, you shall die" (Gen. 2:17). Death was not some far off experience; Adam and Eve immediately realized the separation and loss of fellowship with God. That meant they became spiritually dead to God. It also meant that within their marvelous bodies the "death process" had already begun. Many years later the dying process, as to their physical bodies, would be accentuated by the departure of their souls from their bodies. No matter what religious philosophers would speculate about death, to Adam and Eve it never meant the "termination of their existence," but rather, "a very unpleasant condition of existence."

On this end of human history we find arising an ultimate effort to answer life's questions by removing God from the equation. When the Theory of Evolution was masterfully proposed by Charles

Darwin, the historians were actually surprised at how fast and firmly this doctrine gained credence and acceptance in all levels of society—even by many notable religious leaders. Darwin's doctrine ultimately spelled the "death" of God as the creator and director of all things. It naturally followed that any moral accountability was trampled underfoot as a discarded relic of past superstition. Indeed, the modern theology that there is no conscious torment for the lost and unrepentant at death is the "gospel" for the Christ rejecter. This is the "good news" which excites hardened unbelievers the most, because it calms their fears and chases away doubts about Divine retribution. It is to be expected that some of the cults and liberals in Christendom would reject the doctrine of eternal punishment. However, it is a greater shame that even certain conservative Christians, motivated by their emotions, fall into the trap of propagating this lie as well.

Interestingly enough, when Darwin, himself, was visited by that sober reality of "death," he found it very disturbing. Perhaps the most sober and difficult experience in his life was the death of his very beloved daughter, Annie, whose death deeply moved him. In fact, he found it very hard to cope with the "death" of this child. On the one hand, his own doctrine taught that death was nothing but the natural cleansing process in order for the "survival of the fittest." Therefore, why should there be remorse? Yet on the other hand, that mysterious bond of love had created an inexplicable affection, the breaking of which seemed an unusually cruel misfortune. This would be counter evidence to the moral vacancy which existed in the theory of evolution. Indeed, instead of recognizing the contradiction this reality brought with his theory, in his frustration he became only antagonistic towards the idea of a good and gracious God.

In the superbly written book, *Annie's Box*, by Charles Darwin's great, great grandson, Randal Keynes, he states on page 188—

By contrast with all Christians, some freethinkers among Darwin's friends welcomed the idea that death was the end. Harriet Martineau wrote in *Letters on the Laws of Man's Nature and Development* that she agreed with Mr. Atkinson on '*the fallacy of all arguments for a conscious existence after death'*. People took their wish for a life after death as evidence for it; 'the desire itself is a factitious thing', and '*many* (and this I know) *do not desire it at all'* (emphasis mine, J.L.).

Along with certain clergy who teach disparaging things against the doctrine of conscious existence after death there are also those who commit their doubts to poetry. As if writing to Darwin's daughter, Ann and Jane Taylor gave in *Hymns for Infant Minds*—

> . . . where my living soul would go
> I do not and I cannot know:
> For none was e'er sent back to tell
> The joys of heaven, or pains of hell.

This book you are now reading has been written to collect together the Biblical truths which tell us that there is such a man— Jesus Christ the Lord. Allow me to introduce you to the One, Who "by the grace of God tasted *death* for every man" (Hebrews 2:9). Not only did He explain and distinguish in fine detail the spiritual nature of man apart from his "house of clay," but He also repeated for all a conversation which took place in Hades. Finally He also, Himself, entered through the gates of death, descended into the lowest Hell, opened wide its mysteries for our comprehension, and gloriously arose from the pit of death with the very keys of death and Hell, and ascended into heaven itself, all on our behalf. When Christ died, the Divine Son of God very obviously did not cease to exist! When three days and three nights had transpired He gathered the spirits of the saints in Sheol and ascended before them out of the depths of Hell and into Heaven itself. There He sits in royalty at the right hand of the Father, as the conqueror of *death*!

Therefore this material is designed to make available a vast collection of Biblical data on this subject of which God wishes us to have a clear understanding. We will even hear the voices and messages of the dead, both the righteous and the unrighteous. We will also get a vision of the final climax—when God wraps up His full redemption plan—as if it has already happened. Certainly, for the sake of my own children and grandchildren I intend this legacy of truth about the hereafter, from the pages of God's Holy Word, to be available for their persuasion in these days of withering unbelief.

Throughout this manuscript I have chosen to emphasize primary words descriptive of Hell and of the final Judgment by capitalizing them.

Jack W. Langford, a servant of Christ

SECTION ONE

THE NATURE OF MAN
Spiritual Physiology

"Thus says the LORD [Yahweh],
Who stretches out the heavens,
lays the foundation of the earth, and
forms the spirit of man within him."
Zechariah 12:1

"Foolish ones!
Did not He Who made the outside [of man]
make the inside also?"
Luke 11:40

"Behold, You desire truth in the inward parts,
and in the hidden part
You will make me to know wisdom."
Psalm 51:6

"Therefore we do not lose heart.
Even though our outward man is perishing,
yet the inward man is being renewed day by day."
2 Corinthians 4:16

Translations in this Section
are from the New King James Version
unless otherwise stated.

Many of the references have been
crosschecked with an Interlinear
and/or compared with other translations
to ensure accuracy.

CHAPTER ONE

DEFINITIONS

S ome four hundred years after the last inspired prophet of the
Hebrew Scriptures had spoken, the voice of the Lord Jesus
Christ was heard ministering in the coast lands of Israel. One can
rest assured, He will tell us more about the nature of man and man's
eternal state than anyone else in the Scriptures.

It is important in beginning our exploration of these topics that
we get a clear Scriptural definition of certain words used. Jesus
Christ, Himself, will essentially do this for us.

IMMORTALITY

When Jesus Christ stepped upon earth's scene, He "brought
light and *immortality* to light through the *gospel*" (2 Timothy 1:10).
In fact, it is stated of Christ that He is that ". . .blessed and only
Potentate, the King of kings and Lord of lords, the only One possessing *immortality,* . . ." (1 Timothy 6:15, 16). Thankfully, He is
sharing that immortality with all who place their faith in Him.

Our English word "immortality" is taken from the Greek word
athanasia. The *a* is a negative meaning "no." *Thanasia* means
death. *A-thanasia,* simply means "no death" or "deathlessness." To
not be subject to death means one possesses "*eternal* or *everlasting
life*"—he "*shall never die.*"

Not only does Christ possess *immortality* (1 Tim. 6:16), but during His earthly sojourn He often proclaimed the availability of that *"deathlessness," "eternal"* or *"everlasting life"* to all mankind by means of believing "the gospel" (2 Tim. 1:10). Therefore we must hear that gospel and we shall see the consequent promises of "eternal life," "everlasting life," "shall never perish," "shall never die!"—i.e., have "immortality." Here are a few examples—

"In the beginning was the Word. . . .
In Him was LIFE, and the LIFE was the light of men."
John 1:1 and 4

John 3:16   "For God so loved the world that He gave His only begotten Son, that whoever believes in Him should not perish *but have everlasting life."*

John 3:36   "He who believes in the Son *has eternal life*; but he who does not obey the Son will not see *life*, but the wrath of God *abides* on him" (NASB).

John 4:14   "But whoever drinks of the water that I shall give him will never thirst. But the water that I shall give him will become in him a fountain of water *springing up into eternal life."*

John 5:24   "Most assuredly, I say to you, he who hears My word, and believes Him Who sent Me *has* [present tense] *everlasting life*, and shall not come into judgment, but *has passed* [past tense] *from death into life."*

John 6:47   "Most assuredly, I say to you, he who believes in Me *has* [right now] *everlasting life."* In addition Christ had stated earlier—
". . . but [I] *should* [future] *raise him up* at the last day" (v. 39).
". . . and *I will* [future] *raise him up* at the last day" (v. 40).

". . . and *I will* [future] *raise him up* at the last day" (v. 44).

". . . and *I will* [future] *raise him up* at the last day" (v. 54).

John 10:27, 28 "My sheep hear My voice, and I know them, and they follow Me. And I give them *eternal life*, and *they shall never perish*; neither shall anyone snatch them out of My hand."

John 11:25, 26 "I am the *resurrection* and *the life*. He who believes in Me, though he may die, *he shall live*. And whoever lives and believes in Me *shall never die*. Do you believe this?"

1 John 3:14 "We know that we *have passed out of death into life*, because we love the brethren" (NASB).

1 John 5:11–13 "And this is the testimony: that God has given us *eternal life*, and this *life is in His Son*. He who *has the Son has life*; he who does not have the Son of God does not have life. These things I have written to you who believe in the name of the Son of God, that you may know that *you have eternal life*."

There are many other references, but I will allow these ten to stand as a clear testimony that Christ brought "*immortality to light through the gospel*." Each of these words which I have emphasized demonstrates that this "deathlessness" or "immortality" is *eternal* and is a *present possession* with the *future promise* of a resurrection of the body as well. Consequently there are—

Two Aspects to IMMORTALITY

It is therefore clear that there are TWO ASPECTS TO IMMORTALITY. First of all, Christ gave "*eternal life*" or "*everlasting life*" to believers immediately, right then and there, at the time they believed the gospel which was ministered to them. As stated, it is clearly a present possession. "They *have passed* from death *unto life*" (John 5:24). Furthermore, as to this new life, "*they shall never perish.*" Christ indicated that they "*had passed out of death into life.*" Christ again stated, "*They shall never die!*" This means that though the person dies physically, yet he will go on living. And so Christ stated—"*Though he dies, yet shall he live.*"

Now as stated earlier, to "*never die,*" or to "*never perish,*" or to be "*passed out of death unto life*" or to be "*passed from death unto life*" is the very definition of immortality—*no death,* or *deathlessness.* Consequently this first aspect of "immortality" has to do with man's PRESENT *spiritual condition* or *life* as a result of hearing and believing on Christ, i.e., believing the gospel.

In addition, Christ promised a second aspect to "immortality." Those who believe in Him "*He would raise them up in the last day.*" This is the second aspect of immortality and has reference to man's FUTURE resurrection of his body.

I can say conclusively that if a person does not have the PRESENT immortality of his soul, he is not a true believer (no matter how religious he may be). In addition, he will never have the FUTURE immortality of his body—unless in the future time of this life he truly repents and accepts the finished work of Christ on his behalf.

I will show you in a later chapter where those who believe in Christ "PUT ON THE NEW MAN—the NEW CREATION" right *now* at the very moment they exercise true heart faith in Jesus Christ. This is speaking of our new spiritual person. On the other hand, 1 Corinthians 15 tells us that at the future resurrection of the body the believer will "PUT ON the imperishable body" or "incorruption [i.e., immortality of the body]" (1 Cor. 15:50–54). This is what many false teachers think is the sole event of *immortality.* They totally overlook the present spiritual *immortality* of the new life in Christ.

So there are two aspects to the believer's immortality. The first has to do with his new *spiritual life* in Christ as a present possession and the second has to do with the promise of the future *physical* resurrection of his body.

A Third Aspect To IMMORTALITY

There is a third aspect to this subject of "immortality." Actually, it concerns itself purely with a matter of *terminology*. From the very early centuries of Christianity, theologians saw and believed that the natural, unregenerate person had, from the point of his beginning, *everlasting conscious existence* in a state of "death" by sin or separation from God. They understood this existence as being true both before physical death and after the fact of physical death. They understood that after physical death this existence continued in the residence of Hell until the Judgment. They came to call this fact of *conscious existence* the doctrine of *"the Immortality of the Soul."* The Jewish people of the first century believed this doctrine. It is well-known to have been expressed by the Jewish Historian, Josephus (*Antiquities of the Jews,* Book XVIII, Chap. I, 3), that immortality of the soul was a popular belief of the Pharisees.

As we shall see, they were absolutely right about the fact of the continuous conscious existence of the soul after death in Hell, but the terminology must of necessity be *qualified*. The everlasting existence of the soul after the death of the body is taught in Scriptures, but it is not called "immortality." Unfortunately, many have taken advantage of the terminology used to try and discredit the doctrine. These have eagerly pointed to the Scripture which says Christ alone has "immortality" (1 Tim. 6:16). They further argue that the believer will not share in that immortality until his physical resurrection as promised in 1 Corinthians 15:54. Therefore, these argue, no one could continue to exist in Hell after physical death. Consequently, they call the teaching of "the Immortality of the Soul" a false doctrine.

First of all, these people forget all about the fact that Christ's basic promise in the gospel is "everlasting life," "shall never perish," "have passed from death unto life," and "shall never die," as a PRESENT POSSESSION right now. This means that believers in the gospel of Christ do indeed possess the *"Immortality of the Soul"* both in their lifetime and forever. So then, *"the Immortality of the Soul"*—as far as believers are concerned—is a positive, well-established fact. Indeed, it can be said if you don't have that *immortality* of the soul—you are not a Christian!

Secondly, this subject has been debated for centuries and all know quite well that those who use the expression *"the immortality of the soul"* in a general sense, do so with a careful qualification of the meaning about "immortality" as it applies to the natural man. They have long explained they do not mean "immortality" in the sense of the perfection of life in Christ, but as mere *"continuous conscious existence."* As we shall see, this "conscious existence" is in a state of "death."

So the third aspect to immortality which applies to the whole human family, we should qualify as simply meaning—*the continuous conscious existence of the soul.*

DEATH

Jesus Christ not only brought *"immortality to light through the gospel,"* but He also brought to light a definition of *"Death"* which many people not only do not like, but are horrified at its concept. Those who rebel against a conscious suffering in Hell after death like to define "death" as *"the absence of life,"* meaning—*"the opposite of existence," "cessation of being"* or *"nonexistence."* Therefore they conclude that there could never be a place of conscious existence of the soul after death.

Of course, the Lord Jesus Christ totally ignored this superficial, materialistic definition of death and gave His own. Christ said, as we saw above, "Truly, truly, I say unto you, he who hears My word, and believes Him Who sent Me, has *eternal life*, and does not come into judgment, BUT *HAS PASSED* OUT OF DEATH *INTO LIFE*" (John 5:24, NASB).

Now if "nonexistence" is the proper definition of death, then Christ's words above are absolutely nonsense. How could someone pass into the condition of "LIFE" with God who does not even exist? Even those whom Christ raised from the dead physically— EXISTED. The facts are, in giving these words, Christ is plainly talking to people who are IN EXISTENCE both *physically* and *spiritually*! How then can Christ refer to them as being in a state of "Death"? Here is the answer—we are now to understand that these people who are *physically* alive are considered by Christ to be *spiritually DEAD* to God. Christ is describing their spiritual EXISTENCE as actually being in a *state of DEATH*. He certainly did not mean they were all *physically dead*, because they were standing there listening to Him talk. Christ is offering *spiritual LIFE* to *spiritually DEAD* people. By Christ's words we can understand that in the world today there are millions of "**dead**" people, who are very much *alive* and *conscious* in the flesh. To express it again another way, there are millions of "**living**" *dead people*! In fact, the apostle Paul said, "But she who *lives* in [carnal/physical] pleasure is DEAD *while* she LIVES" (1 Tim. 5:6).

Therefore, we are to now understand that mankind can EXIST in a state of spiritual DEATH. Death is not "cessation of being" or "annihilation." Rather, it is the spiritual separation from the life and fellowship of God. Furthermore, we can conclude that when a man dies physically, that does NOT mean that he ceases to exist spiritually any more than it meant he did not exist spiritually before he died physically. Physical death or physical life has nothing whatsoever to do with any man's spiritual EXISTENCE. That existence is independent of the body's existence. Actually, when you think about it, a physical body does not cease to exist at death, either. The physical body simply eventually changes form (sometimes it takes millenniums). Normally it simply goes back to the dust of which it is composed.

Furthermore, by no stretch of the imagination does "death" mean "*cessation of being*," but rather *death* describes "*the Quality of Being*." Christ said again, "He who believes in Me though he may DIE, he shall LIVE" (John 11:25). Here we have the continuing existence of his new LIFE before and after the occurrence of physical death. In fact, the quality of life is further described by Christ as "Whoever *LIVES* and believes in Me shall never *DIE*" (John 11:26). In other words, the quality of this LIFE is that it is not subject to death; it is everlasting or eternal.

We learn from passages like this that everyone who is confronted with the reality of Jesus Christ and chooses **not** to believe in Him is *EXISTING* in a state of *DEATH*. As another has said, "**Christ's definitions of *death* are as surely Divine revelation as are His**

definitions of *life*" (Maurice M. Johnson, *Eight Kinds of Death*). It becomes obvious that Christ's definition of death is that it is the *absence of HIS LIFE*. "*He who has the Son has LIFE; he who does not have the Son of God DOES NOT HAVE LIFE*" (1 John 5:12). Any person who does not have this "Life" is *existing in a state of "DEATH."*

A better definition of *death*, therefore, would be "*Separation*." As to physical death, it is *separation* of the spirit from the body—James said "the body without the spirit is dead" (James 2:26). Likewise, *spiritual death* is separation from the "Life" in Christ. In the account that Christ gave of the prodigal son, the father stated "My son was DEAD and is ALIVE again" (Luke 15:24 and 32). Obviously, his son was dead in the sense of carnal *separation* from the father. The same is illustrated again by one who came to Christ and said he wanted to first bury his father before he came and followed Christ. To such a one Christ said, "*Let the DEAD bury their own DEAD*" (Luke 9:60). Try and put the definition of "nonexistence" upon this verse—"Let the nonexistent bury the nonexistent." It becomes utter foolishness, does it not?

Christ's definition of Death becomes A Cardinal Doctrine of the Christian Faith

"Death" came upon the whole human race by means of the "Federal Headship" of Adam. Death came in two forms. First, at the moment Adam and Eve sinned against God, they died to God. God had said "In the *DAY* you eat of it you shall surely die" (Genesis 2:17 and 3:3). Therefore we understand they died spiritually that very "day." The fellowship between God and man was instantly broken. Having sinned, they became spiritually "dead" to God. Secondly, the death process began physically and continued until they were both terminated in life as to their physical bodies. This happened, in Adam's case, 930 years later. To emphasize the difference between these two aspects of death, this means Adam actually did not die physically until three hundred thirty nine thousand, four hundred and fifty "days" had passed. That is a long time after "*in the DAY you eat thereof.*"

Through the Pauline Epistles, Christ revealed that this total death passed upon the whole human race—"Therefore, just as through one man sin entered into the world, and *death* through sin, and thus, *death* spread to all men, because all sinned" (Rom. 5:12). And continuing in Romans Paul said—". . . by the one man's offence many *died*, . . ." (v.15), and "For if by one man's offence, *death reigned* through the one, . . ." (v.17), and "so that as sin reigned in *death*, . . ." (v. 21).

More specifically, the apostle Paul was directed to emphasize the spiritual aspect of this death. Ephesians 2:1 and 5 says, "And you [Gentiles] who were *dead* in your trespasses and sins . . . even when we were *dead* in our trespasses, [God] made us alive together with Christ." And once again, Colossians 2:13 reads, "And you, being *dead* in your trespasses, . . ." In 2 Corinthians 5:14 the fundamental principle is again stated with clarity, "If One [Christ] died for all [mankind], then all *died*."

In the book of Jude, the half-brother of our Lord emphasized that those who are guilty of hardening their hearts against acceptance of Jesus Christ as their Savior are "TWICE DEAD" (Jude 12). Here Jude is talking about a further stage in spiritual death. Not only is this person "dead" like "*an autumn tree with no fruit*," but he is now such a tree—"*plucked up by the roots.*" This apparently means he is beyond help. Determining his course, this person has resisted all efforts to help him.

Various "Kinds of Death" Revealed in the Greek Scriptures

Did you notice that I said "*Revealed in the Greek Scriptures*"? There are those false teachers on this subject who claim that the doctrines of the "immortality of the soul," "conscious existence after death," and the nature of "death being separation" are actually derived from Greek mythology and philosophy. Those who make this charge are, in reality, actually blaspheming the truth in the Word of God. All that is being given in the first part of this Bible study on immortality and the nature of man is from the Greek Scriptures—NOT Greek mythology.

Now, I want to bring to your attention at least twelve different kinds or categories of death revealed in the Greek Scriptures. We will see that there are many different aspects to this subject of death as revealed in the Scriptures. These will be divided into two different sections. One section will consist of "Six Kinds of Death" for all mankind who are merely and only members of the "first man's [Adam's]" physical, natural, unregenerate descendants. The second section will consist of "Six Kinds of Death" for those who are vital members of "the last Adam . . . the second Man, the Lord from heaven" and are His spiritual, supernaturally regenerated descendents (see 1 Cor. 15:45–47). This is actually an enlargement of the initial Biblical study done by Maurice M. Johnson entitled *Eight Kinds of Death* which I mentioned earlier.

Six Kinds of Death for the Unregenerated Family

1.   Death "INHERITED" by the whole human family because of Adam's disobedience. This meant total death, both physically and spiritually, which was passed down to all Adam's posterity. All Adam's race are "born in sin" (John 9:34). Thus it is "In Adam all *die*"—1 Cor. 15: 22. All Adam's race receive "sin-natures" because of the original rebellion. Because of these sin-natures, "*death* spread to all men"—Rom. 5:12 and 5:15. "By one man's disobedience many were made sinners"—see also Romans 5:17–19 and 2 Cor. 5:14, etc.

2.   Death "MERITED" by the whole human family because of their own personal sins and disobedience. This compounds the fact of inherited death (number 1. above). "For all have sinned" and "The wages of sin is death"—Rom. 3:23 and 6:23. ". . . every mouth may be stopped, and all the world may become guilty before God"—Rom. 3:19. See also Romans 6:16, 21; 7:5 and 9–13, etc. Thus it is as stated in the prophets—". . . The soul who sins shall *die*"—Ezek. 18:4.

36

3. The UNIQUE DEATH of Jesus Christ the Lord by His voluntary "obedience unto death" — Philippians 2:8. This is the amazing and gracious substitutionary death of Jesus Christ on the behalf of all mankind. Herein Christ died the sinners' death. Christ had no sins of His own, but was "made . . . to be sin for us" (2 Cor. 5:21). Christ voluntarily was "God forsaken" and "con-damned" in our place. Since "the wages of sin is death," Christ paid all the "wages" for all mankind collectively. This was His total separation from God. See 2 Cor. 5:15; 1 Tim. 2:4–6; Heb. 2:9, 14; 1 John 2:2, etc.

4. Those "TWICE DEAD" who, because of "seared consciences," steadfastly refuse the "grace" which was manifested in death number 3. This is a graduation in degree from death number 2. These people are "seared as with a hot iron," "past feeling," "approve [lit., applaud]" ungodliness and of whom it is "impossible" to be "renewed to repentance." See such passages as Jude 12; 1 Tim. 4:2; Eph. 4:19; Rom. 1:32; Heb. 6:4, etc.

5. The actual PHYSICAL DEATH of the lost "*IN THEIR SINS.*" As stated by Jesus Christ, "Therefore I said to you that you will *die in your sins*; for if you do not believe that I AM *HE*, you shall die *in your sins*" (John 8:24). This death marks the end of man's probation on earth. We shall prove later in this study that those who die in this condition are immediately consigned to Sheol/Hades, the temporary "prison house" of the souls of the lost. There in Hell, they await their final Judgment. See such passages as John 8:24; 3:36; Heb. 10:26–31, etc.

6. The "SECOND DEATH." Those who previously "died in their sins" are remaining in the prison house of Hades to be resurrected from the dead at a future time. After the millennial reign of Christ, these dead are said to "LIVE AGAIN" (Rev. 20:5). The inspired text says that both "*Death*" (as to the physical body) and "*Hades*" (as to the souls of the dead) deliver up the dead to stand before God (Rev. 20:13). After the resurrection of the lost to stand before the Great White Throne Judgment of God, the "second death" takes place — Rev. 20:11. Herein the final disposition of the lost is decreed.

Their Judgment and final condemnation is thus called "*the second death*." This death is the permanent separation of the lost (body and soul—Matt. 10:28) from the presence of God. They are sent away to the "Lake of Fire which burns forever." See Revelation 20:6, 10, 11–15 and 21:8.

Six Kinds of Death for the Regenerated Family

Though repentant believers in Jesus Christ are "born again" by the Spirit of God, possess "eternal life" and "shall never perish," nevertheless they still live in their mortal bodies and they still possess their sinful Adamic natures. Consequently there are still different deaths for the believer as well as for the unbeliever. Interestingly enough, when a person believes from the heart the gospel of salvation in Christ, there is not only a new birth, but at the very same moment there is also a *death* which takes place—

1. DEATH in Christ upon believing the gospel. In a person's unsaved life, he is said to be "*alive*" to his Adamic sin-nature and "*dead*" towards God (Rom. 7:9). However, upon believing the gospel, the reverse takes place. He is said to become "*dead*" towards his sin-nature and "*alive*" towards God—Rom. 6:11. This "death" is specifically said to be our identification with Christ in His supernatural "death." Christ's "death" for our sins becomes our "death." And not only that, thankfully, but His "Life" becomes our "life." See Romans 6:3–8; Gal. 2:19 and 20; Col. 3:1–11; John 5:24; 1 John 3:14, etc.

2. DEATH to the appetites of our fallen sin-nature. Not only is the believer said to be "crucified with Christ," but he is also encouraged to "crucify self" and to continue to "put to death" the sinful desires that may still haunt him. This is a daily practice of self-denial through the energy and strength of the Holy Spirit of Christ in our new natures. See such passages as Gal. 5:24; Col. 3:5; Rom. 6:11–12 and 8:13, etc.

3. <u>DEATH by PERSECUTION</u> in our witness for Christ. This type of death is a privilege for God's people and consequently has distinct characteristics in the revelation of God's Word. (A) This is called "The fellowship of His suffering"—see Philip. 3:10, 11; 2 Cor. 1:5; Gal. 6:17; Luke 9:23, 24, etc. (B) There is also an aspect of this "suffering" which constitutes "the sufferings of Christ in us for the church," or on behalf of others—see Col. 1:24 and Philip. 2:17. (C) There is also the Christian's veritable designation, or "baptism" (immersion) into a living death of trials and afflictions which come upon us from the ungodly world—see 1 Cor. 4:9; 15:29–31; 2 Cor. 4:8–12, etc. This kind of death also has a cleansing effect in the believer's life—"He that has suffered in the flesh has ceased from sin"—1 Pet. 4:1.

4. <u>DEATH or separation by broken FELLOWSHIP</u>. This "death" is primarily a figure of speech. It comes between members of the Christian family because of a believer's carnal and ungodly walk which is not repented. This is a disciplinary action that a congregation or individuals must take toward an unruly member of a congregation or family who persists in "disorderly" conduct. Luke 15:20; Eph. 5:8–14; Rom. 6:16; 8:6; 2 Thess. 3:6; 1 Cor. 5:9–13, etc.

5. Physical <u>DISCIPLINARY DEATH</u> sometimes comes in case of the believer's extreme unrepentant sinfulness. This is obviously a step beyond death number 4. This is the actual premature physical disciplinary death of a Christian under the direct chastening hand of God. Such death was sometimes mandated as discipline in certain crucial times—see Acts 5:1–11 and 1 Cor. 11:30–32. See also such passages as 1 Cor. 5:5; 1 John 5:16, 17; James 5:20, etc.

6. "<u>SLEEP IN THE LORD</u>." This is the physical death of a saint, especially those who are walking in fellowship with the Lord. It is called a "sleep" because of the promise of an "awakening" which pertains to the resurrection of the body (Daniel 12:2). The Lord used this expression several times in the Gospel accounts, but it is now used in particular of the saints. See 1 Thess. 4:14; 1 Cor. 15: 6, 18; 2 Cor. 5:1–8; 2 Pet. 1:14, etc.

Thus we have covered at least 12 different kinds or aspects of death. The number 6 is generally recognized as representing the "number of Man" who was created on the "6th day." We saw six aspects of death for the unregenerated person and six aspects of death for the regenerated person. One important obvious fact is that all these deaths demonstrate very clearly a CONDITION of existence and not a termination of existence. Thankfully, the death of a believer, though the outward appearances of its physical aspects seem to be the same as that for the unbeliever, in Scriptural reality involves many quite different aspects from the death of a nonbeliever.

To conclude this section on the various kinds of death, I want to draw your attention to a particular statement by the apostle Paul. Paul was inspired to tell us a very interesting truth which comes about as a result of the Christian's interrelationship with the world. The Christian in his living testimony and demonstration of repentance and faith in Christ often becomes "the aroma of *death* leading to *death*" to the unsaved—2 Cor. 2:16. Now this is an amazing statement and it serves us well to pause and examine it. No one likes the "odor of death." There is nothing as unpleasant as this. How and why should the Christian, who is privileged to bear the message of "good news," also bear this repulsive "odor" of death?

The context of the passage actually says two different things. First it says "For we are to God the fragrance of Christ among those who are being saved *and* among those who are perishing" (verse 15). That means there are two different peoples effected by the fragrance of Christ: i.e., the "saved" and "those perishing." Then in the next verse Paul says "To the one [those perishing] we are the aroma of *death* leading to *death*, and to the other [the saved] the aroma of *life* leading to *life*." The believer's acceptance of the gospel, as demonstrated by his new life, means "life" both **now** and in the **hereafter**. On the other hand, to the rejecter of the gospel, that very message as manifested in the life of the believer becomes the basis of the unbeliever's condemnation both **now** and in **eternity**. By not having what the believer has, the unbeliever is obviously condemned. It has been said by way of illustration, "The bee brings honey to the owner, but stings others." So it is that the Christian's testimony is virtually a reminder to the lost "that it is appointed unto men once to die, but after this the Judgment" (Heb. 9:27). Of course, "the Judgment" herein means "the second death."

What is our Conclusion about Life, Death And Immortality, so far?

We will learn from the Hebrew Scriptures that when persons die, their "spirits" go into the deep "chambers of death." There they consciously exist in "Sheol." It is understood in the Hebrew Scriptures that there is a distinction between man's physical body and his spirit person.

When Christ came into the world, He revealed much more about the spiritual nature of man, about what death actually is and about the reality of "not dying," or this thing we call "immortality."

While Christ walked the dusty trails of Israel, He offered "eternal life" to those who would trust in Him. This is stated many times and in different ways. This life was not something they had to wait for, nor was it something they could only receive at their resurrection from the dead in that final day. On the contrary, it was to be realized immediately right then and there. This clearly meant that the "life" He was speaking about concerned itself with man's inner spiritual nature. In Christ's view this was by far the most important aspect of man's being. To get the soul or spirit in a right relationship with God would guarantee the eventual resurrection of the body.

For the believer, to "have everlasting life" NOW, and to understand it to mean he had passed from "death to life" and that he would consequently "never die," meant the "immortality of the soul." In fact, if a person who professed to be a follower of Christ did not have immortality of the soul, he was actually not a true believer. If he possessed the immortality of the soul, he knew he would eventually get the immortality of his body.

Furthermore, everyone who does not have this "life" is still in a state of spiritual "death." That "death," of course, never means "cessation of being" or "nonexistence." "Death" means separation

41

from the life that is in Christ. Consequently there are millions of people EXISTING in a state of "death." This existence will continue whether they are physically alive or dead. "Eternal Life" is a state or condition of existence in fellowship and association with God. "*Eternal Death*" would simply be the opposite — **the state or condition of conscious existence outside of fellowship and association with God.** This means *death* **is conscious existence outside of life.**

We explored the teachings of Christ about **"Immortality."** Basically, we found there were three kinds of immortality:

No. 1.   The first kind of immortality is eternal spiritual life beginning now, in the present, and existing for all eternity;

No. 2.   The second kind of immortality is eternal physical life in the future at the resurrection of the body;

No. 3.   The third kind of immortality is in qualified terminology only, and has reference to the *eternal conscious existence* of the souls of all mankind.

We also explored Christ's definition of "**Death.**" Basically, Christ taught us that death was a "*condition of existence*" in "*separation*" from the life of God and /or Christ. Death does not, therefore, mean "nonexistence," "cessation of being" or "annihilation." Rather, death should be understood in the sense of "*separation*." Physical death is the spirit's separation from the body. Spiritual death in man is his spirit's separation from the life and reality of fellowship in Christ and/or God. The vast majority of people exist in a spiritually "dead" state of consciousness.

It is to be understood that these preliminary definitions give obvious support to the Biblical doctrine of the essential spiritual nature of man. Man could not possibly have "eternal life" now unless there was a spiritual nature within him which constituted that life. In a similar vein, man could not be said to be "dead" towards God unless there was that spiritual nature within man which constituted that death. Both these conditions have nothing whatsoever to do with man's physical being.

Later in the study of Hell we shall receive with Biblical clarity the definition of "Destruction" or "Perishing." We shall find that the "destruction" of the lost is not the cessation of being, but rather the *condition of being*.

Now let us explore what Christ, Himself, teaches about the nature of **MAN**.

CHAPTER TWO

WHAT IS THE REAL
NATURE OF MAN?

❧

Or Spiritual Physiology

Physiology is that branch of biology which scientifically studies the physical structure and functioning of an organism such as the human body. In my last year in High School I took a college prep course called "Physiology." We studied the human anatomy and function. It was the most interesting course I ever took in High School. Since I had just become a Christian two years earlier, I selected the course thinking at the time of preparing for the Medical Missionary field.

When I began to study the Scriptures outside manmade religious schools, you might say I switched fields. I became far more interested in the spiritual anatomy of man. I call it here—Spiritual Physiology. As I had been captivated by the marvels of man's physical systems, so in reading the Bible and in my interactions among fellow members of God's family, I became even more captivated by the marvels of man's spiritual anatomy and interactions. As I, myself, grew in my new life in Christ, I was especially drawn by the spiritual structure, reality and functioning of the "new creation" in Christ. I found that spiritually the believer goes through a process of nurturing as a newborn baby in Christ, growing up and finally maturing as a full

44

grown adult. I will give more attention to this aspect of the subject a little later in chapter five.

Right now, as if sitting at the feet of our Lord Jesus Christ, we are going to take a short course in Spiritual Physiology. As if being personally tutored by Jesus Christ, we will begin our lesson in the midst of Christ's earthly ministry. He will have more to say to us later through His apostles in another lesson. By the direct teaching of Christ, it will become fundamental to our understanding that man possesses both a physical and a spiritual anatomy. According to Christ, we shall learn that the spiritual anatomy is far more important than the physical anatomy.

The modern scientific world, especially that which is tainted by humanistic philosophy, is totally oblivious to the spiritual realities operating within this world system (2 Cor. 4:18; Eph. 6:12 and 1 Cor. 2:6–8). However, at the very same time, scientists are often haunted by the apparent reality of "out-of-body experiences." Right now, as I write this study, I see another article from the medical field where there is valid ongoing scientific research investigating the evidences of such reality.

According to Christ—The Body is Actually a "HOUSE" for a "SPIRIT" Occupant

In the gospel of Luke, chapter 11, we will stand with a crowd of people who had just witnessed Christ expel a demonic creature out of a man. Verse 14 says, "*And He was casting out a demon, and it was mute* [blunted of hearing and speech]. *So it was, when the demon had gone out, that the mute spoke; and the multitudes marveled.*"

We can well understand why the multitudes marveled. This was probably a well-known man, called in Greek a *kophos*, one who was deaf and dumb. A demonic spirit creature had been inside the man causing this unfortunate condition. The means of curing this condition was by casting this spirit creature out of his body.

45

This was another phenomenal miracle by Christ and the religious leaders lost no time in finding a quick explanation. "He casts out demons by Beelzebub, the ruler of the demons" (v. 16), some of them said. This prompted a response from Christ which most certainly stopped their argument. It was Christ's famous "*house divided*" illustration (verses 17–20). In essence, Christ stated that Satan would not fight against himself lest his own "house be divided" and should fall. This, by the way, was borrowed by Abraham Lincoln in his famous "House Divided" speech which anticipated the eventual American Civil War. This whole event makes us look even more closely at what really constitutes the man—as a "HOUSE."

From accounts like this of demonic expulsion (and there are many others), we learn that man is so constructed as to be capable of control and occupancy by *intelligent spirit creatures*. These evil, fallen creatures, called "demons" (devils), often spoke through the vocal cords of the person they indwelt (see Mark 1:23–26). Sometimes these demons actually controlled the person's whole body and mind in very sinister and cruel ways, so that the person would do abnormal things (see Luke 8:26–30). The demonic spirit creature was, therefore, the real controlling factor from within the physical body of the person. In this account and others Christ talked directly to these demons who were inside the persons (see Matt. 8:28–32). Christ brings us another demonstration of this phenomenon in His next statement (Luke 11:24–26)—

When an unclean spirit goes **out of** a man, he goes through dry places, seeking rest; and finding none, he says, 'I will return to **my house** from which I came.' And when he comes, he finds it **swept and put in order**. Then he goes and takes with him seven other spirits more wicked than himself, and they **enter and dwell there**; and the last state of that man is worse than the first.

Now everyone must admit this is an amazing illustration of truth and reality. There are many important things to learn from this as it applies to the nature of man. (In Matthew 12:45 Christ makes a very sober application of this account to the religious leaders and the history of the Jewish nation at that time.)

First, Christ identifies man's body as just a *"house."* A house, as we all well understand, is for *occupancy*. The *house* is not the *occupant*. The *occupant* is separate and distinct from the *house* in which he is living.

Second, in this case, *"an unclean spirit,"* an *intelligent spirit creature,* had been an occupant of the *"house"* and left it—"goes out of a man."

Third, these spirit beings can thus *move back and forth*. Not finding any other resting place, this spirit being purposes to *"return to his* [my] *house."* It "goes out of" and "enters into"—the body. That means they are existing *independently* of the body, like renters in a rooming house. They are distinct spiritual entities separate from the bodies.

Fourth, these spirit beings *get control* of the "house." As a result "the last condition of this man became worse than the first." The house of flesh is *animated* with physical life. It has blood pumping through its veins giving life to the flesh. But inside the body of the person are nonmaterial spiritual beings which can control the distinctive character or *animation* and attitude and actions of the whole person.

Fifth, the inevitable conclusion is that man is so constructed as to be considered a *DICHOTOMY*; man has two parts. There is that obvious physical outside part (house) and yet there is also that spiritual inside part (the occupant). Man has a physical nature and a spiritual nature. In this case of the man possessed by a demon, the inward spiritual nature spoken of is a separate spiritual demonic being.

The question now arises—**does man possess his own spiritual nature?**

The "INSIDE" and "OUTSIDE" Parts of Man

Christ answers this question for us in this very same eleventh chapter of Luke, verses 37–40. A Pharisee asked Christ to dine with him. On this occasion we are told that the Pharisee marveled that Christ "had not first *washed* before dinner" (v. 38).

We need to understand that this was not just a normal washing of the hands prior to dinner, but rather a *ceremonial cleansing*. The Greek word translated here as "washed" in most of our Bibles is actually in Greek, *baptizo,* which normally should be translated "to baptize." In other words, Christ had not **baptized** His hands in ceremonial preparation for dinner. So the Pharisee was really astonished at Christ's neglect of this religious tradition which had been added to the Jewish customs. Now the Lord knew what the Pharisee was thinking and so He gave another very important lesson—

> Now you Pharisees make the *outside* of the cup and dish [and hands] *clean* [that is, you baptize them for outward, ritual purification], but your *inward part* is full of greed and wickedness [this is an amazing indictment]. Foolish ones! Did not He [God] Who made the *outside* [the physical part of man] make the *inside* [the spiritual part of man] also?

As to the immediate subject of our consideration, it is clear that God has made **two distinct parts to man**. Simply stated—there is the "*outside* part" and the "*inside* part." Just as God made the outward physical part of man, so God also made the inward spiritual part of man. The outward physical part was made from "dust." The inward spiritual part was made of the nonmaterial substance called "spirit." Thus, our deduction that man is a dichotomy is herein confirmed. As Christ indicated, the "*outward*" part of man can be cleaned up to look very nice and pious, whereas the "*inward*" part of man can be just the opposite—dirty as it can be—full of "greed and wickedness."

In this case, Christ was not talking about an inward demonic spirit creature within man. Rather, He was speaking of man's own *inward spiritual nature.* Actually this is nothing new to the theology of Judaism. The Hebrew Scriptures confirm Christ's observation that man is a dichotomy. Here are a few verses of demonstration—

Thus says the LORD, Who stretched out the heavens, lays the foundation of the earth, and FORMS THE SPIRIT OF MAN WITHIN HIM. Zech. 12:1

If He [God] puts no trust in His servants, if He charges His angels with error, how much more THOSE WHO DWELL IN HOUSES OF CLAY, . . . Job 4:18 and 19.

But there is **a spirit** IN **man,** and the breath [Lit., Spirit] of the Almighty gives him understanding. Job 32:8.

Behold, You desire truth in the INWARD PARTS, and in the HIDDEN PART You will make me to know wisdom. . . . Create in me a clean HEART, O God, and renew a STEADFAST SPIRIT WITHIN ME. Psalm 51:6 and 10.

As we shall see in a moment, the Lord's apostles will continue to speak of the body as a "*house*," a "*tent*" or "*tabernacle*" and a "*temple*" in which the spiritual person dwells—1 Cor. 6:19; 2 Cor. 5:1, 2 and 2 Pet. 1:13, 14.

The "INWARD MAN" and the "OUTWARD MAN"

In Romans chapter seven the apostle Paul stepped back in perspective into his natural Jewish experience and stated concerning his relationship to the Law of Moses in the following manner—"For I delight in the Law of God according to *the inward man*" (verse 22). Paul is saying that in his unsaved condition he had an inner consciousness of how good the Law actually was. Paul's problem was that his performance of the Law was hampered by an inward sinful nature. Without going into the rest of this account, I only want to point out this description of Paul's inward person. It is herein described as his "*inward man*." In Paul's regeneration (being born again), this inward man becomes his "New Man," or "New Creation" (Eph. 4:24 and 2 Cor. 5:17). This is another important description of the inner spiritual nature.

In 2 Corinthians 4:16 Paul spoke as one regenerated and said, *"Therefore we do not lose heart. Even though our **outward man** is <u>perishing</u>, yet the **inward man** is being <u>renewed</u> day by day."*

What an amazing revelation! Here we have two MEN in one PERSON! One man, *"the outward man"* (obviously, his physical body), is getting old and dying, whereas the other man, *"the inward man"* (i.e., his spiritual person) is getting stronger every day. We must accept this by faith as revelation from Christ, and rejoice in it. Certainly, in light of a passage like this, no one should want to deny that man is a dichotomy. A stronger proof cannot be made by words. Man is composed of two parts, an outward physical body and an inner spiritual soul or spirit. In this case the inner soul or spirit is called *"**THE INWARD MAN**."* Apparently, to the apostle Paul, the "Inner Man" is far more important than the "Outward Man." This is another case where the two "men" do <u>*opposite*</u> things, so they have to be understood as distinct and separate entities!

The cults have tried to define the word "soul" exclusively by the equivalent of "life." Admittedly, sometimes that is exactly what it means, but not always. They would also like to exclusively define "spirit" as *"wind."* Again, they know good and well that is not the only way the word is used. It is often used to designate God, the angels, demons and the *"inward man"* of every human being. No one would dare suggest that God, angels and demons are just "wind." Likewise, "wind" or "breath" could never be the definition of the "Inward Man." False teachers on this subject have had a harder time defining the expression, *"the Inward Man,"* because that is obviously descriptive of a *personal being*. Some have tried such words as *"personality"* to be its equal. Of course, demons have personality, but mere "personality" could never be the definition of demons. Demons merely affected a person's personality. Man possesses his own personality. No one would suggest that "personality" can be the definition of "The Man Without." Likewise, by no stretch of the imagination is "personality" the definition of "the

Man Within." This type of theological dodge does not work because dogs and all kinds of animals *have* personality, but that does not make them "MEN." The definition of "MAN" is fairly concrete—an intelligent, personal being! "Personality" is but an attribute of man. *"The Inward* **Man**" is the definition of the spiritual life or person indwelling every human being.

Can the "Inward Man" be Totally Separated from the "Outward Man"?

There are many passages which answer that question. We saw that intelligent spirit creatures called "demons" can, within God's allowance, come and go from the body of a person. It is obvious that God created man's body and designed it to be occupied by a spirit intelligence. Many theologians, in studying the subject of demonism, have concluded that at one time in the past these spirit creatures had bodies of their own. However, for whatever reason, they have become *"disembodied spirits."* Consequently, they crave to occupy someone else's body—in this case, man's—or even, at last resort, the body of a beast (Matt. 8:31). Now I am asking the question, "Can man's own *spirit nature* depart from his body, with God's allowance, or in God's own pre-ordained time?" And the answer is a positive "Yes!"

We will also see from the Hebrew Scriptures many evidences of this fact. We will see several texts which state Sheol was full of "disembodied spirits" of the dead. For instance Proverbs 21:16 says, "A man who wanders from the way of understanding will rest in the assembly of the dead." We shall find that this does not mean the graveyard.

However, right now we are going to observe a few select verses from the most popular and obvious passages which clearly teach the distinction and separation of man's spirit from his physical body. Shortly after giving the truth we learned from 2 Corinthians 4:16, Paul continued to say—

1. *2 Corinthians 5:1–9*

*For we know that if our **earthly house**, this **tent**, is destroyed, we have a **building** from God, a **house** not made with hands, eternal in the heavens.*

(This is the promise of receiving an immortal body to dwell in.)

*For in this we groan, earnestly desiring to be **clothed** with our **habitation** which is from heaven, if indeed, having been **clothed**, we shall not be found **naked**.*

(To have died and put off our natural physical body called the "earthly house" is, as it were, for our spirits to take off a garment. And yet not having our "heavenly house," or the immortal body to put on, would constitute our spirits as being "unclothed," or being temporarily in a condition of "nakedness," i.e., an intelligent spirit being temporarily without a body.)

*For we who are in this **tent** groan, being burdened, not because we want to be **unclothed**, but further **clothed**, that **mortality** might be swallowed up by **life** [i.e., the immortal].*

*Now He Who has prepared us for this very thing is God, Who also has given us the Spirit as a guarantee. So we are always confident, knowing that while we are at home **in the body** we are **absent** from the Lord. For we walk by faith, not by sight. We are confident, yes, well pleased rather to be **absent** from the **body** and to be **present** with the Lord. Therefore we make it our aim, whether **present** or **absent**, to be well pleasing to Him.*

(Of course, this means that a believer can be "absent" from his physical body and yet in spirit be "present" with the Lord, until such time as his soul or spirit gets his immortal body.)

For the sake of those who have ignorantly rejected the distinctive and separate spiritual nature of man, like members of the "Watch Tower Society," "Seventh Day Adventists," "Christadelphians" and generally all liberals who oppose even the doctrine of the qualified "Immortal Soul," I want you to honestly note the details of this passage.

First of all, perhaps as important as other words are the pronouns used—"*we*," "*our*," and "*us*." These pronouns represent *personhood*, i.e., in this case the *person* who owns or occupies the "body" like a garment or "tabernacle" which "*he*" is going to "put off." "*We*," the person, is said to be "*at home in the body*." Therefore, the pronouns could not possibly merely represent the physical person because that is the part of man to be "put off." Of necessity, the pronouns must primarily represent the "*Inward Spiritual Person*" who "puts off" his physical body, or is desirous of being in the Lord's presence until such time as he can be "clothed" with an "immortal" body.

Second, as we observed before, there are two kinds of immortality. The first is the spiritual. The person who has exercised faith in the Lord Jesus Christ possesses "Eternal Life." Previously this person was in a state of spiritual "death;" now he has "eternal life." This is the individual who now has within him the "earnest, pledge or guarantee of the [Holy] Spirit" that he will one day receive a glorified body—immortality number two. Obviously, this person, since he possesses "Eternal Life," will go on EXISTING apart from his body at the point of physical death.

Third, this text plainly states the person can be "ABSENT FROM THE BODY" and be "PRESENT WITH THE LORD." Who or what is "absent from the body"? Of necessity, it must be the spiritual person, i.e., the "inward man."

Fourth, to emphasize the fact of this separation is the inspired statement that the believer who is thus "absent from the body" is in a state or condition of being "*UNCLOTHED*" or "*NAKED*." In other words, God Almighty designed man's spirit to occupy a body, and when it does not, it is characterized as being "UNCLOTHED." The sense of "nakedness," in this context, simply means that man is INCOMPLETE without a BODY, either his original natural body, or his promised immortal body. Language could hardly be any plainer than this.

In a similar fashion Paul states the following which I will itemize in parts as (A), (B) and (C)—

2. *Philippians 1:21–25*

(A) *For to me, to **live** is Christ, and to **die** is gain.*

(B) *But if I live on **in the flesh**, this will mean fruit from my labor; yet what I should choose I cannot tell.*

(C) *For I am hard-pressed between the two,*
*having a desire **to depart and be with Christ**,*
which is far better.
*Nevertheless **to remain in the flesh***
is more needful for you.
And being confident of this, I know that I shall remain and continue with you. . . .

The comparisons in this passage are easy to follow and very revealing.

(A)—On the one hand, for Paul to go on "living" would be for the glory of *Christ*. However, on the other hand, for Paul to "*die*" would be his own direct "*gain*." Just here I might ask, how in the world could it be Paul's "*gain*" to "*die*," if "death" meant the "cessation of his existence"?? If "death" is the "cessation of being," as some propose, then they are now going to have to contend that somehow "nonexistence" is "gain"!! They cannot possibly put that manufactured definition upon this passage of Scripture.

(B)—For Paul to go on "*in the flesh*" would be for Christ's service, whereas, since to die would be his "gain," he did not know which "to choose." The question here that needs to be faced is, just exactly WHAT or WHO is "IN THE FLESH"? Obviously it is a person—Paul, himself! Of necessity, this must be a reference to his inward spiritual person. In addition, it is understood that Paul's inner spiritual person is herein SEPARATE and DISTINCT from his FLESH so as to either remain in it, or else depart from it.

(C)—Paul honestly tells us HE wants to "*depart* [from his flesh, i.e., to die] *and BE with Christ*," yet to "*remain in the flesh*" is what is more needful at the present. For Paul to die would simply mean the departure of his soul and spirit from his fleshly body. Paul would obviously still EXIST, but no longer in his flesh. Having departed from his fleshly body, he would "BE with Christ." Paul would not *cease to be* when he died! He would, in fact, *BE* with Christ.

To take the passage literally and at face value positively answers the original question which I asked at the beginning of this series of verses, "Can the 'Inward Man' be totally separate From the 'Outward Man'?" The answer again is—"Yes, absolutely!" There is no other interpretation—unless one was to "wrest the Scriptures to his own destruction" (2 Peter 3:16).

3. *2 Corinthians 12:2–5*

I know a man in Christ, who fourteen years ago—whether in the body I do not know, or out of the body I do not know, God knows—such a one was caught up to the third heaven. And I know such a man—whether in the body or out of the body I do not know, God knows—how he was caught up into Paradise, and heard inexpressible words, which a man is not permitted to speak.

In three passages which we have considered earlier (2 Cor. 4:16; 2 Cor. 5:1–9 and Philip. 1:21–24) the apostle Paul demonstrated that the spiritual part of man, the "Inward Man," can and will be separated from the "Outward Man" at death and still be in existence with Christ. Here in this passage we are told that the apostle himself was also once possibly separated from his body even while he was still physically living. Paul was, in fact, "caught up to the third heaven." It was not only possible, but also probable, that he was outside his body for this experience. His body was in one location on earth, whereas his spirit was in the opposite location — Paradise or the third heaven.

In order for this to be possible, man of necessity must be a DICHOTOMY. If Paul was "apart from his body" on this occasion, then it was his spiritual person, the "Inner Man," who went into Paradise. In the book of Revelation the apostle John was said to be "In the Spirit on the Lord's Day" (Rev. 1:10). He was also actually transferred up into heaven and forward in time (Rev. 4:1).

4. *2 Peter 1:13, 14 and 2 Timothy 4:6*

*Yes, I think it right, as long as I am in **this tent**, to stir you up by reminding you, knowing that shortly I must put off my **tent**, just as our Lord Jesus Christ showed me.*

*For I am already being poured out as a drink offering, and the time of **my departure** is at hand.*

Both Peter and Paul speak of their imminent deaths as a matter of laying aside their bodily tabernacles and/or departing from this earthly station. The only way they could do this is in light of the fact that man is a dichotomy and their spirits would go to be with Christ.

———

Many years ago I picked up the book by Carlyle B. Haynes, the chief apologist for the Seventh Day Adventists, entitled *Life, Death, and Immortality* (1952, Southern Publishing Association). One of his earliest remarks in the book was—

Men have been *falsely taught* that in death the body is like a *garment* laid aside from use, or a *house abandoned*, a *tenement of clay*, while the wearer of the garment and the dweller in the house, that is, the soul, the real man, has gone elsewhere. (Page 44, italics mine.)

Now it just so happens that some of the "men" in the Bible who use this very terminology and teaching are none other than **Job** (4:18, 19), **Jesus Christ** (Luke 11:17–20, 24–26, and 37–40), **Paul** (1 Cor. 6:19; 2 Cor. 5:1–9 and 12:2–5) and **Peter** (2 Pet. 1:13, 14), as we have seen in the previous texts in this chapter. So Mr. Haynes has unwittingly charged them with teaching "falsely." Of course, I hope you have no problem realizing just who the false teacher is! In addition, Carlyle B. Haynes is probably the person more responsible for articulating the basic arguments against the revelation of Christ on this whole subject than any other person in the past generation. His basic contentions are picked up and repeated to the next generation by the more recent false teachers of the same persuasion.

CHAPTER THREE

"SOUL" and "SPIRIT"

The Words "SOUL" or "SPIRIT" used of the "Inward Man"

"Soul" is the English translation of the Hebrew word *nephesh* (Strong # 5315) and the Greek word *psuche* (Strong # 5590). These words have a wide variety of meanings, such as—*a breathing creature, the natural life of the body, animation, the self, a distinctive invisible part of man, a creature, the will, desire, the mind, the person, or some emotion, etc.*

"Spirit" is the English translation of the Hebrew word *ruwach* (Strong # 7307) and the Greek word *pneuma* (Strong # 4151). These words also have a wide variety of meanings, such as—*wind, breath, sensibility, life, a distinct inward nature in man, feeling, desire, perception, character, The Holy Spirit of God, God Himself, demonic beings, angels, disembodied spirits, etc.*

By far the most common expressions used in the Scriptures of man's inward spiritual nature are the words "soul" and "spirit." The cults like to point out that the word *soul* is sometimes used of the animals. Therefore, they would contend that it is never used any other way than just meaning "the life process." As I just stated, the words "soul" and "spirit" are, in fact, used in a wide variety of ways. However, one of those ways is to often designate the separate and distinct spiritual nature of man. This fact, the cults don't want to admit. They must admit, of course, that the word "spirit" is directly used of intelligent spiritual beings, even of God, Himself. It is blatantly dishonest of them to stress only one aspect of the meaning of either of these two words as if that alone is how the word is to be understood.

It is also blatantly dishonest of the cults to quote God's words to Adam in Genesis 3:19 "In the sweat of your face you shall eat bread till you return to the ground, for out of it you were taken; for dust you are, and to dust you shall return," as if this is the ultimate and complete description of man. In reality, this was only an accurate description of man's physical nature—his "house or dwelling place." The cults totally and deliberately ignore the spiritual description of man. To this materialistic fantasy I would simply respond by asking, "Was Jesus Christ merely animated dust?"

I have purposely delayed stressing these words "soul" or "spirit" because I wanted to first emphasize the fact that there are very clear and important descriptive words and phrases concerning man's separate spiritual nature which cannot be circumvented, as is attempted to be done with the word "soul." Christ taught us about man's *"inside"* and *"outside"* parts (Luke 11:37–40) and it was stated that each was specially created by God. These parts are sometimes designated as the *"inward man"* and the *"outward man"* (Rom. 7:2; 2 Cor. 4:16, etc.). We also found that the inward spiritual nature can be so distinct from the physical person as to be in an *opposite* condition and/or going in an *opposite* direction or destination. Indeed, they can be *entirely separate* from each other and yet both are very much in existence.

When the words "soul" or "spirit" are applied to the spiritual part of man we must, therefore, understand them within the context of these clear designations such as "the Inward Man." Shortly we will learn that, for the believer in Christ, this inner nature is also called "the New Creation" and also "the New Man." The *"New Creation in Christ"* is a department in the science of man's spiritual nature which I have reserved for a little later because it is very important and deserves separate scrutiny. I will also reserve for a little later the distinction between "soul" and "spirit." Since the Hebrew word sometimes translated *"soul"* and the Greek word also often translated "soul" have a wide variety of meanings, we must always remember that when they are used to designate man's inner person, they must be defined as "The Inward Man" and not as mere *animation*, *life*, *consciousness* or *personality*. The animal world will also sometimes be described as being "souls." However, by no stretch of the imagination is this the same thing as the "inward spiritual person" in human beings.

No one should doubt that such passages as I quoted at the very beginning of this study are anything other than perfect descriptions of man's inward spiritual nature. Moses cried out to God at a very explosive moment in Israel's beginning, as he interceded on behalf of the nation—"O God, Thou God of the *spirits* of all flesh, . . ." (Num. 16:22 and 27:16). Moses was not as nearly concerned for Israel's "flesh" as he was for their "spirits." That Israel's "flesh" could be destroyed is one thing; that their "SPIRITS" could be eternally endangered is an entirely different matter.

King David was inspired of God to record one of the most important prayers in all human history—the prayer of a repentant heart—"Behold, You desire *truth* in the *inward parts*, and in the *hidden part* You will make me to know wisdom" (Psalm 51:6). It is obvious that man has "outward parts" and "inward parts," just exactly as Jesus Christ explained earlier. Those "inward parts" are more vital than the outward parts in Christ's estimation. How brazenly stupid it would be to even suggest that those "inward parts" are mere *chemical reactions* to outside stimuli.

Both the Hebrew and Greek Scriptures are loaded with references to man's spiritual nature which we are not going to take the time to list, simply because the evidences which are being given are more than sufficient for any honest person.

The Sadducees

Now, the modern vigorous opposition to the doctrines of the separate spiritual nature of man and of eternal conscious punishment is not at all something new. It actually traces all the way back to what we call "New Testament times."

The Sadducees, whom we read about in the New Testament, were those who rejected the Scriptural doctrine about the physical *resurrection*, *angels*, the *spiritual nature of man*, and *eternal punishment* for the lost in a literal *Hell*. In the days of Christ and of the early church it is expressly said about them, *"For the Sadducees say that there is no resurrection—and no angel or spirit;. . ."* (Acts 23:8). Josephus, the Jewish historian who was a contemporary of the times, said the Sadducees believed *"The soul dies with the body"* (Antiq. XVIII, I, 4). And again Josephus says of them, *"They also take away the immortal duration of the soul, and the punishments and rewards in Hades"* (Wars II, viii, 14). In this regard the Sadducees were very materialistic and infidel in regards to the spiritual nature of man and towards eternal punishment. This is just like some of the cults and others today who also reject the doctrine of eternal punishment.

You can see by this that Josephus, as an orthodox Jew, believed exactly as did the Lord Jesus Christ and the early Christians on these subjects. Oppositions to these truths today in our very liberal religious systems are actually not new at all. As you now realize, these false beliefs also flourished in Christ's own day.

You may note that Josephus, himself, qualifies the word "immortal" by the phrase "immortal DURATION of the soul." That means he understood it as the "continued existence of the soul after death," not in the sense of the PERFECTION of the soul.

It is perfectly consistent, therefore, that historical scholars of early Christianity fully understand that Biblical Judaism handed on to Christianity the fundamental truths on this subject which were further developed therein.

Further Scriptures—1 Corinthians 5:4,5

*In the name of our Lord Jesus Christ, when you are gathered together, along with my **SPIRIT**, with the power of our Lord Jesus Christ, deliver such a one to Satan for the destruction of the flesh, that his **SPIRIT** may be saved in the day of the Lord Jesus.*

Here the apostle Paul uses the word "spirit" twice to designate, on the one hand, his own spiritual person, and on the other, the spiritual person of the young man under condemnation. Try and superimpose upon these two occurrences the thought or meaning of *"breath"* as some religious infidels suppose "spirit" should be translated. Would Paul want them to think his special apostolic "breath" needed to be there? Or would Paul want them to think the young man's "breath" was going to be somehow preserved at the judgment? How ridiculous!

Likewise, this is another case where the two parts of man do opposite things. The young man's *"flesh"* would deserve to be destroyed. In other words, his sin would normally bring a death penalty. Under Judaism he would have been stoned to death. Under Christianity, the saints merely recognized him as deserving death, if God so allowed Satan to carry it out. (Thank God, the young man later repented.) However, even if he did die physically, his *"spirit"* was preserved. In other words, he was a saved man who came under the discipline of physical death. The nature of the heinous deeds meant that he did not deserve to live any longer. But as to his spiritual life, that was not to be destroyed.

1 Corinthians 6:19–20 and 7:34

*Or do you not know that your **body** is the **temple** of the **Holy Spirit** Who is in you, Whom you have from God, and you are not your own? For you are bought with a price; therefore glorify God in your **body** and in **your SPIRIT**, which are God's. The unmarried woman cares about the things of the Lord, that she may be holy both in **body** and in **spirit**.*

We have previously found that the human body can be the *"house"* of an evil spirit creature or creatures, called *demons*. How much more can the human body actually be the residence of the very Holy Spirit of God, Who is omnipresent and does dwell in all believers! Hopefully, most Christians do not follow the infidel Watch Tower Society in claiming that the Holy Spirit is only a "force" or "power" like electricity. If you recognize the distinctive personality of the Holy Spirit, then you should have no trouble recognizing that every saved person has residing within him this Divine Person. In addition, and directly because of this amazing truth, all believers should be *"glorifying God"* in both their physical *"**bodies**"* and in their own *"**spirits**."* Once again, therefore, we have two distinct parts to man. Man's "spirit" is just as much a separate distinct being as is the Holy Spirit of God.

2 Corinthians 7:1 and Galatians 6:18

*Therefore, having these promises, beloved, let us cleanse ourselves from all filthiness of the **flesh** and **spirit**, perfecting holiness in the fear of God.*

*Brethren, the grace of our Lord Jesus Christ be with your **spirit**. Amen.*

In both passages the *spirit* of man is treated as a separate intelligent living entity. In the first passage the spiritual part is clearly distinguished from the physical.

Matthew 10:28

*And do not fear those who kill the **body** but cannot kill the **soul**. But rather fear Him Who is able to destroy both **soul** and **body** in Hell* [Lit., *Gehenna*].

Here the word *"soul"* is used to describe the *"inward man."* Clearly the *"soul"* is separate and distinct from the *"body"* or the *"outward man."* This is another passage where these two distinct parts of man are placed in opposition to one another. As Christ stated, another human being can kill the outward physical life of a person. On the other hand, Christ likewise indicated, it is not in any man's power to be able to kill the *"soul."* Of course, if the soul is merely the animation of life of the physical body, and if it is inseparable from man as a unit, then when the body is killed the soul is automatically killed as well, and Christ's words would be nonsensical. Those, who believe that the body and the soul are a singular inseparable unit, declare that when a person dies, his soul dies as well; they say it is one and the same.

Those who oppose the doctrine of man's soul as an everlasting consciously existing entity usually smugly respond to this passage by pointing out that the second part of this passage says that God can "destroy both soul and body in Hell." Therefore they say, the "soul" can be destroyed and consequently it does not have an "everlasting existence." Those who propose this argument forget three things.

First, they ignore the fact that this type of passage clearly teaches that man is a dichotomy. Like many other passages already quoted, it distinguishes between man's body and his spiritual inward part, herein designated as a "soul." That fact cannot be circumvented; they have never successfully been able to answer the implications.

Second, they seem to forget the exact words and doctrine of the passage as it concerns Hell. The word used for Hell here is the Greek word *Gehenna*. It has reference to the final phase of Hell called *"Gehenna,"* and is synonymous with *"the Lake of Fire"* spoken of in the book of Revelation. I will write more about this later because God has ordained a final Judgment before which all the unjust must appear. They are to be bodily resurrected from the dead (Dan. 12:2; John 5:28, 29; Acts 24:15; Rev. 19:20 and 20:13, 14), will be judged and then will be cast *"alive"* (both body and soul) into the *"Lake of Fire."* So this final destruction is for their composite persons—both body and soul. This is precisely the destruction to which Christ was referring.

Third, they forget all about the fact that the "souls," "spirits" or "disembodied spirits" of the lost have been gathering and existing in a place named in the Hebrew Scriptures as ***"Destruction"*** (*Abaddon*) for the last 6000 years (Job 26:5–6; 28:22; Ps. 88:10–11; Prov.15:11; 27:20 and Isa. 14:9, etc.). We shall see that this was in Sheol. And furthermore, during all that time, they did *not cease to exist!* ***"Destruction"*** was a *condition of existence*, not a place of *cessation of being.* All the "souls" of those in the ***"Destruction"*** of Sheol will be reunited with their resurrected bodies and stand before God at the final Judgment and then be cast into Gehenna. Consequently the final Gehenna (Hell) is said to be *"eternal," "everlasting"* and *"they will be tormented day and night, forever and forever"* (Matt. 18:8; Jude 7; Rev. 20:10, etc., etc.). This obviously means a perpetual, unending *"destruction."*

Revelation 6:9–11

And when He opened the fifth seal, I saw under the altar the **souls** *of those who had been* **slain** *for the Word of God and for the testimony which they held.* **And they cried with a loud voice, saying,** *'How long, O Lord, holy and true, until You judge and avenge our* **blood** *on those* **who dwell on the earth?'** *Then a* **white robe** *was given to each of them; and it was said to them that they should* **rest** *a little while longer, until the number of their fellow servants and their brethren, who would be* **killed as they were**, *was completed.*

Later we shall read of the conversations of the lost in Sheol in such passages as Ezek. 32:21 and Isa. 14:9–21. We will hear the conversation of Samuel who was "brought up" and spoke to King Saul—1Sam. 28:13–19. We will also hear the conversation between the rich man and Lazarus in Hades—Luke 16:19–31. Here in the book of Revelation, however, we hear conversation of the *spirits* or *"souls"* of saints in heaven. There is absolutely no reason to not take this passage literally as a prophetic vision of this future event. Again, this positively demonstrates the reality of the separation of the *"soul"* from the body and that the soul remains in conscious existence after physical death.

After the death and glorious resurrection of Jesus Christ, the souls of the righteous dead were transported into heaven (Eph. 4:7–10). Therefore, during the future Great Tribulation, the *"souls"* (the nonmaterial persons) of those who have died consciously exist in heaven. They were situated as *"under the altar"* in the heavenly sanctuary. Many have asked, "Why is this?" These saints had been martyred on earth on behalf of Christ. In the earthly sanctuary, as ordered through Moses, the blood of the sacrifices was to be poured out beside the altar. So it is in this heavenly sanctuary. The saints had been sacrificed, and their blood had been shed on earth because of their testimony for Jesus Christ; therefore their souls are pictured as being situated just beneath the altar in their residence in heaven. They are, in fact, dedicated as an offering to God. So this is a very appropriate situation according to God's own arrangement.

The dead most certainly speak. Their *souls* did not cease to exist as the false teachers on this subject contend. In addition, they are given "*white robes*" which speak of the righteousness of the saints. The modern religious Sadducees contend, in their rationalistic thinking, that nonmaterial beings can't wear *physical* clothing. So they chuckle to themselves and choose to not believe what the Scriptures say! As Christ would say, this is an argument from "*ignorance*," "*not knowing the Scriptures nor the power of God.*" The Scripture does *not* say they wore "*physical*" clothing. It just so happens that the very same book of Revelation pictures God the Father "*sitting on a throne*," "*elders clothed in white robes*," and many other spirit beings with various *appearances* (Rev. 4:8–9). Everyone knows God is a Spirit and so were the elders around the throne; so were all the other spirit beings pictured there. Now, if we realize these are spirit beings, what is so difficult about nonmaterial beings sitting on nonmaterial thrones, wearing non-material clothing with nonmaterial crowns having various nonmaterial appearances?? Furthermore, the Scriptures will and do describe the "*souls*" as NONMATERIAL BODIES which, in this case, John "SAW them," they had "VOICES" and could SPEAK.

There is consistency to Divine revelation and faith in that revelation should be consistent as well.

Acts 2:25–27 and 31

We will look at this passage later concerning Hell; now let us look at it concerning the soul—

For David says concerning Him: 'I foresaw the LORD always before my face, for He is at my right hand, that I may not be shaken. Therefore my heart rejoiced, and my tongue was glad; moreover my flesh also will rest in hope. For You will not leave my soul in Hades, nor will You allow Your Holy One to see corruption. . . .' He, foreseeing this, spoke concerning the resurrection of the Christ, that His soul was not left in Hades, nor did His flesh see corruption.

The "*soul*" is distinguished from the "*flesh*." What was true of David, according to the inspired writer of the Psalm (16:8–11), was also true of the Messiah (Christ), the distant descendent of David. Christ's "*soul*" had been separated from His body at death and went into "*Hades*." His body was laid in an earthly tomb for three days and nights. Christ's "*soul*" was not "abandoned" to "*Hades*," nor did His "*flesh*" see corruption. As we all know, Christ was reunited with His body and gloriously raised from the dead.

The Distinction Between Soul and Spirit

Because of the wide variety of uses of the words "soul" and "spirit" in both the Hebrew and Greek Scriptures, one needs to realize that every time these words are used they may not mean exactly the same thing. Likewise, there seems to be an overlapping nature to the words "soul" and "spirit" which sometimes makes them appear to be used in a similar or interchangeable way. However, as to man's distinct spiritual parts, at least twice the "soul" and "spirit" are clearly differentiated in the same verse. We will quote these two passages. The first is 1 Thessalonians 5:23—

Now may the God of peace Himself sanctify you completely; and may your whole *spirit, soul,* and *body be* preserved blamelessly at the coming of our Lord Jesus Christ.

According to this inspired language, man constitutes a *triune* nature. And why shouldn't man have three distinct parts? The Scriptures clearly tell us that man was created in the "image" of a *Triune* God! The tri-part nature of man bears the likeness of the Tri-unity of the Godhead. Dare I speculate in spiritual caution that the One Who now permanently dwells in a glorified body (Jesus Christ, the Son of God) left His imprint in man's physical *body* when He actually formed man of the dust; and does not God the Father, Who authorized the creation, leave His imprint in man's central being, his *soul*; and does not the Holy Spirit of God, by Whose power the work of creation was done, leave His imprint in man's very own *spirit*?

Furthermore, why is it that these three parts of man are encouraged to be kept "*sanctified*"? Is it not because God has promised to personally indwell man's tabernacle here on this sin-cursed earth? And, when God indwelt the tabernacle in the wilderness, it was to be kept sanctified in its entirety. So it is that our tabernacle must be kept sanctified in its entirety. Remember that the tabernacle in the wilderness, as it was designed by God, *had three distinct parts* — (1) the outer court, corresponding to man's physical *body*; (2) the tent itself was composed of two distinct chambers, the first called "the Holy Place," corresponding to our *soul*; (3) and then the "Most Holy Place," corresponding to man's *spirit*. All three parts of the tabernacle were to be kept sanctified.

The most basic differentiation of man's tri-part nature, of which I have heard or read, is simply the following — 1.) man's physical being is obviously conscious of the physical world; 2.) man's soulish being is conscious of the central self; 3.) man's spiritual being is conscious of God's Holy Spirit, Who communicates with us. To be sure, there are many more things which have been carefully stated regarding the attributes of these three parts of man; however, this should suffice for the present purpose.

The second passage which distinguishes these three parts is Hebrews 4:12 —

> For the Word of God is living and powerful, and sharper than any two-edged sword, piercing even to the division of *soul* and *spirit*, and of the *joints* and *marrow*, and is a discerner of the thoughts and intents of the heart.

In conclusion, because of all the forgoing evidences which have been offered concerning the dichotomy of man's being, I will not go any further to the many, many statements in the Scriptures indicating the differences between man's physical and spiritual natures by the use of the terms "soul" and "spirit."

Two final references which would be appropriate in closing are found in Hebrews 12:22–23 and Numbers 16:22 (see also Num. 27:16)—

But you have come to Mount Zion and to the city of the living God, the heavenly Jerusalem, to an innumerable company of angels, to the general assembly and church of the Firstborn who are registered in heaven, to God the Judge of all, to the *spirits* of just men made perfect.

Then they [Moses and Aaron] fell on their faces and said, 'O God, God of the *spirits* of all flesh, shall one man sin, and You be angry with all the congregation?

CHAPTER FOUR

FURTHER VITAL PROOFS

There is no Greater Proof of the Dual Nature of Man Than The Dual Nature of The Man—Jesus Christ

When Christ spoke of man having both a physical nature and a spiritual nature, we might look at Christ Himself and ask "Where did Your spiritual nature come from?" Christ answers that question through His inspired writers who tell us several things.

First, Jesus Christ the Lord **PRE-EXISTED** *as DIETY —*

John 1:1 "In the beginning was the Word, and the Word was with God, and the Word was God."

Philip. 2:6 ". . . Who [Jesus Christ] being in the form of God, . . ."

John 17:5 ". . . the glory I had with You [God] before the world was."

John 8:58 ". . . before Abraham was, I AM."

Second, Jesus Christ **PRE-EXISTED** *as the SON of GOD —*

Psalm 2:7 "The LORD has said to ME, You are My SON, . . ."

Psalm 2:12 "Kiss the SON, lest He be angry, and you perish in the way."

Prov. 30:4 ". . . what is His name [God the Father], and what
is His SON'S name?"

Dan. 3:25 ". . . and the form of the fourth is like the
SON of God."

Isa. 9:6 "For unto us a Child is born, unto us a SON is given;. . ."

*Third, Jesus Christ was CONCEIVED in the Womb by the
HOLY SPIRIT —*

Matt. 1:18 "Now the birth of Jesus Christ was as follows:
After His mother Mary was betrothed to Joseph, before
they came together, she was found with child by the
Holy Spirit."

Matt. 1:20 ". . . that which is conceived in her is of the
Holy Spirit."

Matt. 1:23 "Behold, the virgin shall be with child, and bear
a Son, and they shall call His name IMMANUEL, which
is translated, 'GOD WITH US'."

Therefore, Jesus Christ had a <u>DUAL ORIGIN</u>

Through the virgin Mary, Christ partook of her linage
back through King David, and past David through Abraham to
Adam — Luke 3:31, 34 and 38, "The son of David . . . the son of
Abraham . . . the son of Adam." Thus, The Divine Son of God truly
became a flesh and blood MAN, a member of the human family, a
descendent of King David, Abraham and of Adam.

*At the very same time He took upon Himself human flesh,
through the agency of the HOLY SPIRIT,* ***He was truly
from HEAVEN —***

John 3:17 "For God did not sent forth His Son into the world
to condemn the world, . . ."

John 6:42 "And they said, 'Is not this Jesus, the son of
Joseph, whose father and mother we know? How is it
then that He says, "*I have come down from Heaven?*"'"

John 8:14 ". . . I know where I came from and where I am going;. . ."

John 8:23 "I am from above . . . I am not of this world."

John 8:42 ". . . I proceeded forth and came from God."

John 13:3 ". . . He had come from God and was going to God."

John 16:28 "I came forth from the Father and have come into the world."

1 Cor. 15:47 ". . . the second Man is the Lord from heaven."

Heb. 1:6 "But when He again brings the Firstborn into the world, . . ."

1 John 4:9 ". . . God has sent His only begotten Son into the world, . . ."

Jesus Christ was consequently DIETY manifested in the FLESH, a DIVINE Eternal Person in a HUMAN BODY—

Col. 2:9 "For in Him dwells all the fullness of the GODHEAD BODILY."

Rom. 8:3 ". . . God did by sending His own Son in the likeness of sinful FLESH, . . ."

1 Tim. 3:16 ". . . great is the mystery of GODLINESS: God [or He] was manifested in the FLESH, . . ."

Heb. 2:14 "Inasmuch then as the children have partaken of FLESH and BLOOD, He Himself likewise shared in the same, . . ."

John 1:14 "And the Word became FLESH and dwelt among us, . . ."

* Those who reject the Scriptural doctrine of the <u>dichotomy</u> of man must, of necessity and in consistency, also reject the <u>Divinity</u> of our Lord Jesus Christ.

One false doctrine usually affects another truth in the Bible. In this case, false teaching about the nature of man—that man is merely animated flesh, that his spirit is only "breath" and that his soul only has reference to his "life"—will of necessity be faced with the need of accurately describing the Lord Jesus Christ. In consistency, the members of the Watch Tower Society deny the Deity of Christ. Others are faced with an insurmountable difficulty when it comes to the man — Jesus Christ.

Whence Then Is — <u>The Origin of Man's Spiritual Nature</u>?

I noted before, from the direct ministry of Christ, that God not only made the outside, physical part of man, but He also made the "INSIDE" part of man (Luke 11:40). This, most certainly, has reference to man's spiritual nature. I also quoted from Zechariah 12:1 which says, "This is the utterance of Jehovah, Who stretched out the heavens, lays the foundation of the earth, and FORMS the SPIRIT of man WITHIN him." Now this passage specifically says God "formed the spirit" inside of man. We understand that God originally and initially did this back at the time of man's creation. In addition, when God originally created man He also designed man to have the ability of pro-creation. All mankind on earth are in fact descendents of Adam and Eve. That is how God has made all mankind. Like the continuation of man's physical life being passed down through each succeeding generation, so it is that man's spiritual life is also passed down through each succeeding generation. Because of rebellion and sin, both man's physical nature and spiritual nature came under the curse. Each succeeding generation inherits fallen natures as to their bodies and souls.

When and how did God originally do this? When we look back at the creation week, we read of God's forming the heavens and the earth for man's habitation. We also see in that account the description of God forming man's physical body out of the "dust" of the ground. I say again, this is how God originally created man. Obviously, it is not how God continues to make man. This original creation is an amazing revelation, and actually petrifies me to even envision it. Scientifically we know that this is exactly what man is physically composed of — an incredibly complex chemical arrangement of nothing more than the elements of clay. But what is even more astonishing is the act of God to enliven that complex arrangement of clay. As I read the account, Christ the Son of God, Who is the member of the Godhead directly involved in this work (John 1:3 and Col. 1:16), after forming man of the dust of the ground, leaned over His work, as it were, to put on the finishing touches and *"breathed into his nostrils the breath of life, and man became a living being* [Lit., *soul*]" (Gen. 2:7).

What did Christ actually do? I don't think any of us are capable of understanding what Christ did. Obviously He enlivened that lump of clay. But—"How exactly did He do it?"—our minds ask. We have never seen anyone else ever do that. No one else can do it! Quite often we natural, Adamic men have breathed on a person and they have moved away from us. Even in our modern enlightened age, scientifically wise experimenters have been trying for over a hundred years to activate a microscopic spot of chemical life. They even shoot electrical currents, heat and radiation into a soupy substance in their laboratories; but the only reaction is a different arrangement of the soupy substance—never any life.

So I ask again, what did Christ actually do? Well, I do know this: I read about Jesus Christ, Who was born of the virgin Mary, walking just outside the Temple in Jerusalem one day (John 9). He spat on the ground and, leaning over, made a little ball of clay. Yes, Christ formed a spit wad of clay. Then, placing the clay on the eye sockets of a blind man whose eyes were deformed from birth, He told him to just go to the pool of Siloam and wash it off. When the blind man did that, he found that his eyes were perfectly whole, and for the first time in his life, he could see. I like to think of this as a little *"touch-up job"* done by the creator of the universe, the very same one Who leaned over and enlivened the original form of clay, whom He named Adam.

Now you may think that I have wandered from my original question—"How did God form the spirit in man?" This is really leading up to that aspect of Christ's work.

On another occasion, after the resurrection of Christ, I read of Him "breathing" on the apostles (John 20:22). Now that is an unusual statement. What exactly did Christ do? The text says, *"He breathed on them, and said to them, 'Receive the Holy Spirit'."* The

74

Greek word for breathed is *emphusao*, which means to puff, blow or breathe. Did Christ puff physical wind at them? No, of course not! The substance Christ "breathed" was *"The Holy Spirit."* This is The Divine Substance or, more accurately, Person. The Greek word is *pneuma*, and it means a current of air, breeze or more often, *spirit*. Obviously, in this case, the text says Christ imparted *"the Holy Spirit (pneuma)"* to the apostles. This was done so that they might understand His instructions. Acts 1:2 explains, ". . . He (Christ) through *the Holy Spirit* had given commandments to the apostles. . . ."

Now I strongly suspect that this is the very same type of *"breathing"* Christ did upon the first man—imparting his spiritual nature inside him. Other Scriptures indicate that this is exactly what happened.

In Job 32:8 we are told, *"There is a **spirit** in man, and the **breath** of the Almighty gives them understanding"* (Lit. translation). This is another amazing statement. The Hebrew word for *"spirit"* is *ruwach*, which means wind or, more often, spirit. The word for *"breath"* is *neshamah*, and means breath or spirit, but more often breath. Many Bibles translate the word *neshamah* on this occasion as "inspiration" because that is the sense intended. Man has a receptive spiritual nature and God breathes in the sense of spiritual inspiration for the purpose of giving understanding to man. This is really the same thing Christ did to the apostles.

However, one step further: Job 33:4 says, *"The **Spirit** of God has made me, and the **breath** of the Almighty gives me life"* (Lit. trans.). Here are the same two words, *ruwach* for "Spirit" and *neshamah* for "breath." In this case the "breath" is not for inspiration or understanding, but for his very *"life."* The *"Spirit"* of God is the agent whereby God (or Christ) made man and gave to him the *"breath"* of *"life."* This *"life"* would, of course, be directly related to the *Holy Spirit*, which would mean man also has *spiritual life.* As the word "breath" in context in Job 32:8 is to be understood in the sense of "inspiration," so the word "breath" in Job 33:4 is to be understood in the sense of spiritual "LIFE," itself.

As confirmation of this we read from Job the following, *"For as long as **breath** is in me, and the **Spirit of God** is in **my nostrils**, my lips will not speak unjustly, nor will my tongue utter deceit"*

(Lit. translation, Job 27:3–4). Once again the same two words are employed—*neshamah* (breath) and *ruwach* (Spirit). Only now it is "The ***Spirit of God*** " Who is in Job's "***nostrils***." That, of course, means that Job not only had physical animation "breathed" into him, but in addition he had the very Holy Spirit breathed into his "nostrils" to give him spiritual life. That means, most certainly, Job had an inward spiritual existence or nature and not just physical animation.

By these words we can understand that Job is reflecting back on God's original creation of Adam and "breathing into his nostrils the breath of Life." It is Job's realization that this same "breath of Life" has been passed down to him and to all mankind as well. When Job was created within his mother's womb he received both physical and spiritual life.

This takes us back to the words of Zechariah, "God FORMS the SPIRIT of man WITHIN him" (Zech. 12:1). How does God do it? Initially God did it directly in Adam. Indirectly, God continues to do it through the supernatural work which He designed in pro-creation. God initially, directly "*breathed*" the *spiritual nature* into man and that nature continues to be pro-created in every generation (Job 33:4 and 27:3).

Now we have made a full circle. When the pre-incarnate Word "*breathed into his* [Adam's] *nostrils the breath of life, and man became a living soul*" (Gen. 2:7), we are to understand this to mean a SPIRITUAL life as well as a PHYSICAL life. I personally don't know if it makes any difference or not, but I understand that the word for "*life*" in this verse is in the plural in the Hebrew, and could be translated "*lives*." The one thing I do know for certain, as a result of reading all these Scriptures, is that **when God made man, He made a spiritual nature as well as a physical nature, and God literally "breathed" that spiritual nature into man.** As God enabled man to pass down his physical nature, so man passes down his spiritual nature as well. After the fall of man through Satan's temptation, both the physical nature and the spiritual nature that is passed down to each succeeding generation are tainted by sin and death.

I also know of another Scripture which says, *"The **spirit** of man is the **lamp** of the LORD, **searching** all the inner parts of his being"* (Prov. 20:27). It just so happens that the word translated "spirit" here is again *neshamah* meaning, literally, "breath." It is understood in this context to be a reference to the *spirit* of man. Likewise, this "spirit" is from "the LORD." In this passage the spiritual nature man has received from God is also acting as man's conscience, which is like a *"lamp,"* *"searching"* through the "chambers of the body" (literal translation). This very same action of *"searching"* is what the apostle Paul was inspired to tell us the very Spirit of God does to God's own Person—*"For the Spirit **searches** all things, yes, the deep things of God"* (1 Cor. 2:10). Likewise, Paul reminds us that man's own *"spirit . . . knows the thoughts of man"* (1Cor. 2:11). Indeed, Paul explains that it is by this very activity that man is illuminated by God—*"Now we have received, not the spirit of the world, but the Spirit Who is from God, that we might know the things that have been freely given to us by God"* (1 Cor. 2:12).

Perhaps this is a companion truth to what is also expressed in the gospel of John 1:9—Christ is *"the **true light** which **gives light to** every man who comes into the world."* According to this passage, not just Adam, but every single human being coming into the world receives a God and/or Christ consciousness in his spiritual nature. All men on earth can thus respond to "the light" which has been given to them by God. And, in turn, "If you [any man] seek Him [God], He will be found of you" (1 Chron. 28:9). "For the eyes of the LORD run to and fro throughout the whole earth, to show Himself strong on behalf of those whose heart is loyal to Him" (2 Chron. 16:9). Therefore God has given to every man an amazing provision, and an even more amazing promise of response.

I also know that when man dies, *"Then the **dust** will return to the earth as it was, and the **spirit** will return to God Who gave it"* (Ecc. 12:7). Here again are the two aspects of man's nature. And here again is that word *neshamah*, literally meaning *breath*, but understood as man's separate and distinct spiritual nature. Consequently, it is often translated "spirit." At physical death, the two parts go in two different directions.

It is noteworthy that the "spirit" of man also seems to mark off his difference from the beasts of the field. Though animals are also called souls (*nephesh*), yet it is never stated that God "breathed" into the animals the spirit (*ruah*). Of man alone it is stated that he was "created in the image of God" (Gen. 2:27). We have certainly seen in these passages a spiritual likeness.

We can also remember that the God Who gave us this revelation did so as stated in the language of 2 Timothy 3:16—"*All Scripture is given by inspiration of God, . . .*" Literally translated—"*All Scripture is God-Breathed* [*Theos-pneo*]." In other words, we are to understand that God "breathed" into the consciousness of the human writers by the Holy Spirit in order to "inspire" them in the duty of composing this sacred volume. But, not only did God "inspire" the human writers, He also "enlightens" the readers by the same Holy Spirit in order for them to understand this sacred volume— 1 Cor. 2:12–14.

CHAPTER FIVE

THE NATURE OF
THE NEW NATURE

❧

The NATURE of the NEW CREATION in Christ

O ne of the most beautiful studies in the Word of God, and certainly apropos to the inward nature of every Christian, is the description of the New Birth called in the Bible, *"The New Creation"* (2 Cor. 5:17). As previously observed from the direct teaching of Christ, man's nature is a dichotomy. Man possesses an *outward physical nature* and also an *inward spiritual nature*. As a result of true heart faith in the gospel of Jesus Christ, there is a "New Creation" which God generates in the inner spiritual life of the believer. He is spiritually said to be, in the words of Jesus Christ, *"Born Again."* This can also be rendered *"Born from Above."* The Scriptures will demonstrate that this is language of spiritual realities. Just exactly what is the nature of this New Birth, or "New Creation in Christ," and how does it relate to the theme before us? To answer this question we must once again start by being seated at the feet of the Lord Jesus Christ as He spoke one night to a religious ruler, a Pharisee named Nicodemus.

1.   John 3:3, 6 and 8 "Jesus answered and said to him, 'Most assuredly, I say to you, unless one is ***born again***, *he cannot see the Kingdom of God*.

That which is *born of the flesh is flesh*, and that which is
born of the Spirit is spirit.
The wind blows where it wishes, and you hear the sound
of it, but cannot tell where it comes from and where it
goes; so is everyone who is **born of the Spirit**.'"

The Greek word for "**born**" is *gennaeo*, which basically
means "to generate" or "to pro-create," such as a father would do.
Consequently, the one generating is a person and the one generated must also be a person. Christ is talking about being *generated*
by God the Holy Spirit. The one generated will thus become a
"*child of God*."

It is also important to emphasize that the only possible way an
individual can see the Kingdom of God is to be thus *generated*.
There are no exceptions. This is emphasized three times, "unless
one is born again—of the Spirit" (verse 3, 5 and 7–8).

Nicodemus, of course, could not conceive of the second birth as
another physical birth, so he asked "How can a man be born when
he is old? Can he enter a second time into his mother's womb and be
born?" In clarification, Christ explained that what was "*born of the
flesh was* [only] *flesh*," whereas, "*what is born of the Spirit is spirit*."
In other words, man must have a *regenerated* spiritual nature in order
to see God's Kingdom. The first birth was simply the issuing forth
by means of the "water" of the womb of the mother in the natural
birth process. That natural process produces a fleshly child, whereas
the second birth is spiritual in nature and is issued forth by means of
the Holy Spirit of God Who produces the new spirit person.

As there was a fleshly birth to enter this present world system, so
there must be a *spiritual birth* in order to enter into a proper relationship with God in His Kingdom system. In the very next chapter
Christ explained that "*God is Spirit*, and those who worship Him
must worship *in spirit and truth*" (John 4:24). In order to worship
God, Who is Spirit, one must be "*born of the Spirit*." This birth is
NOT figurative language any more than the fleshly birth was figurative language. To be "*born of the Spirit*" means one becomes a new
baby, a "*Child of God*," as to one's regenerated spiritual nature. It
will become obvious as we continue looking at passages describing

this creation that it is marvelous and enlightening to the new nature of every real Christian. In addition, this will establish beyond any shadow of a doubt that the inward spiritual nature of the believer in Christ is a distinct part of him which will never cease to exist.

2.   John 1:12. 13 "But as many as received Him [Jesus Christ], to them He [God] gave the right to become *children of God*, to those who believe in His name, who *were born* not of blood, nor of the will of the flesh, nor of the will of man, but *of God*."

No matter how hard men may try, whether by flesh and blood, whether by self-will, or the will of some religious discipline, they can never produce a "new birth." Only God can do it, and does do it when men place their faith and trust in Jesus Christ.

This new birth makes one a "child of God" because the birth was directly "from God" and not from any religious ritual or exercise. "Born" as "children of God" is language which is designed by the Holy Spirit to sound precisely like the physical births. The only difference is that this is talking about the births of real spiritual persons. When one places his true faith in Christ, a new *spiritual child* or person is born. "Congratulations," we should say, "for a new baby has come into existence!"

3.   Romans 6:4 and 11 ". . . just as Christ was raised from the dead through the glory of the Father, even so we also should walk in *newness of life*.
        Likewise you also, reckon yourselves to be dead indeed to sin, but *alive to God* in Christ Jesus our Lord."

Before a person's conversion he was said to be dead towards God and/or "dead in trespasses and sins" (Eph. 2:1). His mind was not comprehending the things of God. It is as if God is far off somewhere out of communication. But at his new birth a whole new world of consciousness opens up to him. Like a new child, everything looks new and interesting—he is *"alive to God."* And above all, this new child enjoys and craves the fellowship of God.

4.   2 Corinthians 5:17, 18 "Therefore, if anyone is in Christ, he is a ***new creation***; old things have passed away; behold, all things have become new. Now all things are *of God, . . .*"

The new spiritual birth is a *"new creation."* The *old creation* is my lost Adamic state of being which I received as a result of being connected, through no choice of my own, to my great grandfather, Adam. My *"new creation"* however, is the result of a direct choice of my own, of faith in the Lord Jesus Christ. As a result of our natural connection to fallen Adam, every man is a recipient of a fallen, sinful, spiritual nature. We also have learned that all men, being without God, are existing naturally in a state of "death" (separation from God)—death due to our connection to the first Adam and also due to our own sins. However, as a result of our faith in Christ, Who is called "the second Man" and "the last Adam," we receive a vital regeneration, a new nature that is "ALIVE" to God. Just as God formed man originally of the dust of the ground as to his physical creation, so it is that God is forming *"new creations"* throughout the world by means of the spiritual message of the gospel of the grace of God.

5.   Galatians 6:15 "For in Christ Jesus neither circumcision [the outward religion of the Jews] nor uncircumcision [the idolatry of the pagan world] avails anything, but a NEW CREATION [avails or is really something]!"

Have you seen happy parents just lift up that new baby and exclaim—"Isn't this something!"? Yes, when a new baby is born, it seems that nothing else matters in comparison. Everything else is to be set aside and we all need to celebrate! There is great rejoicing because this baby is really something! So it is with the "new creation in Christ." We shall see the amazing characteristics of this new child.

6.   Colossians 3:9 and 10 ". . . you have put off the old man with his deeds [evil practices], and have put on the *New*

Man who is renewed in knowledge according to ***the image*** of ***the One Who created him.***"

The first question which usually is asked on the occasion of the birth of a newborn baby is, "Who does he look like?" "Well," we might say, "He is the image of his daddy!" And indeed, the newborn child of God bears the "image" of his Father, as well. This image and likeness is obviously spiritual in nature and just as real as the parent. If the "Creator" is a real person, then so is the creature who bears the "image."

7.   1 Peter 2:2 and 3 "*As **newborn babes, desire the pure milk of the Word,** that you may grow thereby, if indeed you have tasted that the Lord is gracious.*"

Thank God, a newborn child of God does not want or need the artificial religious can or bottled milk. His "taste" is truly for the life-giving Word of God to nurture his soul. I personally vividly remember my thirst for the Word of God when I was first saved. I also remember how that Word of divine nurturing began to change my outlook on life and reality.

Therefore, not only does the newborn child of God bear the "image" of his parent, he also begins to act like his parent—

8.   Galatians 2:20 "*I have been crucified with Christ; it is no longer I who live, but **Christ lives in me;** and **the life** which I now live **in the flesh** I live by faith in the Son of God, Who loved me and gave Himself for me.*"

This is another remarkable Scripture. Some have called it "the one verse autobiography of a Christian." From this passage (and others) we learn that a Christian is NOT one who is merely trying to superficially imitate the life of Christ. Many people do this in a very devout religious way. It is futile and empty. The testimony of "Mother Theresa" is a good example. In her memoirs, she tells us she was taught to imitate piety, and she could do this to perfection, drawing the world's attention to herself. Yet, in all this performance she was never conscious of drawing God's attention. There always seemed to be an intense darkness between herself and God, she indicated. It secretly haunted her all her life. God forbid that any real Christian should ever have that kind of a testimony; I don't believe a real Christian could.

In reality, the only one who is a true Christ-ian is one who has **Christ-in-him**. And, indeed, the believer in Christ can walk in his new life, and others will see Christ living in him. Salvation is not by our religious good works. However, when we are saved, we become *"God's workmanship"*—

9.   Ephesians 2:10 *"For we are His workmanship, **created in Christ Jesus** for good works, which God prepared beforehand that we should **walk in them**."*

To parents, perhaps next in importance to whom our child looks like is the time of his learning to walk. And what a privilege it is for a Christian to be able to WALK. And this is a natural part of our new LIFE. If we never learn to walk, there is something seriously wrong. Though we are not saved by our good works (Eph. 2:8, 9), however "Good Works" are the inevitable RESULT of being saved. As stated, we are *"Created for good works."* In fact, we are going to find out that "Good Works" are the *only kind* of works our New Creation can do—

10.   Ephesians 4:22–24 ". . . that you put off, concerning your former conduct *the old man* which grows corrupt according to the deceitful lusts, and *be renewed in the spirit of your mind, and that you put on the **New Man** which was **created according to God**, in righteousness and holiness."*

It is obvious from this revelation that our "New Natures" are just like that of our spiritual parent—perfectly righteous and perfectly holy! It is always great for parents to see their children develop in their own minds and be able to do their own thinking in a right way. The believer's new "minds" understand and love the things of

Christ. Therefore, we will desire to walk in this new perception and outlook on life. So it is, when we walk in that New Life, we will be walking IN CHRIST'S perfect LIFE. All should agree, this is a LIFE worth living!

11.   <u>1 John 3:9</u> "*Whoever has been **born of God does not sin*** [or practice sin], *for **His seed remains in him;** and he **cannot sin,** because **he has been born of God.**"*

Ephesians 4:24 tells us that our "New Man" is perfectly "righteous" and "holy." Now in 1 John 3:9 we learn that the person "born of God" "cannot" be characterized by "sin" because of the nature or "seed" of God in him. The new nature of the believer is sinless. The new nature can only do what is right in Christ because it is "Christ in us." Therefore, for the believer to be submissive to the "seed" life of God in him enables him to be victorious in life. That New Life can only do what is characteristic of God—perfect righteousness.

12.   <u>1 Peter 1:23</u> ". . . having been ***born again,*** not of corruptible seed but ***incorruptible,*** *through the <u>living</u> and <u>abiding Word of God</u>.*"

This truth and revelation gets more amazing all the time. Not only do we have a "New Man" who "cannot sin," but this New Man is "imperishable." That means he will never die! This, of course, is the same as "eternal Life" which Christ promised to all who would trust in Him. This New Life came by the message in the Word of God.

One time a fellow employee, to whom I had been witnessing, asked if I would be willing to go with him and talk to his priest. He was a Roman Catholic and thought his priest would have all the correct answers to the gospel I had presented. So the visit was arranged and, of course, I brought my Bible, the Word of God. When we walked into the priest's office, the priest immediately spied my Bible. The very first thing he said was, "Now, before you open that Bible, I want you to tell me how you know that it is the Word of God." I started to open my Bible anyway and answer, but he stopped me again and repeated his challenge, "Don't open that

Bible yet! First tell me how you know it is the Word of God. It would be useless to use the Bible if you can't first prove that it is the Word of God!" This actually happened a third time, and I realized the priest was absolutely not going to let me open that Bible until I first answered his challenge.

Now I already knew why the priest was doing this. It is Rome's position that "The [Roman] Church" gave us the Bible, and they are the only <u>authority</u> to tell us that it is the Word of God. And, furthermore, they are the only authority to interpret it. Were I to admit to any of this, then of course, it would make no difference if I quoted the Bible, because they, the Roman Church, were the authority to interpret it. So I finally answered the priest this way—

"Sir, for the sake of argument, let me presume that Peter was the first Pope. Now, the 'first Pope' said that we '*are born again by the Word of God*'—1 Peter 1:23. Now I have read a lot of books and other material, and I can assure you they never changed my life. But, when I heard the message of salvation from this book—I was 'Born Again' exactly as Peter said! My life was changed! That is how I know this book is the Word of God! And now I have a question for you—How do you know it is the Word of God?"

The priest silently looked at me for a moment and then said, "This meeting is over with—get out!" and he very angrily ushered us to the door. My friend was paralyzed with unbelief. Outside my friend exclaimed "What happened?" I then explained to him the Roman Catholic position. Furthermore I said, "It is obvious that the priest cannot say that he really knows the Bible is the Word of God because he can't say he is 'born again' and he is left with only the hearsay of his church."

13.   <u>2 Peter 1:4</u> ". . . by which [Divine power, verse 3] have been given to us exceedingly great and precious promises, that through these *you may be partakers of the Divine Nature*, . . ."

There is no better way to describe the new birth than by the fact that God has granted to us human beings, as members of His family—as His very children—to be actual "*partakers of the Divine*

Nature." No wonder our New Nature "cannot sin"! No wonder our New Nature is "created in righteousness and true holiness"! No wonder that New Nature in "imperishable"! As we grow up in Christ we begin to realize that this New Nature is, in fact, "The Divine Nature"!

14. 2 Corinthians 4:16 "Therefore we do not lose heart. Even though our **Outward Man** is *perishing*, yet our **Inward Man** is *being renewed* day by day."

Not only does the believer in Christ possess a "Divine Nature," but this Nature, also called the "Inward Man," is progressively growing and getting stronger each day. This is happening even as our physical fleshly body grows older and weaker every day. There is that well-known cancerous growth which destroys our physical bodies. On the other hand, according to this revelation, there is that growth which renews our spiritual natures every day forever.

15. Ephesians 3:16 "That He would grant you, according to the riches of His glory, to be *strengthened with might* through His Spirit in **the Inner Man**."

Another description of the increasing progress of the New Nature is this passage from Ephesians. "*Strengthened with might or power*" is not a mere slogan on a vitamin box. It is not some propaganda put out by a super muscle-builder program. Rather, it is the reality of the power of the Holy Spirit of God to make every believer increasingly strong in Christ. Every believer can walk in Christ and be a veritable Samson in his victorious life.

In accord with this truth the apostle Paul encourages Timothy to ". . . exercise yourself toward godliness. For bodily exercise profits a little, but godliness is profitable for all things, having the promise of the life that now is and of that which is to come" (1 Tim. 4:7–8). This type of exercise is simply coordination with our New Nature.

16.   Ephesians 4:13, 14 "*. . . till we all come to the unity of the faith and of the knowledge of the Son of God, to a* **Mature Man**, *to the measure of the stature of the fullness of Christ*; that we should no longer be children, . . ."

Although this passage may be speaking of the growth and progress of the collective body of Christ, the whole Church, yet what it states in principle is also understood to be true of the potential for each individual Christian. It is God's intent that we grow up as Christians into mature adulthood and no longer be "children" who are easily confused by different false teachers. Indeed, Paul says that the believer can "**grow up** in all things into Him Who is the Head—Christ" (verse 15).

Of course, the ultimate maturity for the Christian is his glorification—

17.   Colossians 1:27 "*To them God willed to make known what are the riches of the glory of this mystery among the Gentiles, which* is **CHRIST IN YOU—The HOPE OF GLORY**."

"Christ in us" is a person in us. That Person is in us by the Holy Spirit and this is what constitutes our "new nature." The believer has every reason to rejoice because the *New Life* he has in Christ carries with it the unalterable guarantee of the "*Blessed Hope*" of being "*glorified*" with Jesus Christ. In fact, that hope is so certain that the apostle Paul one time spoke of it in the past tense—". . .whom [the lost sinner who trusts Christ] *He justified* [made righteous], *these He also glorified* [resurrected or raptured, receiving a new incorruptible body]. . . ."—Romans 8:30.

I am sure there are many more Scriptures which exemplify the truths about this New Creation we have in Christ, but these should surely suffice to illustrate the fact that the spirit or soul of the regenerated, born-again person will look forward to an "out of body" experience when he dies.

In Summary

Again I say, there are many more descriptive statements about this "New Creation." However, I believe these will suffice to demonstrate the distinctive persons of our new lives in Christ. Any teacher or modern Sadducee who denies the reality of the separate existence of a spiritual person within our physical bodies must, of consistency, be a denier of the Biblical reality of the "New Birth." All these descriptions would then be nothing more than mere figures of speech and thus lose all their essential value.

These many Scriptures trace the whole process of the newborn believer in Christ from his very birth, growth, development, maturity, and finally to being the divine person clothed upon with a glorified body. Look at them again—*"Born again or from above," "A Child of God," "Newness of Life," "Newborn Babes," "A New Creation," "In the Image of God," "Likeness of God," "Imperishable Seed," "Divine Nature," "The Inner Man," "A Mature Man"* and *"Christ in You."*

Not one of these inspired statements which describes the distinctive inward spiritual nature of every believer comes from some "Platonic dualistic philosophy" of Greek mysticism, as some modern Sadducees might claim. They all come right out of the Divine revelation of the Word of God on the specific subject of what is the true nature of man. These modern Sadducees usually claim that the basic error of the "traditionalist" version of Hell is due to a faulty conception of the nature of man. Of course, just the opposite is true. The error of the modern Sadducees is that they must first destroy the truth about the nature of man in order to justify their elimination of the place of eternal conscious punishment.

"Living" Witnesses

Before we turn to the related subject of Hell, as likewise revealed in the Scriptures, I want to bring before you several witnesses to the continued existence of the soul or spirit long after physical death.

1. Luke 9:29–31; Matthew 17:3 and Mark 9:4 "*As He [Christ on the mount of transfiguration] prayed, the appearance of His face was altered, and His robe became white and glistening. And behold two men talked with Him, who were Moses and Elijah, who appeared in glory and spoke of His decease which was about to be accomplished at Jerusalem.*"

Elijah had been bodily transported into heaven. However, every Bible reader knows that Moses died on Mount Nebo and his body was buried by the Lord outside the land of Israel (Deut. 34:1, 5 and 6). Michael the archangel and the Devil even argued over the body of Moses (Jude 9). And yet, here stood Moses talking with our Lord Jesus Christ about His coming suffering in Jerusalem. Did Moses cease to exist when he died? Of course not! Though his body was hidden by God, yet his spirit person still existed.

2. 1 Samuel 28:3, 14–19 "*Samuel*" came up from Sheol and spoke words of truth and soberness. Everything Samuel said was in perfect accord with the revealed will of God. This was clearly the spirit of Samuel. Samuel was then a living, existing spirit being.

3. Luke 16:19–31 We shall examine closely the account of Jesus Christ wherein "*Abraham*" speaks, as did Samuel, words of truth and soberness from the depths of Sheol/ Hades. Abraham was very real and in conscious existence for 2000 years after his physical death according to this passage.

4. Matthew 22:32; Mark 12:26, 27 and Luke 20:37 and 38—"*Abraham, Isaac and Jacob* . . . He is not the God of the dead but of the living.*"

As we saw before, the Sadducees rejected the teaching about the resurrection of the dead, the existence of angels and of spirits, eternal judgment and the suffering of the lost in Hades. In these last three passages above (#4), we have a combined record of this conversation as indicated below. The Sadducees have proposed a question to Christ concerning the resurrection of the dead. They gave a long entangled problem about death and marriage within a family. They thought for sure they had Christ "stumped." However, in response Christ totally shattered their misconceptions—not only about the resurrection, but also about "angels" and the *spirits* of men in existence after death. In doing so, Christ did not quote well-known passages about the resurrection from the Hebrew Scriptures. Instead He quoted a seemingly irrelevant passage—

> *Jesus answered and said to them, 'You are mistaken, not knowing the Scriptures nor the power of God. For in the **resurrection** they neither marry nor are given in marriage, nor can they die anymore, for they are equal to the **angels** and are sons of God, being sons of the resurrection. But concerning the resurrection of the dead, have you not read what was spoken to you by God, saying, "**I am** the God of Abraham, the God of Isaac, and the God of Jacob"? God is not the God of the dead, **but of the living—for all live to Him**.'*
> (From a combination of Matthew 22:29–32 and Luke 20:34–38)

Now, it is true that this whole response was to answer the specific question about the resurrection from the dead. Nevertheless, one can easily see that there is a great deal *more* to Christ's response than just concerning the physical resurrection.

First he stated their ignorance in two fields—that of ignorance of the Scriptures, and equal ignorance of the power of God. Many infidels put problems before God which they think He could never solve in order to explain away a certain proposition which God has made. They simply don't know, at least in their own lives, the ability of God to overcome seeming impossibilities.

Then Christ gave illumination concerning at least three areas of the Sadducees' confusion. Christ not only corrected their misconception of what it will be like in resurrected bodies, but he also equated that aspect with the existence of the *angels*. That certainly flies in the face of their rejection of the existence of angels. Christ spoke of it very casually, almost as an incidental thought. Nevertheless there it is—the clear statement of a reality about angels which they had rejected.

Finally, Christ used a passage where God stated He was "the God of Abraham, the God of Isaac, and the God of Jacob" (Exo. 3:6) and He drew out of this new realizations of implications deep within the passage. He said that this meant "God is not the God of the dead, but of the living." We might well ask the question, "How does the statement 'I am the God of Abraham, Isaac and Jacob' affect the fact of a future resurrection of the dead?" And the answer would simply be—there must be a *future* resurrection to physical life if God is their God—for God is not the God of dead people!

But that is not all this passage means. Since the passage is in the *present tense*, "*I AM* the God of Abraham, Isaac and Jacob," it means as well that God is *right THEN* their God. And if God is presently their God, then these people ARE NOW IN EXISTENCE; they are "*living*"—"for all men live to Him." And this is what the rest of the passage says according to Luke's account. This answers squarely their false doctrine of annihilation and the nonexistence of spirits. It means that men like Abraham, Isaac and Jacob are spiritually alive to God! This conclusion is just as realistic as the conclusion that there must be a resurrection to physical life.

So now we have the witness of *Isaac* and *Jacob* along with that of *Abraham*, *Moses* and *Samuel*.

5.   Matthew 26:63–65 and Mark 14:61–63 **The High Priest and the Sanhedrin.**

One final word about "witnesses" which demonstrates the existence of individuals after the fact of their physical deaths. Christ made another amazing statement at the time of His trial before the High Priest and the various rulers of Israel. We need to remember that the High Priest was a Sadducee who supposedly did not believe in the existence of the soul after physical death.

Christ would not answer any of the accusations that the various witnesses brought against Him. He really didn't need to since their testimonies seemed to bring more confusion than fact. No doubt, in somewhat of a frustration, the High Priest finally said, "Are You the Christ, the Son of the Blessed?" And to this Christ did respond, no doubt, to their utter amazement! *"I am. And **YOU WILL SEE** the Son of Man sitting on the right hand of the Power, and coming with the clouds of heaven"* (Mark 14:62).

Just think of it! The High Priest himself and all the Sanhedrin, who were then judging Christ, are going to be IN EXISTENCE at the time of Christ's glorious second coming in great power to rule on the earth and they themselves will see that spectacular event. Now we all know that physically they have long been dead. No one believes they are physically alive to this very day, which is some two thousand years later. Nevertheless, according to Christ's words they will be *consciously in existence* to witness that spectacular event! How is this possible if they have long been dead? Some might argue that they will be resurrected from the dead in order to behold this event. That is not the answer because the Scripture reveals that the bodily resurrection of the lost will not take place until after the thousand year reign of Christ—Revelation 20:1 and 12–14. The only possible answer is, of course, what I am going to be contending for in this study—their souls, their non-material persons, would be in conscious existence in Hades at the time of Christ's glorious second coming, and thus they will observe this great event!

No wonder the High Priest tore his garment and exclaimed— "What need do we have of any further witnesses?"

SECTION TWO

THE BIBLICAL DOCTRINE OF ETERNAL JUDGMENT
Hebrews 6:2

"Have the gates of Death been revealed to you,
or have you seen the gates of the deep darkness?"
Job 38:17

"Can you discover the limits of the Almighty?
They are high as the heavens, what can you do?
Deeper than Sheol, what can you know?"
Job 11:7–8

"If I ascend to Heaven, You [God] are there;
if I make my bed in Sheol, behold, You are there"
Psalm 139:8

"Though they dig into Sheol,
from there will My hand take them;
and though they ascend to heaven,
from there will I bring them down."
Amos 9:2

"Sheol and Abaddon [Destruction] lie open before the LORD,
how much more the hearts of men!"
Proverbs 15:11

Most translations in this Section
are from the New American Standard Bible
unless otherwise stated.

Many of the references have been
crosschecked with an interlinear
and/or compared with other translations
and lexicons to ensure accuracy.

CHAPTER SIX

INTRODUCTION

THERE IS A HELL!

"Have the gates of death been revealed to you,
or have you seen the gates of the deep darkness?"
Job 38:17

The passage above is actually a rhetorical question which the LORD asked Job. It was in a series of questions designed by God to illustrate the maximum impossibility of Job, or any other human being, for that matter, to answer. In man's quest for seeing into and beyond the *"gates of death,"* mortals are totally dependent upon God for clear revelation.

One of Job's friends (Zophar) had earlier asked him a somewhat similar question with these words, *"Can you discover the **limits** of the Almighty? They are high as the **heavens**, what can you do? Deeper than **Sheol**, what can you know?"* (Job 11:7–8). To Zophar these two extremes illustrated man's natural inability to even comprehend God. The highest *"Heaven"* on the one hand, and *"Sheol"* (translated "Hell" in most English Bibles) on the other, are both realms which are obviously out of sight and completely out of reach of man's natural capability to explore and know. Interestingly enough, this very comparison is a revelation in itself to alert those who may doubt the reality of Hell or Sheol. No spiritually intelligent person would want to say that "Heaven" does not actually exist, that it is not a real place. Obviously, Heaven exists! This seems to be one thing on which all agree; it is God's dwelling place with all the angelic hosts. In a similar manner, no spiritually intelligent person should want to say that "Sheol" does not actually exist, that it is not a real place with occupants. Obviously Hell exists; no matter what the mystery, gloom or horror it holds, there it is and there it will stay on the pages of Scripture. "Heaven" is not a figure of speech and neither is "Sheol" (Hell) a mere figure of speech.

There is another interesting parallel between the two contrasting places. On the one hand we learn that while Heaven is God's own dwelling place and the dwelling place of innumerable holy angels, yet we discover in the Scriptures that *evil* angelic spirits are also temporarily in Heaven (see Job 1:6–12 as an example). In the process of time we shall learn that the evil angelic beings will be expelled from Heaven (Rev. 12:7–9). That is interesting because in a similar manner we shall see that Hell or Sheol was the residence of the spirits of the dead, primarily the lost. Yet the Scriptures also reveal that as heaven is the temporary residence of evil angelic beings, so Hell was also the temporary residence of the spirits of the *righteous* dead in an area of protection. However, in the process of time (at Christ's resurrection and ascension) the righteous were removed from Sheol to Heaven.

About one millennium after Job, Solomon, by inspiration, affirmed that God alone knows all the answers about "Sheol." Solomon said, "*Sheol and Abaddon* [Destruction] *lie open before the LORD, how much more the hearts of men!*" (Prov. 15:11) In other words, God, Who alone knows all about *Sheol* like an open book and will reveal many things about it, likewise has no problem seeing into the innermost hearts of men. This comparison on Solomon's part raises some important and interesting questions. Everyone can see and interpret the outward expressions made by men in the physical realm. Those outward facial expressions are supposed to show us a person's attitude. That seems to be quite simple. However, often these physical expressions and words may be hypocritical and beguiling to those looking on. Yet there is another realm in man and that part of man is *inward* and out of sight to others. It is known only by the man himself and by God Who looks upon the inward person. The reality of man's heart is no secret to God. The inward heart of man is an intricate maze of complexities all falling within the perimeter of spiritual realities and dimensions. This comparison that Solomon made would indicate to us that Sheol, likewise, is filled with spiritual realities and dimensions which are out of sight to mankind. God alone can know and reveal them to us.

This comparison between Heaven and Hell (or Sheol) is made at least three times in the Hebrew Scriptures. This ratifies the fact that Sheol is a positive reality, and not a mere figure of speech, according to the Thrice-Holy God.

> *Can you discover the depths of God?*
> *Can you discover the limits of the Almighty?*
> > *They are high as the **heavens**, what can you do?*
> > *Deeper than **Sheol**, what can you know?* (Job 11:7–8).

> *If I ascend to **Heaven**, You* [God] *are there;*
> *If I make my bed in **Sheol**, behold,*
> > *You are there* (Psalm 139:8).

> *Though they dig into **Sheol**,*
> > *from there will My hand take them;*
> *and though they ascend to **Heaven**,*
> > *from there will I bring them down* (Amos 9:2).

There we have it! If we believe in Heaven, we must also believe in Hell (Sheol). The Scriptures make it very plain that Sheol is an ultimate place—the opposite of Heaven. As was indicated in the book of Job, no man can discover Heaven, not even by going into outer space. Right now, in our modern age, men have gone only as far as the moon. In light of the actual size of the universe, man's going to the moon is a pitiful reminder of his total inability to get to Heaven. Of course man cannot *"climb into Heaven"* (NKJV). Not even our largest and most powerful telescopes can discern any evidences of Heaven. Heaven is in the spiritual realm, far beyond man's capacity to reach. It is God's dwelling place. Likewise, no one can possibly *"dig into Sheol"* as suggested above. Any hole we would make on the earth would be but a pinprick to the thought of man's descent into the deep *"heart of the earth"* (Matt. 12:40) where Hell is said to be located. The molten bowels of the earth take it totally out of man's ability to explore. It can not be seen with our physical eyes. Like Heaven, Hell is in the spiritual realm. Sheol (Hell) has spirit occupants who are nonmaterial. Both regions are therefore "Off Limits" to mankind with his present limitations. We are totally dependent upon God's revelation for all our information.

Now we know that God's Word reveals a lot about Heaven. However, most of this information is totally beyond our limited capacity to comprehend and appreciate at this time. Likewise, we must totally depend upon God to reveal anything regarding the nature and reality of Sheol, commonly called "Hell" in the English Bibles.

These two zones which are "Off Limits" to man are not "Off Limits" to God. As Heaven is a *Place with realities*—so Hell is a *Place with its own realities*. As Heaven has *occupants*—so Hell has *occupants*. As Heaven is occupied by myriads of *spirit intelligences*—so we shall find that Hell is occupied by myriads of *spirit intelligences*. As we can read in the Bible of *conversations and interactions* in Heaven—so we will read in the Bible of *conversations and interactions* in Hell!

This will NOT be a study of what theologians, philosophers, sociologists, historians, so-called "church fathers," various schools of thought, or pseudo-scriptures have said about Hell. If you are looking for that information, you will not find it here!

This is a BIBLE STUDY of what the BIBLE reveals about the subject. In other words, this is a study which will go directly to the only source giving to us the actual original, inspired, detailed, written information from God about the subject.

I am not saying that the Bible is the only source of revelation about Hell and the afterlife. The Bible itself tells us that the revelations about God and the spiritual realms are also revealed in the physical creation (Romans 1:18–22; Acts 14:15–17; 17:23–31, etc.), in the inner spiritual consciousness of man (Romans 2:14; 1:32; John 1:9; Prov. 20:27: Job 32:8, etc.) and even in the moral and social societies which God has ordained (Romans 13:1–7). Therefore, it is no accident that the consciousness of an afterlife is present in nearly every society on the face of the earth. However, this revelation is often confused and distorted through pagan traditions, whereas the Biblical revelation has remained stable and complete.

In our Bibles we are able to read for ourselves the actual information and ask for God's Holy Spirit to guide our hearts in understanding it. In this study I have gathered enough Biblical information on the subject to make a very comprehensive conclusion about Hell. Amazing as it may seem, God has actually promised to help us make such a discernment—"There is a *spirit* in man, and the *breath* [inspiration] of the Almighty gives him understanding" (Job 32:8).

It is my prayer and purpose that you will appreciate and be sobered by this revelation. To emphasize, throughout this study I will be capitalizing the word Hell and all the other various descriptive names which are given about it. The admonition from the apostle Paul to the young Thessalonian assembly is always apropos—"But examine everything carefully" or "Test [or prove] all things; hold fast to that which is good" (1 Thess. 5:21).

An Introduction to
THE BASIC WORDS

You can rest assured that there are many other words and descriptions concerning the subject of Hell which are used in the Scriptures other than these few basic words. We will discover these other terminologies as we traverse through this study. However, it is essential to get a background knowledge of these basic words which are commonly used in both the Hebrew Scriptures, the Greek Scriptures and even our English translation of the Bible. Like the words for "soul" and "spirit," many false teachers will only point out a one-sided definition of the words for Hell and fail to give their contextual use and definitions as used in the Scriptures on this subject.

In defining these basic words I will start with our own English word for Hell and then go back in order to the Greek and Hebrew words.

"Hell" is an English word which is found many times in our English Bibles. Our English dictionaries say that the word is derived from the old Middle English *helan*. *Helan* originally simply meant *"to cover or conceal."* Some dictionaries will further point out that *Hell* is the English word used to translate the Greek word *"Hades"* which was used in the Greek translation of the Hebrew Scriptures and in the Greek New Testament. Of course this word *Hell* took upon itself a distinctive meaning when it was used to translate the Scriptural words for Sheol or Hades. As a result of the Greek Old and New Testaments, *Hell,* as commonly used today in the English world, has reference to the underworld abode of the spirits of the dead and is a place of punishment by fire for the wicked after death. This is the most popular understanding and definition of *Hell* in the Judao-Christian faiths (and also in the religion of Islam). As in the original meaning of *helan*, Hell is indeed "out of sight" and "concealed" to the eyes of mankind. However, no one should be shallow enough to think that the Biblical "Hell" simply means "to cover, conceal or be out of sight." Like the Biblical word "spirit," though the original Greek simply means "wind or breath," we know it is used in Scripture of personal beings—of God, the Holy Spirit, angelic creatures, demonic creatures and of man's inner self. So it is with the word Hell—the inspired Scriptures give additional specific and unique definitions to the word.

"Hades" is the Greek word which primarily has virtually the same meaning as the English word *helan*. We understand from Greek lexical works that *"Hades"* originally simply meant *"hidden or out of sight."* And interestingly enough, similar to the evolution of the English word *helan*, it was also true that the Grecian world, even long before the time of Christ, came to think of and commonly spoke of *Hades* as the abode of the disembodied spirits of the dead. They came to this understanding and usage completely independent from any Scriptural meaning. It was based upon their own cultural and philosophic persuasion. Indeed, this definition of *Hades,* as the realm of disembodied spirits, had become a native idea in their culture long before Christianity; neither was it derived from the Hebrew Scriptures. This fact has been known in other ancient cultures as well. As I said before, some dictionaries will point out that *Hell* in our English Bibles is the translation of, and the equivalent of, the Greek word *Hades.* Thus the English word *Hell,* both by its basic original meaning and its later theological meaning, became an excellent translation for the Greek word *Hades.*

Some who deny the traditional teachings in Christianity about Hell have tried to say that certain early "church" leaders merely borrowed the pagan Greek philosophers' ideas about the soul of man and Hades and brought them over into Christianity. This is really a blatant falsehood. On the one hand, that certain early so-called "church fathers" borrowed some pagan ideas and brought them over into Christianity, no one doubts. Yet on the other hand, that the Grecian ideas about Hades or the soul of man became the source and origin of the Christian doctrine about Hades and the soul of man is far-fetched, with no actual evidence whatsoever. As we shall see, it is in fact a crafty attempt to deny the reality of the Scriptural source of the teaching.

The fact is that early Christians produced the Greek Scriptures and sometimes used the Greek word *Hades* to describe the abode of disembodied spirits after death. This was done for several reasons. First of all, the Jewish translators of the Hebrew Scriptures into Greek had *already* translated the Hebrew *Sheol* by the Greek word **Hades.** They believed the words basically carried the same meaning. Secondly, the Christian writers (most of them Jewish) of the Greek New Testament understood the *similarities* between *Sheol* of the Hebrew world and *Hades* of the Greek world. Since the Greek translation of the Hebrew Scriptures previously employed the use of *Hades,* which already had a similar understanding which the Greek world had about *Hades,* the inspired writers of the New Testament simply were led to retain its use. Of course, *Hades* in the Greek translation of the Hebrew Scriptures and in the Greek New Testament must be understood in the light of its usage in those Scriptures and not by any pagan extremes or distortions.

I say again, the Grecian world already believed that Hades was the realm of disembodied spirits of the dead. Since that is the inherent meaning of the Greek word as used in the New Testament, this has become a hard pill to swallow for those disenchanted with that meaning. In fact, one lexicographer (Bullinger, *A Critical Lexicon And Concordance To The English and Greek New Testament*, page 367), openly bemoaned the fact that the writers of the Greek New Testament used what he called a "heathen" word (Hades), which "was surrounded with heathen traditions," and was already loaded with meaning which he did not believe was inspired of God (Bullinger did not believe in the traditional view of Hell). Of course, if the New Testament writers did this, then they certainly were not inspired by the Holy Spirit in their choice of words. However, I think most Christians believe that those writers of the New Testament Scriptures were indeed led of the Holy Spirit in their choice of words—including *Hades*. Therefore men who believe like Bullinger on this subject must remain with their enigma.

Of course, this was not the only Greek word the writers of the New Testament used, but it was an important one. We shall see later, among many other descriptions, they also used the word *Gehenna* for a final aspect of Hell and once the word, *Tartarus*. We will explore the definitions of those words when we come to Part Two: the Greek Scriptures.

"Sheol"—As *Hell* is the English translation of the Greek word *Hades*, so it is that *Hades* is the Greek translation of the Hebrew word *Sheol*. Consequently, the definition of *Sheol* would be the same as *Hades—the abode of the disembodied spirits of the dead*. However, I will give an extensive definition and explanation of this Hebrew word *Sheol* in chapter seven, and a very complete Scriptural definition in chapter eleven. For now it is important to remember that even before Christianity came upon the scene, the Hebrew Scriptures had been translated into the Greek language which was the international language of the time. For several hundred years before Christ, many of the Jewish peoples had been scattered throughout the world and no longer spoke the Hebrew language. Once the Hebrew Scriptures were translated into Greek, the Jews of the dispersion could read the

Scriptures in that language. This was done approximately 200 years before Christ. In addition, many Gentile peoples in the Grecian and Roman worlds wanted to hear the beauty of the Hebrew prophets in the language they could understand. This translation was called the Septuagint and is also spoken of as the LXX. In that translation the Greek word *Hades* became the consistent rendering of the Hebrew word *Sheol*. In other words, the Hebrew translators recognized the Greek word *Hades* as the equivalent in meaning of the Hebrew word *Sheol* which was often used in the Hebrew Scriptures to describe the abode of the spirits of the dead in past ages. This, of course, is not the only description used in the Hebrew Scriptures for this residence, but it is certainly the most important one. When we study the Hebrew Scriptures we will note at least fourteen other designations for Hell or Sheol.

Herein we have the derivation of several of the most important words on the subject—*Sheol*, Hebrew; ***Hades***, Greek; and ***Hell***, English. The final form of Hell is expressed by the Greek word ***Gehenna***. Some would prefer to classify only Gehenna as Hell. In this Bible study I will say that *Gehenna* is the final form of Hell. As I stated above, I will give more attention and explanation of that word and its equivalent description when we come to the revelation from the Greek Scriptures.

In the Bible itself, the subject of *Hell,* though sometimes spoken of as the residence for the righteous after death, is most often associated in context with the themes of death, destruction, wrath, judgment, punishment, eternal condemnation and, as we shall see, is sometimes associated with and described as a suffering in flames of fire.

Because of the extremely sensitive nature of this subject you can well believe that there are many objections to it and/or different versions of it. Atheists, rationalists and humanists rail against Hell as a base superstition of a barbaric *god* who sadistically enjoys torturing people forever. Sad to say, certain "Christian" groups believe the same thing. Efforts have been made by certain religious, liberal and cultic groups to eliminate it altogether. Some other professed orthodox believers have attempted to make certain qualifications of it, or have reinterpreted the subject to fit what they believe would be a more satisfactory balance of justice by a loving and gracious God. Thus it is, in addition to "The Traditional View," there have come to be what is called "The Conditional View" and "The Metaphorical View" and other combinations. In this Bible study I want to do everything in my power to discover and ascertain "**The Biblical View.**"

In addition, we have understood that there are other subjects which are interrelated with the subject of Hell which we have already dealt with—such as "What is the nature or full composition of man?" We have already seen that when God created man, he did not merely animate a pile of dust. We saw that man possesses a spiritual nature which consciously exists after death, apart from the body. We discussed "immortality" and what exactly is the nature of death itself. We saw that "death" does not mean "annihilation" or "cessation of being." We will yet explore the question of what exactly do the words "eternal" or "everlasting" mean, and "can God be justified in sending people to Hell?" Last, but not least, we must know how the gospel of Christ relates to the subject of Hell. And this issue of the *gospel,* I think, is more important than most students of the subject realize. Therefore, we will begin our study with—

THE GOSPEL OF CHRIST

Make no mistake about it; the Bible reveals—there is a Hell! And today the only occupants of Hell are the lost or unsaved. But equally clear is the remarkable revelation that *no one will go to Hell directly because of his sins*! In the body of the revelation of Scripture is the gospel of Jesus Christ the Lord. That gospel tells us that Jesus Christ intervened on man's behalf and **paid the direct and full penalty** for all the sins of the entire world for all the ages (John 1:29 and 1 John 2:2). Yes, indeed, Christ actually took the sinners' place! On Him was placed all the guilt and penalty of sin (Isa. 53:6). In fact, "He [God] made Him Who knew no sin to be sin on our behalf, so that we might become the righteousness of God in Him" (2 Cor. 5:14–21). Yes, the Bible reveals that Jesus Christ was "cursed" by God as our substitute, that we might not "perish" (Gal. 3:13 and John 3:16–17).

On the singular most climactic day of each year on Israel's liturgical calendar, called the great Day of Atonement, the "scapegoat" had all the sins of Israel placed upon it and was led out bearing those sins into the wilderness of abandonment (see Lev. 16). Israel thereby received ritual "atonement" for another year. So it is, the Scriptures reveal that *"once at the climax of the ages"* (Lit. trans., Heb. 9:26) the antitypical scapegoat, Jesus Christ, had placed upon Himself all the sins of mankind, and He bore them out into that wilderness of abandonment in Hell, cursed and forsaken by God.

Thus, the Eternal, Divine Son suffered the equivalent of a universal death in the sinners' place for all mankind. The wrath of God poured over His soul (Matt. 27:46; Ps. 42:7 and 88:6) until the just punishment against sin was satisfied in the court of Heaven. Through the Divine sacrifice of Christ, God was both *"just and the justifier of the one who has faith in Jesus"* (Rom. 3:26). God's justice against sin was manifested in the person of our substitute Who suffered in our place. For all who put their faith and trust in this sacrifice of Jesus Christ on their behalf are consequently exempt from the guilt and penalty of sin and are thereby said to be "justified," and "shall not come into condemnation" (John 5:24).

This is the everlasting gospel. It was foreshadowed for four thousand years of human history through the animal sacrifices practiced by nearly every nation and society on the face of the earth. The grace and merciful kindness of God was likewise seen in the testimony of creation and also in the inner consciousness of mankind. Christ is thus *"the true light that enlightens every man who comes into the world"* (See NASB footnote, John 1:9). Thus, the Creator of heaven and earth, Who chose to allow sin to enter into the world in the first place, also chose to take total responsibility for sin by paying the direct penalty for it Himself, through the agency of His "only begotten Son," the antitypical "Lamb of God Who takes away the sin of the world" (John 1:29). So, I say again, amazing as it may seem, no one is going to go to Hell directly because of his sins; Christ was God-forsaken, damned and paid the penalty for sin as the sinners' substitute. This is the revelation of the Gospel.

Why Then, Will People Today Go To Hell??

Notably, there was *one sin* that Christ did not die for; that is the sin of unbelief and rejection of God's merciful kindness. It makes no difference how that grace has been revealed to him—whether by the Scriptures, creation or conscience. Even the Scriptures reveal that God's merciful kindness has been available to all ages and societies (Romans 10:18 and Psalm 19:1–4). And now my friend, if anyone goes to Hell it is only because he chooses to "not receive the love of the truth" (2 Thess. 2:10). That "truth" is the revelation of God's grace for salvation. No one goes to Hell accidentally! No one goes to Hell inadvertently! No one goes to Hell except *by choice*!

The revelation of God's will that "none should perish" (2 Pet.3:9) is abundant throughout all history and time. In addition to the revelation of the Hebrew and Greek Scriptures, the mercy of God on the sinners' behalf is also revealed in the very consciousness of every soul (Rom. 2:14, 15). As said earlier, Christ "is the light that enlightens every man who comes into the world" (John 1:9). The character and grace of God is likewise revealed in all the physical creation (Ps. 33:18 and Rom. 1:19–22). So, it is a fact that no one goes to Hell by chance—*but by choice. "This is the judgment that the light has come into the world, and men loved darkness rather than light."* (John 3:19).

Consequently, in the gospel of Jesus Christ not only can the sinner be "justified" in the sense of being "made right" (salvation), but God is also "justified" in the sense of being "declared right" (1 Tim. 3:16; Rom. 1:16; 3:4 and Luke 7:29) in all His counsels and provisions concerning the destiny for mankind. In reality, therefore, no one goes to Hell except by choice—the conscious choice to reject the goodness and mercy of God's gracious provision—and continue in his sins and rebellion.

Some People Need Convincing!

Many people in the world, and in this country in particular, don't even think they are sinners. Yet we realize that right here in this great, civilized, so-called "Christian" nation, the United States of America, there has been the veritable blood bath of over 45 million unborn infants aborted in the last 35 years. The womb of the mother, instead of being the God-ordained *chamber of life*, has become instead the *chamber of death*. This holocaust comes because of a blinding selfishness and is the inevitable result of a hedonistic society which has capitalized on the pleasures of the sexual act, while evading the God-ordained responsibility for the life or new creation, which comes as the result of that act. Thus the *act of pro-creation*, in our enlightened, pleasureful society, has become for many the *act of pro-abortion*. Does anyone really think America will not have to answer for this perverse wickedness? Do you really think the Scriptures warn in vain—"*Do not be deceived, God is not mocked; for whatever a man sows, this shall he also reap*" (Gal. 6:7)?

Germany was one of the most—if not the most—educated, enlightened nations on the face of the earth in the 1930s and 40s. Nevertheless, it experienced a veritable baptism of fire upon most of its fine cities by the end of World War II. Historians have recorded the consciousness of thousands of Germany's citizens who instinctively recognized that this "fiery hell" they were experiencing was the equitable consequence of their merciless destruction of six million Jews. Do we, here in this United States, really think that since our abortions were carried out under the guise of "pro-choice," with clinical sanctity and silence, that we have evaded the judgment from God because of this? Is this stupidity not the ungodly result of a prosperous nation which, instead of being "thankful" (Rom. 1:21, 22), became ungrateful and hedonistic? Millenniums ago God spoke by the prophet saying, "*Behold, this was the iniquity of . . . Sodom: . . . pride, fullness of bread and abundance of idleness, . . .*" (Ezek. 16:49, NKJV). And I might add that such perversions as were in Sodom and Gomorrah are in this country also reaching the magnitude of judgment.

By God's matchless grace and overruling providence, the atonement of every single one of those aborted babies has been secured by the virtue of Christ's substitutionary sacrifice, which none of those infants could ever have rejected. Likewise, all the infants of Sodom are safe from the eternal condemnation of Hell. Yet, the very liberal, modern propagandizers who perpetuate this perverted, philosophical *"freedom of choice"*—this wicked crime of hypocritical clinical murder—will go to the destiny of their *"free choice"* as well; for to "choose" the clear violation of God's law and to consciously reject the gospel of Christ is, indeed, to "freely choose" eternal damnation. Merely to choose the destruction of *another*, is potentially to choose *your own*. When men reject the payment Christ made for their sins and choose to abide in their sins, they will die *"in their sins"* and suffer the consequence of their rejection according to the magnitude of their sins.

At the conclusion of the second world war, an investigator stood outside one concentration camp through which he had taken a tour. He happened to be an atheist. He shook his head as if to rid himself of the horrible, unbelievable and unbearable sights he had seen and smelled. He had seen firsthand the utter depravity of man—the vile depths of man's inhumanity to man—by the most educated, enlightened nation on earth, at this apex of human history. Then he was overheard to say, "there may not be a heaven—

—but there has to be a Hell!"

This expression represented the instinctive inclination in man to demand a just retribution for those responsible for such wickedness. Indeed, the very combatants in the Second World War realized that such retribution was forthcoming. Even before the war was over, proclamation was issued by the victorious forces that justice would be brought to those responsible for the atrocities which were being discovered.

Actually one shall find that our modern civilization's own judicial system is patterned after the judgment of Hell as revealed in the Bible. Some people may be shocked to realize this; nevertheless, it is true. Normally when one in our society, who has committed a heinous crime, is caught by the police he is placed in a *temporary* jail or confinement. He normally remains in very undesirable and sometimes very unpleasant conditions until such time as his trial. At the conclusion of his judgment his final sentencing is made. Then *permanent disposition* in prison is assessed and assigned based on the magnitude of his crime. He will be isolated from society, of course, out of socio-cultural necessity.

So it is in the Biblical descriptions concerning Hell. There is, first of all, the *"prison house"* for the disembodied spirits of mankind after physical death. In the Hebrew Scriptures this is most often called *"Sheol."* In the Greek Scriptures it is called *"Hades."* Up until the glorious resurrection of Christ from Hades and death, there was also a section of Sheol or Hades which was the holding place for the souls of the righteous. However, they remained in quiet and comfort. At Christ's ascension, they were taken by Him and transferred to heaven. All the rest of the souls of mankind remain in Hades or Hell and more are gathered there every day until the final Judgment. At the *"Great White Throne Judgment"* the Bible reveals that the final sentencing will be made. Then righteous judgment will be made so that the lost will suffer only according to their iniquity—some more, some less. At that time all those souls will be cast into the final and *"eternal"* Hell called *"Gehenna—the Lake of Fire."*

As I said before, no one could do away with the reality of Hell any more than he could do away with the reality of Heaven. Now I will also say, one could no more do away with the reality of Hell than he could do away with the reality of civilization's necessary execution of judgment and the establishment of prisons of confinement for the law breakers who are, then and thereby of necessity, segregated outside law-abiding society; only thus can society be preserved. Without the necessary proper judgment and confinement, society would end up with a total lack of fear and respect, and the inevitable total defilement, barbarity and ultimate catastrophe would occur. Just think what would happen if we resurrected all the world's devil-inspired conquerors, like Adolph Hitler, Joseph Stalin, Mao Tse-Tung, etc., and then emptied all the prisons all over the world and said to all the liberated ones, "enjoy yourselves." I think most of us would want a transfer to Mars, if that were possible. In like manner, think of this universe if evil were not thus segregated.

To me, one of the most amazing things revealed in the Bible about the ultimate Hell is that though evil is totally segregated out of the New Heavens and Earth, ye*t evil does not cease*—for it is said, *"He who is unjust, let him be unjust still; he who is filthy, let him be filthy still. . .outside are dogs and sorcerers and sexually immoral and murderers and idolaters, and whosoever loves and practices a lie"* (Rev. 22:11, 15, NKJV). Like most men in prison, their evil dispositions may not be changed, but nevertheless, they are confined with their own society. Yes, the final Hell will not be a purifying place; instead it will be the continuation of all that is ungodly and unholy in confinement and judgment. Yes, those who have rejected the Lord Jesus Christ, and/or the revelation of God's merciful kindness, have indeed the association of their choice. Of course, without Jesus Christ it is, most certainly, not the paradise of their delusion, but rather the opposite.

One atheistic evolutionist "summarized" his philosophy of life, based upon his evolutionary views, this way—"There are no gods, no purposes, and no goal-directed forces of any kind. There is no life after death. When I die, I am absolutely certain that I am going to be dead. That is the end of me. There is no ultimate foundation for ethics, no ultimate meaning to life, and no free will for humans, either. What an intelligent idea." (Evolutionary biologist William Provine of Cornell University—*Origins Research 16(1):9*, 1994, by W. B. Provine.)

What a surprise Dr. Provine is going to have! This is not only a stupid unreality in this life, but most certainly for the next. The "intelligent idea" he has come to embrace is actually a modern day dope or drug, which brought him into a stupor as to the realities of what life and death actually are. The purpose of this Biblical study is to look upon things Provine cannot see through his laboratory microscope or through his philosophically tinted glasses.

However, you would be surprised at how many cults (the so-called "Jehovah Witnesses," the "Seventh Day Adventists," the "World Wide Church of God," "Christadelphians," etc.) and how many supposedly orthodox "Christian preachers" are now advocating this view of death—that death simply means cessation of being, the very end of it all—the opposite of life. Consequently, these loving, sweet, tender preachers are happy to tell us there is no real penalty for rejecting God's grace, other than death itself, which, by the way, is the common end of everybody.

My friend, if this view of death were true then I, too, would reject any notion of God, or any idea of an ultimate purpose to life, or any thought of consequence for disobedience. At least the atheistic evolutionist is consistent!

Yes, there is a "Hell." The Bible exposes its inner domain. In the Scriptures we are told of its location, contents, torments and final stage. The reader of the Scriptures will even be allowed to hear conversations by its occupants. We shall also see that the most loving person on the face of the earth, Christ Jesus the Lord, talked about it and warned of the consequences of rejecting the offer of God's forgiveness and cleansing more than any other character in the pages of Scripture.

"Shall not the Judge of all the earth do right?"
Genesis 18:25

"O God, the God of the *spirits* of all flesh, . . ."
Numbers 16:22; and 27:16

"Behold, You desire *truth* in the *inward parts*,
and in the *hidden part* You will make me to know *wisdom*."
Psalm 51:6

Are You Ready To Take a Tour— Of the Biblical Revelation?

PART ONE

THE HEBREW SCRIPTURES

CHAPTER SEVEN

WELCOME TO SHEOL

❧

Welcome to "SHEOL"—
that is, the study of Sheol

TRANSLATIONS

The singular most important word in the Hebrew Scriptures which designates the place of conscious existence of the spiritual natures of mankind after physical death is the word "Sheol." We shall see that at least seven times "departed spirits" are said to be in "Sheol." *Sheol* is not the only word in the Hebrew Scriptures used in this regard, but it is the first and primary one. For our examination, therefore, I will list all the passages wherein that particular word is used. You can go back and read the context for each passage as you have time and interest. As we go along we will note other words and descriptions of Sheol which are used in the same context. We will study them carefully because they add to and complement any conclusion to be made. In fact, I will not make a formal definition of Sheol until we have concluded our survey of its use in the Hebrew Scriptures. After this investigation I think there should be no doubt in anyone's mind as to its meaning.

Recently I opened a web site by a reputable Seventh Day Adventist organization. The organization stated rather emphatically that "Sheol" simply means *"grave."* What they should have said, if they were at all honest about the subject, is that some people today have translated the word on *certain occasions* as "grave," but this is not at all the primary definition which Hebrew lexicons give. Nor could "grave" possibly be the definition if, as I have previously stated, the Greek word "Hades" was its equivalent.

Probably the translators of the King James Version of the Bible caused a lot of unnecessary confusion. The same word *Sheol* is used 65 (some say 66) times in the Hebrew text and the King James translators rendered it "Hell" 31 times, the "grave" 31 times and the "Pit" 3 times. There is actually no firm basis for these differences other than the translators' perceptions and/or what appear to be superficial presumptions. Remember, as I stated earlier, the Hebrew translators rendered the word into Greek almost always by the Greek word *Hades*. To the Hebrew translators, this word was very consistently understood to carry the modern meaning of our present word "Hell." However, other English translators, even some modern ones, fumbled as well, if not worse (namely, those translating the New International Version) than the King James translators.

However, the Revised Version and the American Revised Version of 1901 caught and began to arrest the errors. The New American Standard Bible and the New Revised Standard Version continue to set the pattern for consistently transliterating the word into English as "Sheol." These are excellent translations of the Hebrew Scriptures. By doing this, the revisers were extremely helpful to those reading the sacred text, because in truth and by the Holy Spirit's illumination, as we shall see, there is uniformity as to its meaning. All the passages consistently refer to the same place and condition.

In addition, by now the currant various Jewish translations have returned to the actual Hebrew word "Sheol" in their English translations as well. (Why the N.I.V. did not translate correctly, I and others do not know. Someone on their translation committee must have had a theological agenda.)

It is interesting to note the gradual change in the Jewish translations away from the supposition left by the King James Version of 1611. In 1853 Isaac Leeser made his translation for the English speaking Jewish world. He lowered the rendering of "Sheol" as "grave" (or "tomb," once) to only 16 times and raised up the rendering as "Nether World (world beneath), Hell, the Deep or Perdition" some 46 times, and "Pit" the remaining 3 times. In 1917 the Jewish Publication Society made a new translation and maintained approximately the same division—"Grave" or "Pit" 18 times, and "Nether World" or "Sheol" 47 times. Then the Jewish publication Society made another new translation between 1962 and 1982, and consistently rendered the word as "Sheol" (or "Nether World," once) 64 times, and "grave" only once. In Israel they have recently published a Hebrew-English translation called *The Jerusalem Bible*, Koren Publishers Jerusalem, 1997 and have done the same—"Sheol" (or "Nether Word," once) a total of 63 times, and "grave" only twice. The translators have thus made a full circle back to the Septuagint translation of approximately 200 B.C. wherein the Jewish scholars rendered "Sheol" into Greek as "Hades" (Hell) 62 times, "death" twice and "plundered" once. Never did the Septuagint translators render it "grave." As any Hebrew lexicon will tell you, "grave" in the Hebrew has its own separate and distinct word—*queber*.

Since it is obvious to every reader of the Bible that this word "Sheol" is loaded with the most deeply sensitive intimations, the modern Jewish translators felt it best to simply render it the same way in most cases. They knew its primary meaning of "Hell" as was understood in 200 B.C., yet they would allow the modern reader to make up his own mind and conviction as to the meaning. The Hebrew translators of the Scriptures into the Greek language were consistent in nearly always translating Sheol as Hades in the Septuagint translation. We would do well to recognize that uniformity. They most certainly lived closer to the understood meaning and doctrine inherent in that Hebrew word as used in context in the Hebrew Scriptures.

Oh, yes, theologians and miscellaneous religious groups have debated over different ideas as to how they think this word can be translated. Some have commonly wanted to always call it "the grave." That, however, is obviously impossible in many cases as we shall see. In addition, as I stated earlier, there is clearly another Hebrew word for grave, namely, *queber*. "Sheol" has different properties which I will show at the conclusion. Consequently, some, realizing these different properties, have selected the idea of "gravedom" or "deathdom" for the understanding of *Sheol*. We shall see later that none of these maneuvers will work with consistency.

Etymology of the word "Sheol"

The etymology of the Hebrew word *she'ol* is understood by some prominent Hebraists as taken from *sa'al,* which means simply "to ask." Also in light of the context of some of the references where it is used (like Prov. 27:20 and 30:15, 16), it means "to ask for" in the sense of being *"never satisfied"* or *"insatiable."* If this is the case, then "to ask" was modified to become a name for this place of the dead.

Another strong suggestion is found in the Hebrew Lexicon by Gesenius. He believes it may be taken from the Hebrew word *so'al,* which means "a hollow." This, he says, fits the idea of a subterranean "hollow" or gathering place for the souls of the dead. If this definition is correct then "a hollow (place)" becomes the actual definition or origin of the word "Sheol." Gesenius strongly believes this more surely answers all the various circumstances where the Hebrew word *Sheol* is used.

Because of the immediate association of "Sheol" nearly always with death, some have been led to conclude that it means nothing more than "the grave," at least on some occasions. This, of course, turns a deaf ear to all other contextual facts associated with this realm of the dead. As I stated earlier, the Jewish translators of 200 B.C. never translated the word as "grave."

Perhaps we can only make a complete and accurate assessment of the meaning of this place called "Sheol" after a careful review of its use in the Scriptures. We will go through the Scriptures where Sheol is found. As we go, we will be making assessments. In addition, I will list these references, sometimes taking into consideration a literal interlinear of the Hebrew text for accuracy's sake.

It is amazing to me that one writer today who supposedly wrote an exhaustive research on the subject of Hell, at least from the perspective of the "Conditionalist" position, and whose work is sometimes considered the "definitive" work on the subject, has actually spent the vast majority of his research on what *others have said about the subject*, and then made what amounts to be a very shallow investigation of what the Scriptures themselves actually say (*The Fire That Consumes* by Edward William Fudge). Sometimes people consider this Biblical scholarship. This amounts to being scholarship, but only on what "everybody else" says about Hell. This is certainly not scholarship on the Biblical exegesis of the subject. I can assure you that the conclusion of this kind of investigation can and will be very confusing and totally misleading.

I invite you to follow now as we take a very careful survey of exactly what the Scriptures say about all aspects of this important subject. I believe you will be surprised to find that the Scriptural revelation is far more informative and comprehensive than what most people are told. No doubt, certain religious teachers, who think they are more "loving" than God, would actually want to eliminate the doctrine altogether.

SHEOL OF THE BOOK OF JOB

We are going to start our investigation with the book of Job. Many people don't realize that the book of Job is thought by many Biblical scholars and Bible students to be the oldest book in the Hebrew cannon. Though it is true that Moses was inspired to write about the original creation of Adam and Eve and the beginnings of civilization, yet it is a fact that Moses did not put his hand to the pen until about 1500 B.C. with the exodus of Israel out of Egypt. On the other hand, the great age of Job, who lived 140 years after the death of his first ten adult children (Job 42:16) and fathered a second family, places Job at approximately 200 years of age or more. This would mean that Job probably lived in the days of Terah, the father of Abraham. This would also mean that Job's recorded story is of more ancient origin. Indeed, even Hebraists speak of the book of Job as the most ancient of the Hebrew dialect and much more difficult to translate.

Since the book of Job was most probably first recorded hundreds of years before Moses, we will start there. Sheol is mentioned eight times in the book of Job. In addition, other important information and descriptive terminology is given in accordance with it.

After reading these eight occurrences you will begin to note that Sheol is always used in the *singular.* In other words there is only one common Sheol, not many. In fact, throughout all the Hebrew Scriptures, Sheol is never used in the plural. This leads us to the conclusion that though there are many graves (*quebers*), there is only one Sheol. Consequently, Sheol is not "a grave."

1. The Setting for Job

In the book of Job, reference is made to the flood which took place a few hundred years earlier. Job spoke of "waters" which were sent out by God "to inundate the earth" (Job 12:15), and Eliphaz spoke more specifically of the *"wicked men"* who were "swept away" by the flood and warned—"Will you keep to the ancient path which *wicked men* have trod, who were *snatched away* before their time, whose foundations were washed away by a flood [literal translation]?" (Job. 22:15–17). No doubt this was common knowledge to all in Job's day, because a look at the Biblically revealed chronology will show that Noah and Shem were still living at the time of Job (see Genesis 9:22 and 11:10–32).

Why do I bring this up? Simply because the identity of these "wicked men," and what happened to them after their physical drowning, was especially common knowledge not only to Job's generation, but also to the later Hebrew generations who wrote further commentary about them. This will also have vital connections to the very setting for the whole account recorded in the book of Job.

In the Mosaic account of the flood, which was also probably handed down by way of Noah, Shem, Ham and Japheth, we are told about these "wicked men" in these words—

Now it came about, when men began to multiply on the face of the land, and daughters were born to them, that the *sons of God* saw that the daughters of men were beautiful; and they

took wives for themselves, whomever they chose. . . .The
Nephilim [giants] were on the earth in those days, and also
afterward, when the *sons of God* came in to the daughters of
men, and they bore children to them. Those were the ***mighty
men*** who were of old, ***men of renown***. Then the Lord saw
that the ***wickedness of man*** was great on the earth, . . .
(Genesis 6:1–5).

First of all, no doubt Job knew precisely who *"the sons of God"*
were, because they form *the very introduction to his book.* They were
the angelic beings, some of whom were wicked and in compliance
with Satan (the name Satan means *Adversary*), the very adversary
who brought Job's pains and heartaches upon him (see Job 1:6 and
2:1). Among the "sons of God" was none other than Satan according
to the book of Job. The "wicked men" were the outstanding "men
of renown," "mighty men" or "giants" in the earth, who were the
offspring of the cohabitation between some of these fallen angels
and the beautiful daughters of men.

According to the apostle Peter and Jude, the half-brother of
Jesus, these fallen angelic beings had been plunged into a special
abode called *Tartarus* (or Pit of darkness) to await their final judgment. But not only that, the *"spirits"* of wicked people who rejected
the ministry of Noah were likewise gathered into a holding *"prison"*
to await their judgment as well. Let us read it—

The *angels* who did not keep their own domain, but abandoned their proper abode, He [God] has kept in *eternal bonds
under darkness* for the Judgment of the great day. (Jude 6)

For if God did not spare *angels* when they sinned, but cast
them into *Hell* [*Tartarus*] and committed them to *pits of
darkness*, reserved for Judgment; . . . (2 Pet. 2:4)

. . . the *spirits* [including the wicked men] now in *prison*,
who once were disobedient, when the patience of God kept
waiting in the days of Noah, . . . (1 Pet. 3:19, 20)

It becomes evident from these inspired commentaries that certain of the fallen angelic beings called *"the sons of God"* were, after the flood, confined by bonds in the part of Hell called in the Greek, *Tartarus*. In addition, the *"spirits"* of the wicked men were likewise *"imprisoned"* (from the time of that flood until the very moment Peter was writing) in what would be *Hades* in the Greek or *Sheol* in the Hebrew.

Now all this information from the books of Job, Jude and Peter also means that in Job's day there existed this place of the residence of the *"spirits"* of the disembodied wicked and of the fallen angels. As we shall see, Job was most certainly not ignorant of this reality. In the book of Job this place of confinement was designated as *"Sheol"* and *"Abaddon."* We will explore this as we come to the verses in Job.

First, let us note Job's understanding of the nature of man—

2. Job's Understanding of the Nature of Man

Some people seem to think that the early generations of mankind were Neanderthalic in their understanding of what we have come to call in our modern times the doctrine of Anthropology, i.e., "the nature of man." Such was not the case.

Job was fully cognizant of spirit intelligences in God's creation. After all, God, Himself, is a spirit being—the supreme Spirit intelligence and creator of all things. In fact God spoke directly to man at the end of the book of Job. The book of Job, as we just read, talks about the angelic "sons of God" who were *spirit* creatures. There were other "spirit" intelligences indicated in the book of Job. Eliphaz had placed his whole contention with Job upon a message from such a being—"Now a word was stealthily [with secrecy] brought to me, . . . from the visions of the night, . . . Then a *spirit* passed by my face; . . . a form was before my eyes; . . . Then I heard a voice: . . ." (Job 4:12–17).

Not only did Job know of such spirit intelligences but he was likewise cognizant that man, himself, was a dichotomy. That is, man possessed a spiritual nature which was separate and distinct from his body of mere physical animation or breath. For instance in the book of Job, Elihu spoke—". . . The *spirit* within me constrains me" (Job 32:18). Indeed, in the very same chapter we are told—"But there is a *spirit in man*, and the breath [or inspiration] of the Almighty gives them understanding" (Job 32:8).

This is a fundamental truth which never loses its power throughout the ages. It is added upon, but never diminished. The apostle Paul spoke the very same truth when he said—"For to us God revealed them through the Spirit; For the Spirit searches all things, even the depths of God. For who among men knows the thoughts of a man *except the spirit* of the man *which is in him*? Even so, the thoughts of God no one knows except the *Spirit* of God" (1 Cor. 2:10–11).

According to these passages in Job and in 1 Corinthians, the spirit in man is that faculty within him which can receive communication from the greater Spirit being—God. It is stated earlier in Job—"He [God] has put no trust even in His servants; and against His angels He charges error. How much more *those who dwell in houses of clay, . . .*" (Job 4:18, 19). This is, no doubt, the original statement in the Bible describing man's physical body as a mere "*house*" in which the real man dwells; see also Christ's words in Luke 11:24–26 and 37–40; 2 Cor. 5:1–9; 2 Pet. 1:13, 14, etc. In addition, Job stated these discriminating words about man, "Only his flesh *while upon him* will keep aching, and his *soul within him* will keep mourning" (Job 14:22, literal rendering).

All this is in perfect accord with Solomon who spoke of man at death, "Then the *dust* will return to the earth as it was, and *the spirit* will return to God Who gave it" (Ecc. 12:7). Zechariah concurs in the dichotomy of man with the words, "Thus declares the LORD Who stretches out the heavens, lays the foundation of the earth, and forms the *spirit of man* within him" (Zech. 12:1). Christ said to the religious rulers of His day, "You foolish ones [or unreasonable people], did not He Who made the *outside* [part of man] make *the inside* also?" (Luke 11:37–40). Christ also said, "Do not fear those who kill the *body* but are unable to kill the *soul*; but rather fear Him Who is able to destroy *both soul* and *body* in Hell" (Matt. 10:28). In this context we must understand the *soul* to be that spiritual nature existing within man. In addition, as we have already seen, it is consistently revealed in other places as well that man's spirit can and does exist apart from his body. As examples — 2 Cor. 12:2–5; 2 Cor. 5:1–9; Philip 1:21–24; 2 Pet. 1:13, 14, etc.

Therefore "death" to Job would be no different than it was to James some 2000 years later, who said, "For just as the body without the *spirit* is dead, . . ." (James 2:26). Death was merely the *separation* of the spirit of man from his house of clay. Likewise we shall see that it is in the book of Job where the unique word *raphah* (disembodied spirit) is first used and directly related to the occupants of Sheol.

3. Truly, God Opens the Doors on Death

The LORD asked Job the questions of maximum curiosity and impossibility for man to answer in order to demonstrate man's utter reliance upon God for revelation. "Where were you when I laid the foundation of the earth . . . when . . . the sons of God shouted for joy?" (Job 38:4 and 7). Of course neither Job nor any other human being was anywhere around. Then God asked, *"Have the **gates** of **death** been revealed to you, or have you seen the **gates** of the **deep darkness**?"* (Job 38:17 and 2 Peter 2:17). Of equal impossibility was man's ability to look into the world of death.

Most certainly there was no secret concerning what happens to men physically when they die; their bodies are buried in tombs or graves and return to the dust. This was never a secret and needs no special revelation.

However, this whole study is all about the question God asked Job. Here in Job 38:17 God spoke of death from another perspective. It is as if death was a vast secret chamber and a person must pass through the *"gates"* or *"doors"* to enter into this chamber. Earlier Job himself had identified the "gates of death" as being *"the gates of Sheol"* and stated in his frustration — "Where now is my hope? And who regards my hope? *Will it go down with me to Sheol?* Shall we together go down into the dust?" Job 17:15, 16. To die and return to the dust is one thing, but going through the "gates of Sheol" is an altogether different event. The one has to do with man's body;

the other pertains to man's spiritual nature and, as we shall see, his continued conscious existence. King Hezekiah used the same terminology when he said, "In the prime of my life I shall enter the *gates of Sheol*" (Isa. 38:10, literal trans.). Solomon, with unique wisdom and divine inspiration, likewise spoke concerning the path of immorality as being ". . . the way to *Sheol*, descending to the *chambers of death*" (Prov. 7:27). So now we have learned from these several Scriptures that Sheol has "*gates*" and those gates open into "*chambers*." Of course, we all know that "chambers" are made for *occupants*.

Earlier in this very passage Job had said, "If I look for *Sheol* as my *house*, I make my bed in darkness; . . ." Job 17:13. In this larger context Job spoke about the two aspects of death. On the one hand there is physical corruption of the body into the dust; on the other hand is this residence having "*gates*" or "*doors*" which lead into a "*house*." The word "*house*" and Solomon's word "*chambers*," of course, represent an entirely different kind of dwelling place than the "dust."

4. Job Foresees Ultimate Liberation

Yes, Sheol is designed for occupants. Job, himself, on one occasion asked to be a resident there. In the midst of Job's anguish he asked God with these words, Job 14:13—

*Oh, that You would **hide me in Sheol**, that You would **conceal** me until Your wrath returns to You* [or, is past], *that You would **set a limit for me**, and **remember me!***

I think this is one of the most amazing verses in the Bible. On the one hand, Job asked to be "*hidden in Sheol*," which in itself would make Sheol for him a place of residence outside the sight of man and away from the pains of this life. However, in addition, he also asked for God to "set a limit" for him being there, and "*remember*" him there, implying a time of release! This is amazing, is it not? Here we are at the very beginning of our study on Hell, and the very first book in the Bible to describe it, and here are Job's words which actually take us all the way across the ages to the highlight of the revelation placed upon the subject by Christ's work of redemption. For the New Testament reveals that the "*set time*" of the liberation of the saints from Sheol was at the glorious resurrection and ascension of Jesus Christ, when He ascended from "*the lower parts of the earth*" (Sheol or Hades) and "*led captivity captive*" (Eph. 4:8–10). That is, Christ emptied Sheol of all the righteous occupants at the time of His ascension. This is when Job would get his "*set time*" and be "*remembered*."

In a similar way, no one doubts that Job saw the time of his eventual physical resurrection as well, for he said—

Oh, that my words were written!
    Oh, that they were inscribed in a book!
That with an iron stylus and lead,
    they were engraved in the rock forever!
As for me, I know that my Redeemer lives,
    and at the last He will take His stand on the earth.
Even after my skin is destroyed,
    yet from my flesh I shall see God;
Whom I myself shall behold,
    and Whom my eyes will see and not another.
[How] my heart faints [yearns] within me (Job 19:23–27).

5. God Alone Knows All About Sheol

We have seen that God's revelation alone will open to us the secrets concerning Sheol, the world beneath. Job stated emphatically, "***Sheol*** is naked before Him [God], and ***Abaddon*** [Destruction] has no covering" Job. 26:6. In other words God sees all, even the world that is outside the sight of man. Solomon, in all his God-given wisdom made a similar statement, "*Sheol* and ***Abaddon*** [Destruction] lie open before the LORD; how much more the hearts of men" (Prov. 15:11). This is an interesting statement, as I have previously discussed in my introduction.

One of the amazing things that the four gospels record for us are the occasions when our Lord Jesus Christ knew and read what was going on in the hearts of men, even though those men were often disguising their inward thinking by their outward flattery. On one such occasion, recorded for us in the gospel of Luke (7:36–50), the Pharisee Simon had invited Christ to a feast and no doubt made Christ the honored guest. Actually this was an example of polite, dignified hypocrisy. An uninvited person came in who was a notorious woman of disrepute. No doubt, she was an embarrassment because she placed herself at Jesus' feet weeping and washing His feet with her very tears of shame. What an embarrassing situation! And there sat Simon, thinking inwardly, with a secret attitude of contempt, "If this man [Christ] were a prophet he would know who this woman is." In other words, Simon was thinking that anyone who knew about this woman would never let her even touch him. But the facts were, Christ not only knew who the woman was, but He also knew what Simon was actually thinking. In reality therefore, Christ was more than just a prophet; He was Jehovah Who, as Solomon stated, knew "the hearts of the children of men."

In a similar manner, the world of Sheol, which is out of sight to men, is not out of sight to God. And furthermore, it is God's good intent to reveal to His people many of the important details about Sheol which we would otherwise never know.

6. Additional Revelations in Job About Sheol

I said that Sheol was mentioned eight times in the book of Job. So far we have read four of those occasions—Job 14:13; 17:13; 17:15,16 and 26:6.

Permanence   The first time Sheol is mentioned in the book of Job it is simply stated "He who goes *down* to Sheol does not *come up*. He shall not return again to his *house*, nor will his place know him anymore"—Job 7:9. This is a simple principle that once a person goes into Sheol he does not return into this life. No one leaves this place of confinement. Sheol is generally a permanent place. Of course, there is the exception of Job's own ultimate hope of the "*set* *time*" of his "*remembrance*" (Job 14:13), which implies his (and the rest of the righteous people) eventual release from Sheol.

Dwelling   These Scriptures reveal an interesting fact that Job actually had two different "*houses*" which he could occupy. As stated in this verse (7:9), the first house was on earth to which he could never return once he had gone to Sheol. However, in chapter 17, Sheol itself was also spoken of as his "*house*" (verse 13). Houses are, of course, *dwelling places*, and that is precisely the meaning which the Spirit of God wants to convey to the understanding of the reader of the Scriptures; Sheol is a dwelling place for existing, conscious spirits.

Down   Another question which emerges from this passage is the question; just exactly where is this "house," in particular, the house of Sheol? The "house" on earth is a given. We naturally know it is on the surface of the earth. But Sheol is herein and always said to be "DOWN." But let not the reader assume this simply means "six feet under," because it most certainly does not. Nor does it mean a real deep pit or even a deep cavern, because that is not to be understood, either. "*Down*" as used here, and as we shall see, is the ultimate depth, the very *opposite* of Heaven. Other Scriptures will say it is in the bowels (lower parts) of the earth. Jewish translators of the Hebrew Scriptures will often use the expression "the nether world" or "the world beneath."

The second time Sheol is mentioned in Job, it is placed only within "the limits of God"—"Can you discover the limits of the Almighty? They are as *high* as the heavens, what can you do? *Deeper* than Sheol, what can you know?" Job 11:8. In other words, Sheol is obviously beyond man's capability in which to literally dig. This takes it totally out of any equation with a physical grave of some kind on the earth. Nor is the book of Job the last to make this comparison. The Psalmist made a similar statement—"*If I ascend to heaven, You* [God] *art there; If I make my bed in Sheol, behold, You* [the omnipresent God] *art there*" (Psalm 139:8). Sheol is the opposite of Heaven. Heaven is beyond our starry heavens. Sheol is in the opposite direction; it is within the depths and bowels of the earth. Amos 9:2 says *"Though they dig into Sheol* [which they could never do], *from there will My hand take them; though they ascend up to heaven* [which they could never do], *from there will I bring them down."* No one can escape from God.

Wicked   The last two references in Job indicate that the wicked are most certainly going to Sheol. <u>Job 21:13</u> *". . . and suddenly they* [the wicked] *go down to Sheol."* <u>Job 24:19</u> *"Drought and heat consume the snow waters; so does Sheol those who have sinned."* So we certainly know that Sheol is for the wicked and it will be a time of being *"consumed."* Being *"consumed"* in Sheol, as we shall see, does not mean the wicked cease to exist. Verse 30 of Job 21 expressly says, *"For the wicked men are reserved for the day of destruction; they shall be led forth at the day of fury* [wrath]." Though this may be speaking of the end of the wicked on this earth, yet this is also a truth which will be their ultimate Judgment in eternity as well.

7. *"Sheol" and "Abaddon"*

Before we leave the book of Job, let us look once again at <u>Job 26:5 and 6</u>. I will quote this passage first from the New King James Version and then we will look at a literal translation more carefully.

> The **dead tremble**, *those* under the waters and *those* inhabiting them. **Sheol** is naked before Him [God], and **Destruction** has no covering.

The *first* thing we want to examine is the question of just exactly WHO or WHAT goes to Sheol? As we stated earlier, Job most certainly believed in the dichotomy of man. Man possesses an inner spiritual nature. Job believed he would go to Sheol after his physical death. Later commentary by the apostle Peter says that the *"spirits"* of the wicked before the flood were in this *"prison"* (1 Pet. 3:19, 20). Now, in this last passage about Sheol in the book of Job, it is clearly demonstrated that it is the inward spiritual natures of men which occupy Sheol. The word used here, often translated as the *"dead,"* is really a unique word and is used only eight times in the Hebrew

Scriptures; and it does not have reference to a dead, lifeless *physical body*. The Hebrew Lexicons say this word is *raphah*; it specifically means "ghosts, shades, or disembodied spirits residing in Sheol" (see *Gesenius Hebrew Lexicon*, *Brown-Driver-Briggs Hebrew and English Lexicon*, *NASV Hebrew Dictionary*, or Strong #7496). They explain that the word is taken from the Hebrew *rash,* which carries the idea of something "feeble, weak, flaccid, or to tremble." Furthermore, out of the eight occurrences where this word is used, four of the times it is specifically associated in context with Sheol: Job 26:5, 6; Psalm 88:10 (see context of verses 3, 4 and 6); Prov. 9:18 and Isa. 14:9. In addition, in Prov. 21:16, it is designated as the *"assembly of the dead [raphah],"* or literally, *"the assembly of the spirits* [of the dead]." The other three references are Prov. 2:18 and Isa. 26:14 and 19. Thus it is clearly proven that it is the inward spiritual natures of men which are destined to occupy this subterranean Sheol. The literal rendering of the passage is as demonstrated in the New American Standard Bible—

> The *departed spirits* tremble, . . .
> Naked is *Sheol* before Him [God],
> and *Abaddon* has no covering.

The second important truth about this passage in Job (26:5, 6) is the introduction of a new word, *"Destruction,"* or literally, *"Abaddon."* It appears to be used as a synonym or complementary word to "Sheol." Indeed, *Abaddon* is used in equal force in the following three passages: Job 28:22 *"Abaddon* and *Death* say [they heard a report about] 'wisdom'"; Job 31:12 ". . . [a judgment] *fire* that consumes to *Abaddon"*; and Psalm 88:11 "Will Your lovingkindness be declared in the grave, [or] Your faithfulness in *Abaddon*?" As in Job 26:6 above, so again, in Proverbs 15:11 and 27:20, Abaddon is directly linked with Sheol: *"Sheol* and *Abaddon* lie open before the LORD" and *"Sheol* and *Abaddon* are never satisfied."

Finally, in the last book of the Bible, Revelation, *"Abaddon"* is clearly identified with *"The Bottomless Pit,"* the realm of demonic spirits—Rev. 9:1–12. In addition, the word is now also personified. Rev. 9:11 says, "They [the demons] have a king over them, the angel of the abyss; his name in Hebrew is '***Abaddon***,' and in the Greek he has a name, '***Apollyon***' [destruction]." Both the Hebrew and the Greek carry the meaning as "Destruction," and are generally understood as synonyms or further complements for Sheol or Hades. Since Sheol is referred to as containing "*the chambers of death*" it would appear that there is that part of Sheol which would make it a place of ***destruction*** and suffering. Later Scriptures will add further evidence to this as it pertains to the suffering of the wicked.

This is obvious confirmation to the fact that Sheol is the place of the departed spirits of the dead. This is also the place of the general "destruction" (*Abaddon*), by means of a "fire" (Job 31:12) on the disembodied spirits of the lost or unrighteous. There is likewise a section of Sheol for the demonic spirits referred to as "*the bottomless pit*" in the book of Revelation. There is that section of Sheol for the unrighteous and for demonic spirits; so also at that time there is that understood section of Sheol for the righteous, like Job. In fact, Jesus Christ, Himself, will enlarge upon and explain this more thoroughly in Luke 16:19–30 (the account of the death of the rich man and Lazarus).

There is another passage in Job, though it does not specify Sheol, which most believe has a clear reference to this subterranean place called Sheol; that is Job 10:21 and 22. In expecting his death Job stated,

*Before I go—and I shall not return—to **the land of darkness** and deep shadow, the land of utter gloom as darkness itself, of deep shadow without order, and which shines [or, where even the light is] as the darkness.*

This, indeed, seems to be a general and common designation befitting this subterranean chamber.

IN SUMMARY FROM JOB

Since we have spent so much time in the book of Job it may be appropriate to make a summary. Most of what we have discovered are basics and will simply be added to as we traverse through the rest of the Hebrew Scriptures.

1. Job was aware of the "Sons of God" who were angelic spirit creatures, some of whom were wicked and antagonistic to God and God's purposes. The truth in Job is consistent with the revelation by the apostle Peter that both the "**sons of God,**" who polluted the earth, and the "**wicked men,**" who were destroyed by the flood, are presently confined in Sheol.

2. In Job, the dichotomy of man is understood. Man has both a physical **body** and a **spirit-nature** residing in that body. At physical death the spirit departs from the body.

3. In Job, Sheol is for the "*disembodied spirits*" (*raphah*) of mankind.

4. In Job, Sheol is spoken of as "*a land of darkness*," having "*gates*" or "*doors*," and is as a "*house*" or dwelling place to which people enter after death.

5. In Job, Sheol is "*down*" within the earth in the sense of being the maximum or ultimate depth, the very *opposite of Heaven*.

6. In Job is the beautiful revelation that Job hoped for an "*appointed*" "*set time*" when he would be "*remembered*" in Sheol, so as to be liberated.

7. In Job, Sheol is a place of *permanent confinement* till a day of Judgment for the unrighteous.

8. In Job, Sheol is *especially* the destination for the *wicked*.

9. In Job, Sheol is for the continuous *"consumption"* and/or *"destruction"* of the wicked, as in a *"fire."*

10. This last point is very important! In Job we are introduced to the word *"Abaddon"* as a complementary word to *Sheol* and/or of a compartment in Sheol. The truth regarding *Abaddon* will be summed up in the very last book of the Bible.

Herein we have a remarkable fact presented before us. *Abaddon* is presented in the very first or oldest book of the Hebrew Cannon and it is also taken up in the very last book of the Greek Cannon of Scripture. It is understood that from the time Job lived to the time Revelation was written spans nearly 2000 years. In addition, the context for mentioning *Abaddon* in the book of Revelation is the prophetic event of the second coming of Jesus Christ; that spans another 2000 years of our present age. Then, John in the book of Revelation indicates that Abaddon will continue to exist for another 1000 years after the second coming. Thus in the revelation from our Scriptures *Abaddon* has existed and will continue to exist for at least 5000 years. This of course, does not take into consideration how long *Abaddon* was in existence before Job. Since it is the residence of certain fallen angels and the wicked from the time of the flood in Noah's day, it had to exist some 500 years before Job. And, no doubt, it goes all the way back to the fall of man. So *Abaddon* probably spans the whole time of man's probation on earth. In fact, if it includes some of the rebellious angels who were with Lucifer in his original insurrection against God then the existence of *Abaddon* long antedates the fall of man.

Now, as we saw, *Abaddon* means **"DESTRUCTION"**! That means that "Destruction" is in existence for a minimum of 7000 years. Furthermore, the occupants of "Destruction," both angelic spirits and human spirits, *still exist as spirit beings throughout the whole time* from their entrance into Abaddon. They never change. Consequently, **"Destruction"** for the wicked and for the fallen angelic beings could absolutely never possibly mean *"Annihilation"* or *"Cessation of Being."* We must understand that "destruction" as it pertains to the lost suffering in Sheol means a *Condition of Existence* and not the *Termination of Existence.* This is precisely the observation made by W.E. Vine in his *Expository Dictionary of New Testament Words*; the Greek word for destruction is *Apoleia*, "indicating loss of well-being, not of being."

As one should be able to see from the information we have gathered from the book of Job, a whole new world has been opened to us on the subject of Sheol. It becomes absolutely clear that Sheol is a subterranean gathering place for the disembodied spirits of the dead, both the righteous and the unrighteous. For the wicked it appears to be a fearful place of continuous destruction in fire, and yet there is that reservation for the Day of Judgment. There does not appear to be any suffering for the righteous, but only an awaiting for a future release.

CHAPTER EIGHT

SHEOL OF THE TORAH
(The Five Books of Moses)

&

GENESIS

"Gathered to His people"

The first expression which draws our interest in the book of Genesis is not the word Sheol; nevertheless, it must be, and is, *directly related*. The expression, "*gathered to his people*," is noteworthy in the book of Genesis when one of the fathers had died.

For instance, at Abraham's death, he was said to be "*gathered to his people*" (Gen. 25:8). The first thing we think of by the words "*his people*" are either his own physical relatives who have died before him, or else those of like precious faith with him who had gone before in death. If this is merely a figure of speech, not to be taken literally, then it simply means he died like all the rest of mankind and thereby joined the whole human race in the dust. That idea does not find much resonance in anyone's thinking. Other than Lot, all Abraham's relatives or ancestors were living in the land of Mesopotamia. So he certainly was not "*gathered*" to them physically because Abraham was very plainly buried right there in the Land of Promise. His body was not taken all the way back to the land of Mesopotamia to be interred with his physical relatives. However, as was stated in the book of Job, it must have the same meaning as

135

to pass through the gates of Sheol to a permanent resting place (Job 17:15–16 and 38:17).

There are obviously two aspects to death. Abraham was to be "buried at a good old age" (Gen. 15:15); that took care of his body. Yet in the very same passage it was first promised—". . . *you shall go to your fathers, . . .*" Since they buried Abraham's body right there in Canaan, how then could he "go to his fathers," or be "gathered to his people"? The action of being "*gathered to his people*" speaks of the person who has died as actually being collected together with a group of people who are in some way related to him. The only revealed fact that would fit in clarity was the reality that the spirits of the righteous were *gathered in Sheol*. Indeed, this is precisely the answer the Lord Jesus Christ gave to us in the Gospel account of Luke 16:22 and 23. There Christ specifically said Abraham was in *Hades* which is the Greek translation of the Hebrew *Sheol*. So, for Abraham to be "gathered to his people" meant that his soul went to Sheol and was united with all the souls of the righteous who had gone before him.

Also, at the moment when Jacob died down in Egypt he was said to be "*gathered to his people*" (Gen. 49:33). Yet it was months before Jacob's body was actually buried up in Canaan with his physical fathers (Gen. 49:29 and 30). Therefore he certainly was not immediately buried with them. So this is talking about the action upon his spirit, not his bodily remains. See also Gen. 25:17; 35:29 and 49:29 where this expression is used.

In Deut. 32:50 the expression is used again in reference to Moses. Remember, Moses' body was privately and secretly buried—Deut. 34:6. So Moses was not gathered to anyone physically. Yet Moses was collected together with "his people," i.e., the souls of the righteous dead.

These expressions, therefore, must have reference to the souls of these men who, at the actual time of their separation from their bodies, went into Sheol, the subterranean (always "down") gathering place for them. This will be further confirmed as we look at the following passages—

"Sheol"

Gen. 37:35   "Surely I [Jacob] will go down to *Sheol* to my son mourning" (Literal trans.).

Jacob had just heard the report that his son Joseph was torn to pieces and probably devoured by wild beasts. Consequently there would be no burial or grave for Joseph's body. Yet Jacob says *"I will go down to . . . my son."* That means that where Joseph is, in *"Sheol,"* Jacob will eventually go, himself. Obviously, this is not into some tomb or sepulcher. This fits perfectly the previous statements about those who died being *"gathered to their people."* In this case, when Jacob was to eventually die, he would, in fact, be *"gathered . . . to Joseph in Sheol."* Consequently, being gathered to one's people at death has reference to their souls gathering down in Sheol.

Gen. 42:38   ". . . then you will bring my gray hairs with sorrow to Sheol."

Gen. 44:29   ". . . and you will bring my gray hair down to Sheol in sorrow."

Gen. 44:31   ". . . will bring the gray hair of your servant our father down to Sheol in sorrow."

In each of these cases it should be understood that the "sorrow" in Jacob's soul was probably because most of God's promises to him and his sons were centered around their inheritance of the land of Canaan and their consequent prosperity there. Jacob was hoping to realize those promises in his lifetime with his sons. The thought of their demise brought sorrow to his soul. Now in his old age ("gray hairs") the thought of another son lost (Benjamin) would compound his "sorrow."

"Fire"

The first time that *fire* is spoken of in Genesis is in chapter 19 with the destruction of those two notorious cities, Sodom and Gomorrah (Gen. 19:24). The fiery judgment was an expression of God's utter wrath against the depravity of those communities. Today there still remains what some say is the largest potash industry in the world at the lower end of the Dead Sea area. Actually, throughout the Bible, fire remains as the emblematic judgment of God against sin and wickedness. We saw in the book of Job the expression of God's wrath as "fire that descends even into Sheol." The prophets speak of more fiery judgments to come upon the world. They are so designated numerous times.

The second time *fire* is mentioned in the book of Genesis was in the sacrifice of Isaac (Gen. 22). Most people know quite well the test that God gave to Abraham to offer up his own beloved son as a sacrifice. However, the realization that Abraham was to offer him as a **burnt** sacrifice is not always remembered. The words of Isaac to his father are really quite shocking—"Behold, *THE FIRE* and the wood, but where is the lamb?" (Gen. 22:7). The answer of Abraham is truly amazing. As his answer pertained to the lamb, Abraham said, "God will provide for Himself *the Lamb* for the *burnt* offering, . . ." (22:8). We all know now that this answer actually looks down through the corridors of time to *"the lamb of God Who takes away the sins of the world."* However, the question we can ask in view of the subject before us is—"Why would God want Abraham to *BURN UP* his son?" Would not the simple sacrifice of physical death be enough? Why does God demand that the body, either of the lamb or of Abraham's own son, be burned up with a consuming fire? Was it not a picture of Christ's suffering as the antitypical Lamb?

As in the first case of the destruction of Sodom and Gomorrah, there is no secret about the purpose of fire as it is used in the animal sacrificial system. It is used as an expression of wrath and judgment and purging against sin.

LEVITICUS—The Burnt Sacrifices

As we just saw, Isaac was to be offered as a "burnt sacrifice." In the book of Leviticus we are given the details about the "*Law of the Burnt Sacrifices*" (Lev. 1 and 6:8–13). Obviously the most important thing about the "burnt sacrifices" was the fact that *after* the animal was slain, it was to be placed upon an altar to be *wholly consumed by fire*. The redemption of any individual was not completed at the time the animal was slain. On the contrary, in order for the atonement to be made, the animal must be totally consumed by fire. Thus, the major act in this sacrificial system was the *burning* of the sacrifice to depict the actual total judgment of God against sin.

The overwhelming number of times that fire is mentioned in the Scriptures is specifically concerned with judgment upon ungodly idols, people, or cities, or nations, or even the earth itself. The words commonly associated with fire are "*punishment, torment, fury, vengeance, anger, consuming, wrath, jealousy, purification from sin, etc., etc.*" Fire is thus depicted throughout the Scriptures as the judgment of God against sin. This is basic and fundamental. Everyone who reads the Scriptures admits to this reality.

All admit these sacrifices spoke of the redemption the sinner obtains through the substitutionary sacrifice of our Lord Jesus Christ. Though the death of Christ on the cross is often used to epitomize our redemption, yet by no stretch of the imagination did Christ's physical death on the cross complete the basis for our atonement. We must always remember that Christ's death was a three day and three night death, wherein he descended into the lower region of the earth called Sheol/Hades—Matt. 12:40; Jonah 2:2; Acts 2:31; Psalm 16:10; Eph. 4:9, 10 and Rom. 10:6, 7. In this three day death Christ was bearing our sins under the judgment hand of God. That meant *bearing our sins under the curse of God* in the fiery Hell. Because the fire of the burnt sacrifices has its obvious **complement** in the judgmental fire of Hell where Christ went, theologians, using their natural, soulish minds, have been thrown into controversy ever since. Please read in the closing chapters of this book—*The Sufferings Of Jesus Christ Even To The Depth Of Hell.*

As positive proof that the burning of the sacrifice depicts the sufferings of Hell, let us look at the most important sacrifice in the revelation given to Moses—

"Into A Land of Separation"

The goat shall bear on itself all their iniquities
to a solitary land; . . . (Lev. 16:22).

When one explores the sacrificial system given to the nation of Israel through the prophet Moses, it is like walking into a great memorial museum and passing before numerous paintings displaying the struggles and passions of the nation as manifested in their sacrificial system of blood, death and fire. Yet, the result of putting away sin brought forgiveness, life and redemption with victories and hopes for the future. As we walk along we finally come to stand before the last grand work which is a massive panoramic scene named "*The Great Day Of Atonement*" (Lev. 23:26 and 27). You gaze upon it as if mesmerized in an attempt to fully comprehend the details of its meaning.

Here in the book of Leviticus we do, in fact, enter into the sacred halls of Divine revelation. These halls (chapters) portray before us the many sacrifices which speak of the story of sinful human beings, on a sin-cursed earth, being reconciled to the Creator of heaven and earth on the basis typified by the sacrifices. Finally in chapter 16, we stand before the most important sacrifice of Israel's sacred year calendar. Here is the sacrifice of all sacrifices. There is none other like it and there is none other of equal importance. *Amazingly, here is a sacrifice which is actually not sacrificed!* Here is a living animal which does not die and is not burned up! Yet this live animal *represents the burning* which would normally take place in all the burnt sacrifices.

Note carefully—here portrayed before us will be the sacrificial *afterlife existence* of a substitute bearing away the sins of mankind into the horrible wilderness of the dead. Here it has been said by some Jewish sages, "**all life is in a state of death** and only **death is alive**." What the Jewish sages of old were talking about was simply *conscious existence after death* in a wilderness of isolation or separation.

The Hebrew word translated herein as "*solitary land*" is actually somewhat of a mystery in itself. It is found only one time in all the Hebrew Scriptures and that is right here with this particular unique sacrifice where the goat is taken out, in seclusion, bearing the sins of the nation, to an uninhabited wilderness. Strong gives it the number 1509 and indicates it is taken from 1504 which is "a prime root (meaning) *to cut off*." Therefore, Strong will indicate that 1509 carries with it the idea of "separation." Rotherham says that it means "land of seclusion or cutting off." Therefore, the New American Standard Bible comes very close by the words "solitary land." Of course, we will discover that this land was intended to be the residence of "*Azazel*," whom we shall recognize as another description of the Devil or Satan. We will look at this in detail shortly.

Here is where the total story of the price paid for our redemption is spelled out in unusual detail. Let us explore those details as it pertains to the subject before us.

1. Explanation

On the tenth day of the seventh month of Israel's sacred year calendar, a very special High Sabbath was held. It is literally called "The Sabbath of Sabbatism" (Lev. 16:31). More commonly, this day was known as the great "Day of Atonement" (*Yom Kipper*) or simply "The Day" (*Yoma*); see Lev.23:26. This day represented the culmination of the Levitical sacrificial system. It is also referred to as the "climax" of all purificatory sacrifices and ordinances. On this day the sins of the nation of Israel would be "atoned," in a ritual or ceremonial manner, for another year. The importance of this day is also demonstrated in that once every fifty years this day was selected as the day upon which the great "*Jubilee*" release would be announced (see Lev. 25:9).

This would be the one and only time of the year that the High Priest had access to "the Holiest of All" section of the Tabernacle, or later, the Temple (Lev. 16:2). This was virtually going into the very presence of God as represented by the Shekinah glory over the Mercy Seat. As a consequence of this sacrifice the sins of the nation of Israel would be put away, covered and/or atoned for. In turn this particular day would bring to an end the special sacrificial calendar of Judaism which would not open again until the spring sacrifice of the Passover lambs.

This day clearly represents the most mysterious and yet significant of all Israel's sacrificial services. In particular, this sacrifice will explain, by an outward visual demonstration, the deep hidden spiritual realities of how God has put away, for all eternity, all our sins by the antitypical "Scapegoat," the Lord Jesus Christ. The inspired writer of the book of Hebrews would say, "But now, once at the *climax* of the ages, He [Christ] has appeared to put away sin by the sacrifice of Himself" (literal translation, Heb. 9:26). Most certainly at this particular sacrifice, strange and unusual things took place. Only by this putting away of sins could AT-ONE-MENT with God ever be achieved. Here we will see Christ die and shed His precious blood, and yet beyond His immediate death, we will see Christ bearing the horrible guilt and penalty of sins upon His soul into a wilderness of despair and abandonment where the only inhabitants are the spirits of the wicked dead and the demons of Hell.

2. Procedure—The Two Goats

Because of the importance of this day no ordinary priest could officiate—only the High Priest. In addition, the High Priest was instructed to bathe his flesh in water prior to putting on the special priestly garment for the occasion (Lev. 16:3, 4). Outside the sanctuary and throughout the whole land of Israel, the people would be "afflicting their souls" all day long. Anyone who would not thus "humble himself" (16:29 and 31) was under threat of being *"cut off and destroyed"* from the nation (23:29). Some of the major passages are—Lev. 16:1–54; 23:26–32; Exo. 30:10; Num. 29:7-11; Hebrews 9:6–12 and Hebrews 9:24–28.

Though there are different sacrificial offerings made on this day pertaining to the different people involved in the ritual, yet the focus of attention will concern the offering of two goats representing the nation. All commentators, whether Jewish or Christian, agree that these two goats represent ONE singular sacrificial offering. Each goat will represent a different aspect of the special offering which brings the ceremonial remission of the nation's sins. The congregation will present these two goats which, according to tradition, looked very much alike. They would be the same size and color to look almost like twins. The two goats would be taken by the High Priest (Lev. 16:3, 5 and 6) and would be presented "before the Lord" (Lev. 16:7) at the doorway of the tent of meeting.

One may remember earlier in the book of Leviticus the ritual service regarding the cleansing of the leper, where two birds were selected for that sacrifice (Lev. 14:1–9). Only one bird was slain, and the second bird was then dipped into the blood of the slain bird and set free to fly away. In a very simple and beautiful way, this is the picture of both the death of Christ for cleansing and then the resurrection of Christ as the basis for giving new life as well. As we shall see in the case of these two goats in Lev. 16, one will die and the other will be taken away but not, by any stretch of the imagination, to a blissful freedom. Therefore, in this case of the two goats, the departure of the second goat does not depict resurrection, but the actual existence of the sin bearer in the destruction of Sheol.

3. Procedure—the Two Lots

When these two goats are presented before the Lord, an interesting procedure takes place. "Lots are cast" on behalf of these two goats (Lev. 16:8–10). The casting of lots was a custom in the times of Israel to determine or make selection for whatever purpose was involved. "Lots" were simply objects such as, in this case, two stones or two pieces of material upon which an inscription was made on each object to represent one of the two parties for the selection. These lots were either placed in a container and thrown out, or somehow cast forth by the High Priest, who could not see the inscription or the objects. This was the means by which the two goats were differentiated and selected, each for its particular assignment in the sacrificial ritual. Though this is considered as ONE sacrifice, yet this selection is necessary in order to depict the two important stages which are to form the total picture of what is necessary in order to dispose of the nation's sins.

Let us look at what is inscribed upon the two lots. The text says one lot is for "Jehovah." That would mean that the name in Hebrew called "the tetragram," "*YHWH*," was inscribed on one of the lots. The other lot was said to be for "*AZAZEL*" (literal, not *scapegoat* as used in later tradition). The Hebrew is *AZ* (goat) and *AZEL* (departure). The basic meaning is "goat of departure." However, most interpreters point out that "AZAZEL" stands in opposition to "YHWH" which would mean that it stands as a personification of another person. Furthermore, since this goat will depart into "a land not inhabited," or "the wilderness desolation" from which they make sure the goat will never return, AZAZEL came to represent a goat demon (Lev. 17:7) or an evil spirit or Satan, himself. Further reason for this is the fact that throughout the Scriptures the wilderness itself represented all that is "great and terrible" (see as examples Deut. 1:19; 8:15 and Jer. 2:6). Evil things were said to inhabit the desolate wilderness, even demons (see Isa. 13:21; 34:14; Matt. 12:43; Lk. 8:27; 11:24 and Rev. 18:2). Consequently, the goat head came to represent or stand as a symbol for Satan. (Satanists' cults, even today, still use the emblem.) From one of the oldest books of the Pseudepigrapha (book of Enoch), Azazel was a half goat and half Satan. This ancient Jewish tradition was also found in the Dead Sea Scrolls. In the Pesher (ancient Jewish commentary), Azazel was the goat-headed Satan. Thus we can see that the tradition of associating this goat as being designated for Satan existed even long before the time of Christ. In the middle ages of the Christian era, up to and beyond the 15th century, Jewish commentaries continued to depict this goat as being offered or sent to Satan in the wilderness.

4. Procedure — The One Sacrifice

Remember that these two goats represent a singular sacrifice. Tradition says that with the casting of the lots, they tied a red cloth around the *neck* of the goat selected for YHWH. This goat alone was to be actually killed. Then they attached a red cloth to the *horn* of the goat selected to be sent into the wilderness for AZAZEL. They slaughtered the first goat which was designated for YHWH. Silently, part of his blood was taken into the Holiest of All by the High Priest and sprinkled before the Mercy Seat (Lev. 16:15–17). No one else was allowed in the Tabernacle or Temple while this was being done.

As to the sacrifice of the live goat (Lev. 16:20–22), the text says *"Aaron shall offer the live goat."* However, the live goat, designated for AZAZEL, is not slaughtered. Since these two goats represent ONE sacrifice, this goat is considered as *already dead* by virtue of the death of the first goat. Therefore it remains alive in order to depict the remainder of the ritual. The High Priest would now approach the goat designated for AZAZEL and place *". . . both of his hands on the head of the live goat, and confess over it all the iniquities of the sons of Israel and all their transgressions in regard to all their sins; **and he shall lay them on the head of the goat**, . . ."* (Verse 21). Normally this procedure would have been done with an animal to be slaughtered. However, since these two goats represent ONE sacrifice, it is the second of the two goats which will actually bear the guilt of the sins of the nation upon itself. In that this second goat is *still alive,* it will depict the actual transportation of the sins of the people into a place of condemnation and judgment. *"The goat,"* it is stated, *"shall bear on itself all their iniquities to a solitary land; . . ."* (verse 22). The Divine application of this event is expressed in the inspired words of Isaiah—*"But the LORD has laid upon Him* [Jesus Christ] *the iniquity of us all"* (Isa. 53:6, NKJV).

The two goats also, therefore, represent the *two aspects* of the nature of man. The goat which was slaughtered represents the *body* being put to death. The live goat represents the *soul or spiritual* nature of man which remains *in existence* separate from his body.

5. Procedure—The Awful Trek

Many have painted the beginning of the awful trek of Christ bearing His cross to Golgotha. And many have made depictions of the awful sufferings of Christ on the cross when He died. That would be like painting a picture of the goat which was actually slaughtered on this Day of Atonement. But no one (that I know of) has ever painted a picture of that awful trek of Christ after death, bearing the sins of the world into Hell. And in God's reality, this is the most important part of the sacrifice, for herein are our sins actually disposed. In reality it was a three day trek into the wilderness of "Hades/Sheol," a place *originally made* for Satan—AZAZEL (Matt. 25:41). The Scriptures make it very plain that Christ did not cease to exist the moment He physically died. At the point of physical death, Christ actually delivered His "spirit into the hands of God" (Luke 23:46) Who, in turn, sent Him (His soul) into "Hell" (*Hades*, Acts 2:27 and 31). Like the goat which was now sent out into the wilderness bearing upon itself the sins of the nation of Israel, so the antitypical scapegoat, the Lord Jesus Christ, was sent away bearing the sins of the world into the "land of separation". Make no mistake about it, though the thief on the cross was safe "with" Christ in the "paradise" (Luke 23:43 and 16:22) section of Hades, yet Christ, Himself, was bearing our sins in the flames of Hades. This scene is, of course, "out of sight" to the human eye, but herein it is vividly represented by the trek of the scapegoat.

Now some men perceived and have painted pictures of this awful trek of the "scapegoat." They are not intended to be beautiful paintings, but dismal scenes of despair and sorrow. In the Biblical account an "*appointed man*" (vs. 21 and 22, or *strong man*, NKJV) is needed to lead this goat away into the wilderness bearing upon itself the indignity of being accursed. The obvious reason a special man is needed is because this goat is going into a place to which it instinctively does not want to go; the goat hates it and resists it—yet becomes resigned to it. Truthfully, this trek must have been most solemn and sad. They passed away from any people or other animals, away from any green fields or shrubs, beyond any source of water and out into the midst of a blazing heat, dry rocks and crevices. One could often see the goat vainly attempting to go back. The trek goes on through deeper canyons and desolations. The only life is the nervous lizards and soaring vultures; finally the goat is disoriented and lost. Then quickly the strong man leaves the goat behind and makes his escape. In the later years of Israel's history, the goat was taken out of Jerusalem into the desolate Judean wilderness and sometimes even pushed over a cliff. There are even drawings in late Jewish commentaries of the goat falling into the clutches of an awaiting demon or devil called AZAZEL.

Perhaps the most vivid example of this wilderness was made not too many years ago by the modernistic preacher, Bishop Pike, of the Episcopal Church. He thought he would try personally to find some evidences of the "historical Jesus," because he was not at all satisfied with the Christ of the Bible. Amazing as it may seem, he came into this same Judean wilderness to try and find caves or places where some proofs of his idea of what he thought Jesus should be could be found. He thought archaeologists might have overlooked certain evidences. He wandered through the desolations by himself and got lost. Many days later search parties eventually found his body in some canyon. He died a decidedly unpleasant death of thirst, with his tongue swollen to almost fill his mouth. How sad it was that he had rejected the antitypical "Scapegoat."

6. Conclusion and Revelation

The trek of the goat selected for AZAZEL is a vivid picture of the desolations of "Sheol." The first goat which was actually sacrificed represented the physical death of Jesus Christ. This is all that the world looking on could see. The second goat actually had all the sins placed upon it and bore this great burden into a hellish place of oblivion and *living death*. This is the portrayal from the Hebrew Scriptures of what happened to the spirit of Jesus Christ after His physical death and burial. Christ spent three days and nights in the "chambers of Sheol." If you didn't know what Sheol was before, certainly you do now! It is not a pleasant place.

Thank God, the court of heaven was satisfied with the supernatural sufferings of Christ, God's Divine Son. The guilt and penalty of the sins of the world were "taken away." As John the Baptist said, *"Behold the Lamb of God Who **takes away** the sin of the world"* (John 1:29). God has thus left for us a visual representation of what was done in the substitutionary sacrifice of Christ. "Hades" of the Greek Scriptures is the "Sheol" of the Hebrew Scriptures. In addition, in this typology we have preserved for us the reality AND CONDITION of Sheol as being the reception place to which the spirit and/or soul of our substitutionary Sacrifice descended.

Since Sheol, Hades or Hell was originally designed by God for Lucifer and his fallen angels (Matt. 25:41), the designated goat for *Azazel* would indicate that God would now banish the sins of the world back into the very residence of those who originally were responsible. In no sense whatsoever is this a sacrifice to Satan, because the sacrifice was initially made to God for the forgiveness of Israel's sins. As those sins were borne into Hell, God accepts the punishment for those sins as paid in full, and in turn forgives the sinner by His marvelous grace. However, the sins have now been deposited back to the eventual habitat of Satan for his shame, humiliation and disgrace.

Why is it that most of the studies on the subject of Hell (Sheol), especially by those who reject it as a place of conscious torment, totally ignore this vivid picture which God has designed so long ago for our understanding? I think the answer is obvious. The stark desolation of the Judean wilderness was allowed by God to be a sober reminder to the Jewish people of that ultimate desolation of Hell.

NUMBERS and DEUTERONOMY

Num. 16:30   "But if the LORD brings about an entirely new thing, and the ground opens its mouth, and swallows them up with all that is theirs, and they descend alive into *Sheol*, . . ."

Num. 16:33   "So they and all that belonged to them went down alive to *Sheol*; and the earth closed over them, . . ."

This was a phenomenal event, which was a "once in human history" occurrence. There was serious rebellion against the leadership of Moses. The rebellion was composed of the very leadership of the nation—"two hundred and fifty of the leaders of the congregation" under the heads of Korah, Dathan and Abiram. God's revealed judgment upon them was going to be severe; "an entirely new thing" would happen. As stated above, the earth would literally "open its mouth and swallow them up . . . and they would descend *alive* into Sheol. . ." If this was merely the earth opening up and people falling into a pit or canyon, then we could say that it actually has happened quite often before as during an earthquake. And the only thing unusual about it on this occasion was that the earth gave way directly beneath them. But even that is not totally unusual because throughout time people have sometimes suddenly fallen into unexpected sink holes. In fact, animals, carts and whole houses on occasions have abruptly fallen in. That is obviously not what happened on this occasion. It is obvious that no one has ever gone down ALIVE into Sheol! Therefore Sheol is not simply a grave, sinkhole or canyon—it is understood to be in another category altogether.

<u>Deut. 32:22</u>   "For a *fire* is kindled in My anger, and burns to the *lowest part of Sheol,* and consumes the earth with its yield, and sets on fire the foundations of the mountains."

This is the last book of the Law. It concludes with a prophetic "song" which would remain throughout Israel's history as a sober reminder of the nation's apostasy and subsequent judgment from God. God's wrath is spoken of throughout this song, but in this particular verse it is epitomized as "*a fire*" that "*burns to the lowest part of Sheol.*" This should leave no doubt in anyone's mind that there is "**fire**" in Sheol! The fire in Sheol is the epitome of God's wrath. This would be the same "*fire*" as mentioned in Job 31:12 which "*consumes to destruction* (Abaddon)."

CHAPTER NINE

SHEOL OF THE PROPHETS

ꙮ

Following the order in the Hebrew Bibles, we will next look at those books under the classification or section called "The Prophets."

1 Sam. 2:6   "The LORD kills and makes alive; He brings down to *Sheol* and *raises up*."

This is obviously an interesting statement and deserves our attention. Hannah made this statement in a prayer of thanksgiving after God gave to her a son who was to become Samuel the prophet. God had thus taken away her reproach of childlessness by her conceiving and giving birth to Samuel. This was likewise a prophetic prayer which spoke of the second coming of the Messiah (verse 10). The statement in verse 6 by Hannah can also be understood as prophetic truth. Note the following—

The "Bringing Back" of Samuel

In 1 Sam. 28:1-24 we have an unusual account which further enhances and complements all that we have learned so far about Sheol. At the end of this account we will realize that the facts of the story are totally consistent with what the collective body of Scriptures has so far given to us. Thus, this story gives confirmation to the teaching of the conscious existence of the spirits of men after death within the regions of Hell or Sheol. As a result, this particular story is either totally ignored, as it is by Edward Fudge in his recent book *The Fire that Consumes*, or it is brazenly mocked as a mere account from a witch which should not be believed by anyone (*Answers to Objections*, by the Seventh Day Adventist, Francis Nichol, pages 354, 355).

I will also state at the outset, that there is no question about the fact that the activities of witchcraft had been outlawed in the nation of Israel and enforced by the death penalty—see Lev. 20:27 and Deut. 18:9–12. In addition, King Saul, himself, will be guilty for even resorting to a witch for help—see 1 Chron. 10:13. However, we cannot successfully discount what happened on this occasion merely because a witch was used by Saul. In fact, we must remember that the king of Moab, Balak by name, employed the false prophet Balaam, as recorded in Numbers chapters 22, 23 and 24, to come and curse Israel. Instead of allowing Israel to be cursed, God overruled and put one of the most spectacular series of prophecies in Balaam's mouth. These prophecies became a great blessing for Israel instead of a curse. So it is here in the case of the witch of Endor. More than anyone else, she was the one to be totally surprised because God overruled and did bring up Samuel. Not only that, Samuel gave nothing but the absolute truth as we shall see. Everything which was stated by Samuel was absolutely true and consistent with his message and attitude towards Saul; it was also prophetically fulfilled. One can rest assured that the witch of Endor would never talk like this. Therefore, a conscientious Bible reader will accept this event at its face value.

After the death of the prophet Samuel, the weak and disobedient King Saul came to dire straits in Israel's war with the Philistines. Every attempt by King Saul to receive communications from God for directions failed. He called upon God but there was no answer. He asked for communication through the priesthood, but there was still no answer. In addition, there was no prophet available. In desperation Saul told his servants to search for a medium (or witch) even though they had been outlawed by his own decree. They found a medium of Endor who was known to them to be able to communicate with the dead. Saul disguised himself and promised the woman protection if she would but call up Samuel.

This demonstrates on the face of it that Saul, and all others for that matter, recognized the continued existence of the spirits of the dead in Sheol. One who has ceased to exist could obviously never "be called up." However, God did not want Israel to trust in mediums, who were devilish or demonic and often added fakery to their magic spells to deceive the people.

The text says—

Now Samuel was dead, and all Israel had lamented him And *buried him in Ramah, his own city* (1 Sam. 28:3).

This is a clear statement as to the placement of Samuel's physical body in a grave in his home town of Ramah. King Saul obviously did not go back to Ramah and ask for the physical resurrection of Samuel. His understanding was the same as Job's and all that was so far revealed in the Law; man's soul or spirit exists apart from his body in the lower parts of the earth in Sheol.

In this case the medium, not knowing that this was King Saul in her presence, apparently went through her routine; to her own total surprise and shock, Samuel "came up." In other words, God overruled in this situation and allowed a saint to arise out of Sheol. As we noted earlier, Samuel's mother, Hannah, had stated that God could "bring down" or "bring up" from Sheol as He wished. And now, indeed, God "brought up" Samuel himself, for whom Hannah was so thankful.

No doubt, mediums sometimes faked and mimicked their communication with the dead. But in this case, the text tells us, the medium herself was totally surprised because Samuel actually came up—

When the woman saw Samuel, she cried out with a loud voice; and the woman spoke to Saul, saying, 'Why have you deceived me? For you are Saul (verse 12).

I do not believe for one second that God would allow a saint to so respond to a medium's enchantments unless it was within His perfect will. With Samuel's actual emergence from the realm of the world beneath, the witch realized that she had been deceived and the real identity of the one who had made this request of her was none other than King Saul, himself. The witch then looked at King Saul in bewilderment, as Saul encouraged her to continue without fear of punishment. King Saul calmed her down and gave assurances that she would not die. He then asked her what she was seeing. The witch's first response was amazing—

I see a *divine being* coming up out of the earth (v. 13).

In the King James Version it is rendered, "I saw gods ascending out of the earth." This translation reflects the literal Hebrew word for God, *Elohim*, which is used in this text. *Elohim* is in the plural and can be translated *gods* when it has rare reference to angels, judges or man. Jesus Christ, Himself, reminded the Jews of His generation that the Scripture has referred to men in some cases as *gods*—See John 10:34 and 35, with Psalm 82:6. However, the rendering, "a divine being," from the New American Standard Bible, reflects more upon the truth of 2 Peter 1:4 that the fact of the new birth makes every believer "a partaker of the divine nature." We should understand that the "new birth" is common to all ages. Therefore Samuel, himself, was a partaker of the "divine nature." Consequently, what the witch saw in Samuel was very accurate indeed. She saw a "saint," or one with "the divine nature."

When King Saul asked further "What is his form?" she answered—

An old man is coming up, and he is wrapped with a robe (v.14).

This meant to Saul that he was once again in the presence of Samuel the prophet and "he bowed with his face to the ground and did homage" (v. 14). Can anyone imagine King Saul doing this if it was commonly understood in the Hebrew religion that there were no such things as disembodied spirits of the dead?

As recorded in the sacred text, Samuel then spoke directly to Saul and said, "*Why have you disturbed* [or disquieted] *me by*

153

bringing me up?" This meant that Samuel was in a condition of rest and comfort in contrast to the lost in Sheol who are in a condition of suffering. Samuel was perfectly contented with his rest in Sheol and didn't like being disturbed. Saul rehearsed the situation where God was not answering any of Saul's requests. And Samuel responded appropriately, "*Why then do you ask me, since the LORD has departed from you and has become your adversary?*" Samuel then reminded Saul of God's past warnings, "*The Lord has done accordingly as He spoke through me; for the LORD has torn the kingdom out of your hand and given it to your neighbor, to David*" (v. 17). In addition Samuel added the following message to Saul—

> As you did not obey the LORD and did not execute His fierce wrath on Amalek, so the LORD has done this thing to you this day. Moreover the LORD will also give over Israel along with you into the hands of the Philistines, therefore tomorrow you and your sons will be with me. Indeed the LORD will give over the army of Israel into the hands of the Philistines! (verses 18–19). King Saul "immediately fell full length upon the ground. . . ." (v. 20).

Of course every single thing Samuel said to Saul was absolutely true, consistent to the facts and realities, and prophetically happened exactly as stated. Obviously, everyone should realize this is not the way a fraudulent deceiver operates. Therefore, what happened on this occasion was authentic and in accordance with God's revealed will. In addition, this event with King Saul plays a genuine part of the revelation about *Sheol*.

As we have already learned, Sheol was down within the earth. The language used in this case was additionally specific—to "bring up," "coming up out of the earth," "coming up" and "bringing me up." In addition Samuel specifically said Saul and his sons would join or "be with" him (Samuel, in Sheol) the very next day.

Such revelation can never be circumvented except to one's own confusion, frustration and predicament—just like that of King Saul.

King David and his son

When King David sinned and committed immorality, a child was conceived by Bathsheba (2 Sam. 11:5). After the total exposure of David's sin of the adultery and the murder of Bathsheba's husband, Uriah, judgment was placed upon David which included the death of the infant who had been conceived. Sometime after the birth of the child, it became seriously ill. David sincerely pleaded for the child, fasted and lay all night upon the ground. Several days later the child died. David's servants were afraid to even tell him of the fact out of fear of increasing David's sorrow. When David finally realized that the child had died, instead of worse expressions of sorrow, he washed and anointed himself, put on other garments, went into the house of the Lord and worshipped. Then he returned to his own palace and ate.

David's servants were dumfounded by the apparent irregularity of his actions. When asked for an explanation, David said—

> *While the child was still alive, I fasted and wept; for I said, 'Who knows, the LORD may be gracious to me, that the child may live. But now he has died; why should I fast? Can I bring him back again?* **I will go to him,** *but he will not return to me'* —2 Sam. 12:22–23.

Of course, the language here is similar to that which Samuel used. He spoke of Saul and his sons being with him shortly. This also meant that when the child died, it did not cease to exist. The *spirit* of the child was automatically safe. This safety was by virtue of the fact of Christ's death for all the sins of the world; this meant that Christ's supreme sacrifice covered all the inherited sin-natures as well. That substitutionary sacrifice in God's merciful plan could never be rejected by the child; the soul of the child would be safe as a result. Therefore David knew that one day he, as a saved and forgiven man, would be with his child. This passage also sheds light on all the infants who die in their infancy or pass out of this life in innocence. Those who die in innocence, who have not rejected God's merciful kindness, are positively safe.

2 Sam. 22:6   "The chords of *Sheol* surrounded me; the snares of death confronted me."

This is a Psalm of David wherein he rejoiced in being delivered from physical death and from being pulled down to Sheol prematurely.

1 Kings 2:6   ". . . and do not let his gray head go down to *Sheol* in peace."

1 Kings 2:9   ". . . and you will bring his gray hair down to *Sheol* with blood."

These statements were made in King David's counsel to his son, Solomon. Though Joab was the commander of David's army, yet he had committed certain crimes for which he needed to suffer punishment. David therefore wanted Solomon to order the execution of Joab. The same was true of Shimiel who had cursed David at the time of Absalom's insurrection; he also must pay for his sins.

Some references of this nature (1 Kings 2:6, 9) could possibly be understood to merely mean the grave if this was all we knew about Sheol. However, the context does not actually demand that it be understood as a mere grave! And in the light of all the other facts revealed about Sheol, it is by far more consistent to understand *Sheol* as the same in every case. Thus did the Hebrew translators who wrote the Greek Septuagint.

The Book of ISAIAH

Isa. 5:14–16   "Therefore *Sheol* has enlarged its *throat* and opened its *mouth* without measure; and Jerusalem's splendor, her multitude, her din of revelry, and the jubilant within her, *descend into it*. So the common man will be humbled and the man of importance abased. The eyes of the proud

also will be abased. But the LORD of hosts shall
be exalted in *judgment*."

There is no mistaking *Sheol* as a place of judgment for the rebels
of Jerusalem. In this passage of Isaiah, Sheol is personified as some
great subterranean monster which swallows down its prey. For the
souls of the wicked there is no honored funeral service or long procession of mourners. Rather, it is a humbling mass descent "down"
into the stomach of Sheol.

Isa. 14:9–20

This next passage from the prophet Isaiah begins as a very sober
prophecy of God's judgment upon the nation of Babylonia. However
its major aim is to focus upon the ultimate destruction of Lucifer.
The king of Babylon is mentioned in the foreground or beginning,
but will become the mere backdrop for the future destruction and
judgment upon Lucifer, himself. We need to read the following
passages carefully. This is clearly a major passage on the subject
of Sheol in the Hebrew Scriptures. Again, this is totally consistent
with everything else we have learned so far about Sheol. There is no
need, therefore, to try and explain it away as many try to do, who
do not appreciate a literal understanding of the subject of Sheol as
revealed in the Scriptures.

This is the second time we will hear conversation from those in
Sheol. Samuel came up and spoke truthfully about the future death
of King Saul. His words were not the words of a lying deceiver, but
of accurate spiritual rebuke and a correct foretelling of the future.
Now, here in the prophecy of Isaiah, the "spirits" of the kings
of the earth in Sheol form a *reception committee* for the king of
Babylon and beyond him, ultimately for Lucifer, himself, in the far
distant future—

Isa. 14:9   (9) "***Sheol from beneath*** is excited over you
                   [*king of Babylon*, verse 3; *Lucifer*, verses 12 &
                   13] to meet you when you come; it arouses for
                   you the **spirits of the dead**, all the leaders of the
                   earth; it raises all the kings of the nations from

their thrones. (10) They will all respond and say to you, '*Even you have been made weak as we, you have become like us.* (11) *Your pomp and the music of your harps have been*

Isa. 14:11   *brought down to **Sheol**; Maggots are spread out as your bed beneath you, and worms are your covering.'*
(12) How have you fallen from heaven, *O Star of the Morning* [or Morning Star, Lucifer], *Son of the Dawn!* You have been cut down to the earth, you who have weakened the nations!" (Verses 13 and 14 tell of Satan's original rebellion.)

Isa. 14:15   (15) "Nevertheless you will be thrust down to **Sheol**, to the recesses of the **Pit**. (16) *Those who see you* will gaze at you, they will ponder over you, saying, '*Is this the man who made the earth tremble, who shook kingdoms,* (17) *who made the world like a wilderness and overthrew its cities, who did not allow his prisoners to go home?'* (18) All the kings of the nations lie in glory, each in his own tomb. (19) But you have been cast out of your tomb like a rejected branch, clothed with the slain who are pierced with a sword, who go down to **the stones of the Pit** like a trampled corpse. (20) You will not be united with them in burial, . . ."

As it relates to the spirit world, this is an incredible passage. *Sheol* is clearly the residence of the departed "spirits of the dead" (verse 9). As stated earlier, the Hebrew word *raphah* means "shades," "disembodied spirits" or "ghosts" of the dead (see Strong, Young, or Gesenius). Eight times this word is used in the Hebrew Scriptures. Four of those times it is used in connection with Sheol or Abaddon—Job 26:5–6; Psalm 88:10–11; Prov. 9:18 and here in Isa. 14:9. In this passage of Divine revelation the occupants of Sheol are *conscious* and *talking*, yet they are spoken of as being "*the dead*." Consequently "death" as it applies to Sheol does not mean and cannot mean "cessation of being" or "non-existence." Rather, the word "death" should be understood as "separation"—separation, first of all from the life of God, and then separation of the spirit from the body. Never in the context of Sheol should "death" be thought of as nonexistence. Rather, we learn from passages like this that "death" is actually a ***condition of existence***, separate from the life of God, and/or separation of the soul from the body.

Some have taken this to merely be an animated description of physical death because of the mention of "maggots" and "worms." However, the context clearly specifies the "spirits of the dead" and the eventual presence of the spirit creature—Lucifer, himself. Furthermore, Jesus Christ also spoke of "worms" that "never die" in relationship to Hell (see Mark 9:44, 46 and 48).

In addition, this passage actually looks past the destiny of the king of Babylon to the future time when Lucifer will be cast out of heaven to the earth (Isa. 14:12; Luke 10:18 and Rev. 12:7–12). And then a very short time later Lucifer will be cast into the *Bottomless Pit* (Isa. 14:15 and Rev. 20:1–3). No one doubts that Lucifer is an intelligent spirit creature who will thus end up in Sheol, Hades or Hell. Even this will not be his ultimate destiny.

Amazing as it may seem, we have here a fitting judgment upon Lucifer. If we will remember, at the original creation of Lucifer, many great and magnificent things were said about him. In Ezekiel 28 we are informed that Lucifer was *"the anointed Cherub who covers"* and that he *"walked back and forth in the midst of the stones of fire"* (28:14). These stones of fire represented God's very dwelling place in the "mountain of God" (see also Exodus 24:9, 10 where they are referred to as a pavement of *"sapphire stones"*). These stones literally radiated beauty. But now, at his inglorious end, Lucifer has instead nothing but *"the stones of the Pit"*—the just result of the rebellion of pride. Also in the justice of God, He has determined that it will be equitable for all those who have rejected His grace and mercy, shown for them when Christ "died for our sins," to allow them to now "die IN their sins."

According to this passage of Scripture, Lucifer is obviously not the only one to be in Sheol. According to the revelation of the passage, many other spirit beings have been long in residence in Sheol. The aroused dead are leaders and kings who have lived in the past on the earth, but are now residents of Sheol. They seem to greatly anticipate this event. They form, as it were, the *"welcoming committee"* for Satan. They will speak to him as portrayed by the text. So here again is an accurate and inspired look inside the depths of *Sheol* in the Hebrew Scriptures.

Isa. 28:15   "Because you have said, 'We have made a covenant with death, and with *Sheol* we have made a pact.'"

Isa. 28:18   "Your covenant with death will be canceled, and your pact with *Sheol* will not stand; . . ."

In the context of these two passages, some of the rulers of Judah had mocked God's warning of impending judgment. They pretended to not be worried about death and Sheol. However, God says otherwise. In this case there is the evident distinction between "death" (physical) and "Sheol" (their spiritual destiny).

Isa. 38:10   "[Hezekiah said] In the middle of my life I am to enter the gates of *Sheol;* . . ."

Isa. 38:18   "For *Sheol* cannot thank You [God], death cannot praise You; those who *go down to the Pit* cannot hope for Your faithfulness."

Hezekiah did not want to die at this time in his life. Therefore he spoke despairingly of Sheol. If we keep in mind that Israel's primary hope was in the realization of God's blessings to them "in the Land of Promise," we can better appreciate their reluctance to go to their holding place in Sheol.

In the context of the following passage, Isaiah gave God's word of strong rebuke to rebellious, idolatrous and hypocritical Israel who pretends to serve God, but in obvious deliberate mockery shows contempt instead. In response God sent their "envoys down to Sheol."

Isa. 57:9   "[The evil people of Israel who had mocked God] You have sent your envoys a great distance and made them *go down to Sheol.*"

Continuing in the Prophets

In the context of the following Scriptures from Ezekiel 31, God warned Pharaoh in Egypt about their haughty pride. God exhorted them to look at the judgment He brought upon the Assyrians in their day of pride.

Ezek. 31:15   ". . . On the day when it [Assyria] went down to *Sheol* I caused lamentations; . . ."

Ezek. 31:16   ". . .when I made it to go *down* to *Sheol* with those who go down to **the Pit***; . . ."

Ezek. 31:17   "They also went down with it to *Sheol* to those who were slain by the sword; . . ."

God further warned the Egyptians in chapter 32. The statements in Ezekiel 32 are **major statements** and we will look at them in context more carefully later under the designation of *"the Pit."* I have emphasized several times the use of the word "pit" in connection with Sheol. Actually several different Hebrew words are used for "Pit" and we will investigate each of them when we get there.

Ezek. 32:21   "The strong among the mighty ones shall *speak of him* [Egypt] and his helpers from the midst of *Sheol,* . . ."

Ezek. 32:27   ". . . who went down to *Sheol* with their weapons of war, . . ."

Hos. 13:14   "Shall I ransom them from the power of *Sheol*?
              Shall I redeem them from death? "

Hos. 13:14   "O death, where are your thorns? O *Sheol*, where
              is your sting?"

Here in Hosea is the third reference to the deliverance of the
saints out of Sheol. The first was clearly intimated in the book of
Job—Job 14:13, the second in 1 Sam. 2:6.

Amos 9:2   "Though they dig into *Sheol*, from there will My
              hand take them; though they ascend to heaven,
              from there will I bring them down."

Jonah 2:2   "... I cried for help from the depths of *Sheol*;....(6)
              I descended to the *roots of the mountains*. The
              earth with its *bars* was around me forever, but
              You have brought up my life from the *Pit*, ..."

Here, Jonah was impersonating the three day and three night sufferings of Jesus Christ in Sheol. This well-known event is referred to
by Christ Himself in the Gospels. The other designations used in this
passage along with Sheol indicate its depth within the earth. "The
roots of the mountains" would indicate the lower strata of earth and
not just some deep grave. "The earth with its bars" is indicative
of a prison. "From the Pit" tells us that no matter where a person
physically dies, whether on the ground or in the ocean, he still goes
to the "Pit." "The Pit" could not be a mere deep hole in the ground
since Jonah was near death in the depths of the ocean.

This is the final passage specifically mentioning Sheol from
the Prophets—

Hab. 2:5   "[The drunkard] enlarges his appetite like *Sheol*,
              and he is like death—never satisfied."

CHAPTER TEN

SHEOL OF THE WRITINGS
And OTHER DESIGNATIONS
(This is the third section of the Hebrew Scriptures.)

The Book of PSALMS

<u>Psalm 6:5</u>   ". . . in *Sheol* who shall give You thanks?"

<u>Psalm 9:17</u>   "The *wicked* will be turned to *Sheol*, even all the *nations* who forget God."

<u>Psalm 16:10</u> "For You will not abandon my soul to *Sheol*; nor will You allow Your Holy One to undergo decay."

Here is the fourth time in the Hebrew Scriptures where special deliverance from Sheol is mentioned concerning the righteous. In this case it has to do with King David. However, the apostle Peter observes that herein is a prophecy which applies to Christ (Acts 2:27). Therefore when Christ died, we are to understand that His "soul" went into "Sheol." The second Person of the Tri-unity did not cease to exist at physical death. Sheol became His soul's residence for three days and three nights according to the Scriptures. As this particular Scripture testifies, God did not "abandon" Christ's soul in Sheol, but reunited His soul to His body before it would decay. Consequently, once again we observe that physical death does not mean annihilation of the person's soul or spirit. Sheol is a real place for the existence of the spiritual natures of the dead.

Psalm 18:5   "The cords of *Sheol* surrounded me; the snares of death confronted me."

Psalm 30:3   "O LORD, You have brought up my soul from *Sheol*; You have kept me alive, that I would not go down to the *Pit*."

David was fearful of death and going to Sheol. God spared his life several times. By now you have noticed the words *"the Pit"* used many times as a synonym for *Sheol*. As I said before, we will examine these later because they are very strong and give further information concerning the existence and conditions of Sheol.

Psalm 31:17   "Let the wicked be put to shame, let them be silent in *Sheol*."

Psalm 49:14   "As sheep they [the wicked] are appointed for *Sheol*; death shall be their shepherd; . . ."

Psalm 49:14   ". . . and their form shall be for *Sheol* to *consume*. . . ."

Psalm 49:15   "But God will redeem my soul from the power of *Sheol*, for He will receive me."

This passage in Psalm 49:15 is either speaking of God preventing one from going to Sheol or it could possibly be the fifth reference to the eventual redemption of the righteous from Sheol. The same is true of Psalm 71:20 which states, "You Who have shown me many troubles and distresses will revive me again, and will bring me up again from the depths of the earth."

Psalm 55:15   "Let death come deceitfully upon them; let them go down alive to *Sheol*. . . ."

Certain enemies of the righteous were deserving of the same judgment of Korah, Dathan and Abiram in Numbers 16. When a person died his spiritual nature separated from his physical body and went into Sheol. In the case of Korah, Dathan and Abiram there was no separation. Their spirits and bodies all descended alive into Sheol.

Psalm 86:13   "For Your lovingkindness toward me is great, and You have delivered my soul from the depths of *Sheol*."

Psalm 88:3   ". . . and my life has drawn near to *Sheol*."

Psalm 89:48   "What man can live and not see death? Can he deliver his soul from the power of *Sheol*?"

Psalm 116:3   "The cords of death encompassed me and and the terrors of *Sheol* came upon me; . . ."

Psalm 139:8   "If I ascend to heaven, You art there; if I make my bed in *Sheol*, behold, You are there."

Psalm 141:7   "As when one plows and breaks open the earth, our bones have been scattered at the mouth of *Sheol*."

A great deal of commentary could be made on each of these passages. However, they speak fairly well for themselves for the purpose of this study.

The Book of PROVERBS and SONG of SOLOMON

Prov. 1:12   ". . . let us swallow them alive like *Sheol*, even whole, as those that go down to the *Pit*."

This is yet another reminder of the fate of Korah, Dathan and Abiram.

Prov. 5:5   "Her feet go down to death, her steps take hold of *Sheol*."

Prov. 7:27   "Her house is the way to *Sheol*, descending to *the Chambers of Death*."

In the book of Job the "gates" of *Sheol* were discussed. Here Solomon speaks of the "Chambers of Death." We learn from other Scriptures that there is a variety of different spirit occupants in Sheol; some are human spirits and some are angelic and demonic, each within an apparently different section or "chamber."

Prov. 9:18   "But he does not know that the dead are there, that her guests are in the depths of *Sheol*."

Prov. 15:11   "*Sheol* and *Abaddon* lie open before the LORD; how much more the hearts of men."

Prov. 15:24   "The path of life leads upward for the wise, that he may keep away from *Sheol* below."

Prov. 23:14   "You shall strike him with the rod, and shall rescue his soul from *Sheol*."

Many have thought that in this last passage *Sheol* must mean "death" simply because the correction applied can effectively be a warning to a child, guiding him away from possible physical death later on. Of course, parents have often implemented discipline for the very purpose of avoiding physical death. However, in the very same sense, the lessons of discipline for the child in this life are also effectively designed to warn them of the ultimate penalty of Hell in the afterlife. Indeed, there are many judgments in this life which stand as effective warnings of judgment in the afterlife.

Prov. 27:20   "*Sheol* and *Abaddon* are never satisfied, . . ."

Prov. 30:15–16 "There are three things that will not be satisfied,
. . . *Sheol*, . . ."

Ecc. 9:10   ". . . for there is no activity or planning or knowledge or wisdom in *Sheol* where you are going."

From this passage we would learn that the various activities and
projects which characterize life on earth will no longer be applicable
in the prison house of Hell.

Song of Sol. 8:6 ". . . jealousy is as severe as *Sheol*; its flashes
are flashes of fire, *the very flame of the LORD*."

This can be understood as another reference to the fact of
fire in Sheol.

It might be added that the New American Standard Version
has one more occasion for the use of "Sheol" and that is in Job
33:18—"He keeps back his soul from the Pit, and his life from
passing over into *Sheol*."

It can be stated that not one single passage containing the word
Sheol absolutely demands that it be understood as something other
than the residence of the spirits or souls of the dead. In other words,
there is actually no need to try and arbitrarily determine where the
Hebrew word *Sheol* should mean eternal Hell and where it should not.

Other Important Designations

We have reviewed all the passages that use the designation—
SHEOL. These can be studied more carefully as you have time.
At the end of this Section I will be making a summary concerning
Sheol and the other descriptions as they are used in the Hebrew
Scriptures. Some of the other designations for the subject of *Sheol*
are as follows—

1.   We have also already noted the designation, ***ABADDON***. See again Job 26:6; 31:12; Prov. 15:11; 27:20 and Rev. 9:11. We have noted that the Hebrew word *Abaddon* means **destruction.** However, since Abaddon is a place of destruction for some, and yet the occupants continue to exist for thousands of years, we would understand that this does not mean their *extinction* of being. Abaddon therefore describes a condition of existence and not the extermination of existence.

2.   We also pointed out the expression, ***The CHAMBERS OF DEATH,*** from Proverbs 7:27. In the book of Job God asked the question—"Have the gates of death been revealed to you, or have you seen the gates of the deep darkness?" (Job. 38:17). As we can see from the many passages in the Hebrew Scriptures on this subject, God is opening the doors or "gates" on "the chambers of death" for the believer's investigation. And we shall see that those doors will be opened even wider by the Lord Jesus Christ.

3.   Another expression used is ***The LAND OF DARKNESS.*** A few of the passages which refer to the darkness of Sheol are Job 10:21, 22; 38:17 and Psalm 88:6.

4.   ***PRISON* and *PRISONERS*** are also used in regard to Sheol; see Isa. 14:17 and 24:22. A further description of Sheol (Jonah 2:2) is intimated in Jonah 2:6 as with "the earth with *its bars*." It will be further referenced in 1 Peter 3:19. It is also stated in the famous passage of Isaiah 61:1 that Messiah, at His first coming, will release the *"prisoners."* And then, in Ephesians 4:8 we are told that when Christ "ascended on high" from "the lower parts of the earth," "He led ***captive a host of captives***." This appears to be a reference to the righteous souls imprisoned in Sheol until the glorious redemption victory and ascension of Christ out of Sheol (see also Psalm 68:18 and 1 Samuel 30:18–20).

5.   Another expression which is used to describe Sheol's location is ***The LOWER PARTS OF THE EARTH***. Thus it is described in Ezek. 26:20 and 32:24. Ezekiel 31:16 connects *"Sheol," "the Pit"*

and "*in the earth beneath*" all together. This is the similar expression used by the apostle Paul in Ephesians 4 to describe the work of Christ in delivering "captivity." Paul said "*What does it mean but that He also had first descended into the lower parts of the earth?*" (Eph. 4:9).

6.   Last, there is the word ___PIT___ which deserves special attention because it is used so many times—approx. 32 or more times in reference to Hell or *Sheol*. On at least 18 of these occasions it is directly linked with Sheol—note the following passages.

"The PIT"
And "The Lower Parts of the Earth"

• The first word in the Hebrew for Pit is *be-er,* and it simply means a *well* or *pit*. This word is used many times of just an ordinary pit dug and used by man for various purposes. However, it is also used as another reference for Sheol.

Psalm 55:23   "But You, O God, will bring them [the wicked] down to *the Pit of Destruction*; . . ." (In verse 15 is the word *Sheol*.)

Psalm 69:15   (Prayer that God may not allow catastrophe to come upon him) ". . . nor *the Pit* shut its mouth on me."

• The second Hebrew word for Pit is *bo-or,* and it means a cistern sometimes used as a prison. This likewise is often used in reference to Sheol.

Psalm 28:1   ". . . I will become like those who go down to *the Pit*."

Psalm 30:3   "O Lord, You have brought up my soul from *Sheol*; You have kept me alive, that I would not go down to *the Pit*."

Psalm 30:9   "What profit is there in my blood, if I go down to *the Pit*?" (Sheol is mentioned in verse 3.)

Psalm 88:3–4 ". . . and my life has drawn near to *Sheol*. I am reckoned with those who go down to *the Pit*."

Psalm 88:6   "You have put me in *the lowest Pit*, in dark places, in the depths." (Verse 3 is Sheol.)

Psalm 143:7   ". . . will I become like those who go down to *the Pit*?"

Prov. 1:12   "Let us swallow them alive like *Sheol*, even whole, as those who go down to *the Pit*."

Isa. 14:15   "Nevertheless you will be thrust down to *Sheol*, to *the recesses* [or depths] *of the Pit*."

Isa. 14:19   ". . . who go down to the stones of *the Pit*. . . ." (See Sheol, v. 15.)

Isa. 24: 21–22 "So it will happen in that day, that the LORD will punish the host of heaven on high, and the kings of the earth on earth. They will be gathered together like **prisoners in the Pit** [or dungeon] and will be confined in **prison**; and after many days they will be *punished*."

A look at this whole chapter from Isaiah will show a fearful description of the impending judgment on the earth at the time of the second coming of Messiah. Verse 23 concludes with *"For the LORD of hosts will reign on Mount Zion and in Jerusalem and before His ancients gloriously"* (NKJV). From the book of Revelation we learn that fallen angels will be cast out of Heaven and together with the wicked of earth will be placed in confinement until after the thousand year reign of Messiah (see Rev. 20:1–3 and Matthew 25:31,

32, 46). Thus, the earlier reference in Isaiah 24 describes Sheol as a
pit-prison.

Isa. 38:18   "For *Sheol* cannot thank You, death cannot praise
              You; those who go down to *the Pit* cannot hope
              for Your faithfulness."

Ezek. 26:20   ". . . then I shall bring you [the wicked of Tyre]
              down with those who go down to *the Pit, to the
              people of old*, and I will make you dwell in *the
              lower parts of the earth*, like the ancient waste
              place, with *those who go down to the Pit*, so that
              you will not be inhabited; but I will set glory in
              the land of the living."

Here is a very important passage on the subject. According to
this passage of Scripture the occupants of Sheol or *the Pit* have been
gathering there from ancient times and now the wicked of Tyre shall
join them in this desolate place in *"the lower parts of the earth."*
In addition, the domain of the dead stands in stark contrast to *"the
land of the living."* Consequently, we have the two realms clearly
spelled out for us where "people" dwell. The one is in "the land
of the living," which means living people here on earth. The other
is those occupants of "the Pit" or "the lower parts of the earth"
which includes "the people of old." We have learned about the past
occupants (the "ancients"), the present (the wicked of Tyre) and the
future occupants (those who will be so placed at the second coming
of Messiah).

Ezek. 31:14   "For they have all been given over to death, to
              the *earth beneath* [or *nether parts of the earth*],
              among the sons of men who *go down to the Pit*."
              (See *Sheol* in vv. 15 and 16.)

Ezek. 31:16   "I made the nations quake at the sound of its fall
              when I made it go *down to Sheol* with those who

> *go down to the Pit* . . . all were comforted in the
> *earth beneath* [or ***the nether parts of the earth***]."

Ezek. 31:17,18 "They also went down with it to *Sheol* . . . unto the
earth beneath [or ***the nether parts of the earth***]."

EZEKIEL 31 and 32, under the word "Pit"

Chapter 31 of Ezekiel prepares the way for similar facts being
brought out in the next chapter (32). Here in chapter 31 another
description of Sheol has been given as either "*in the earth beneath*"
or in "***the nether parts of the earth***" (R.V.). This is similar to "*the
lower parts of the earth*" as found in Ezek. 26:20 and 32:24. These
descriptions are mingled with "*down to the Pit*" (verses 14 and 16),
and "*down to Sheol*" (verses 15 and 16). In chapter 32 these facts
will be enlarged upon.

Ezek. 32:18   "Son of man, wail for the hordes of Egypt and
bring it down, her and the daughters of the powerful nations, to ***the nether world***, with those who
go down to *the Pit*." (See *Sheol*, vv. 21 and 27.)

Ezek. 32:23   ". . . whose graves are set in the remotest parts of
the Pit." (See *Sheol*, vv. 21 and 27.)

Ezek. 32:24   ". . . who went down uncircumcised to ***the lower
parts of the earth*** . . . with those who go down
to *the Pit*."

Ezek. 32:25   ". . . (although their terror was instilled in the
land of the living), and they bore their disgrace
with those who go down to *the Pit* . . . ."

Ezek. 32:29   "There also is Edom, its kings and all its
princes . . . with those who go down to *the Pit*."

Ezek. 32:30   "There also are the chiefs of the north . . . with those who go down to *the Pit*."

Ezekiel 32:17–31 is one of the more interesting passages on the subject of Hell in the Hebrew Scriptures. God told Ezekiel to lament for the land of Egypt because punishment by the hand of the king of Babylon is coming upon her. Babylon has already conquered many nations and Egypt sits as a beautiful queen, but she is about to be destroyed as well (v. 19).

There is to be noted a certain continuous repetition in this whole passage. God will call each of the nations to witness to the Egyptians that they are soon going to be joining them in *"Sheol—the Pit."* So the destruction of Egypt, and of the various nations before her, was actually twofold. On the one hand, their strong armies were, of course, slain with their graves scattered about. Each of those nations was once strong themselves and had much power *"in the land of the living"* (verses 23, 24, 25, 26, 28 and 32). Nevertheless, each of the nations will now also be joined by the Egyptians who descend into *"Sheol,"* or *"the Pit,"* or *"the nether* [lower] *parts of the earth."* Therefore, there will emerge here a contrast between death in "*the land of the living*" and a further descent into "*the nether parts of the earth*," which is *Sheol* or *the Pit*. In both realms the people are understood to be *animated* and *conscious*. Obviously, those alive on earth are physically and spiritually intact. Obviously, as well, those in Sheol are yet spoken of as alive and cognizant, and in one case will be called upon to speak to them *"out of the midst of Sheol."* Amazing, is it not?

First, the Egyptians shall be *"cast down"* into *"the nether parts of the earth with them that go down into the Pit"* (verse 18). The Egyptians will die by the sword (v. 20). Then *"the strong among the mighty ones shall speak of him* [Egypt] and his helpers from *the midst of Sheol, . . ."* (v. 21).

Next, the Assyrians are there in Sheol as well. On the one hand, they are said to be *"slain by the sword"* with *"the graves all around"* (v. 22). Yet on the other hand their *"graves are set in the remotest parts of the Pit"* (v. 23). This may be the only verse in the Bible where we have "graves" in Hell. Job spoke of making *"his bed"* in

"the darkness of Sheol" (Job 17:13). The Psalmist did the same—
"If I make my bed in Sheol, You are there" (Psalm 139:8). Of course,
"bed" is understood as a metaphor and, no doubt, this use of *"grave"*
is also to be understood as a metaphor. There can be "graves" for
the bodies on earth and "graves" for souls in Sheol. This would also
further illustrate that the word "grave" could never actually be the
same as "Sheol" because here we have "graves" in Sheol.

Next is Elam. There are all *"her hordes slain by the sword"* in
their graves. Yet they are also gone down *"into the lower* [nether]
parts of the earth" and *"down to the Pit."* They at one time caused
"terror . . . in the land of the living" (verses 24–27).

Next are those of Meshech, Tubal and their multitudes. Their
graves are all around them. They also caused *"terror in the land of
the living."* But now they *"went down to Sheol with their weapons of
war and whose swords were laid under their heads; but the iniquity
rested on their bones, . . ."* Here we have a mixture of terms between
the physical and the spiritual parts of death for punishment (v. 26).
In Sheol these men cannot shake loose from their instruments of
death nor from their iniquities. In other words, there are memorials
of their crimes which follow them into Hell.

Then the Edomites and the Sidonians who once caused terror in
the earth are now with them *"that go down into the Pit"* (vv. 29, 30).

Finally "Pharaoh wi*ll see, and will be comforted for all his
hordes slain by the sword."* And now he also *"shall be made to lie
down among the uncircumcised. . . ."* (v. 32).

• A third Hebrew word for Pit is **shachath** and it has reference
to *corruption, a trap* or *pit*, i.e., to *corrupt*. This is another use of
"Pit" as a synonym for Sheol.

Job 33:18   "He keeps back his soul from *the Pit* . . .
              from passing into Sheol."

Job 33:22   "Then his soul draws near to *the Pit, . . .*"

Job 33:24   ". . . 'Deliver him from going down to *the Pit, . . .*'"

Job 33:28   "He has redeemed my soul from going to *the Pit, . . .*"

Job 33:30   "To bring back his soul from *the Pit, . . .*"

Psalm 103:4   "Who redeems your life from *the Pit, . . .*"

Isa. 38:17–18 "It is You Who has kept my soul from *the Pit of nothingness . . .* for *Sheol* cannot thank You, . . ."

Jonah 2:6   "I descended to the roots of the mountains; the earth with its bars was around me forever; but You have brought up my life from *the Pit,* O LORD my God." (See Sheol, v. 2.)

See also *"Pit"* and *"Bottomless Pit"* in Revelation 9:1, 2, 11; 11:7; 17:8; 20:1 and 3.

Other Related References

Daniel 7:11

In the seventh chapter of his book the prophet Daniel received a revelation of four "beasts" arising out of the sea of humanity which represented four great world empires. Most all interpreters recognize that the last beast represented the Roman Empire. In the vision the final phase of that empire will be headed by a "horn" who is generally recognized as the one we call "Antichrist" (Dan. 7:8 and 9). Daniel also beheld the final "destruction" of that beast in the form of the world leader who opposed God. Daniel 7:11 says,

> *. . .I kept looking until the beast was slain, and its **body** was **destroyed** and given to **the burning fire**.*

Now in the last book of the Bible, the book of Revelation, this same event is further described by John (Rev. 19:20) in the following manner:

*And the beast was seized, and with him the false prophet
. . . these two were thrown **alive** into **the Lake of Fire** which
burns with brimstone.*

So now we can understand that the *fire* Daniel beheld was
actually a glimpse of the final form of Hell, which is designated
as *"the Lake of Fire"* (which is also called *Gehenna*). In addition,
in the vision of Daniel the beast is spoken of as being *"slain"* and
"its body destroyed." Apparently, this does not mean that the beast
ceased to exist because in the Revelation account we are expressly
told that the beast was *"alive"* in the Lake of Fire. And furthermore,
in Revelation 20:1–10, we understand that after being in the Lake
of Fire for the duration of the 1000 year reign of Messiah the "beast
and false prophet" *"ARE"* still in existence in the Lake of Fire. In
other words their *"destruction"* is an ongoing, conscious destruction.

Daniel 12:2

*Many of those who sleep in the dust of the ground will
awake, these to everlasting life, **but the others to disgrace
and everlasting contempt**.*

This passage of Divine revelation is highly important for two
reasons. First of all, notice the word "awake." What does this have
reference to? Obviously it looks back in the sentence to those *"who
sleep in the dust of the ground."* Spirits do not sleep in the dust of the
ground. All that we have learned so far tells us that the spirits of the
dead go to Sheol. However, the physical bodies of the dead are said
to return to the dust. Therefore the "awaking" of those who "sleep
in the dust" pertains strictly to the physical bodies of the dead. It
means that at a future day, as described in the context, the bodies of
the dead will be raised from the dust of the earth and reunited with
their spirits to constitute "living" once again.

Second, there are clearly two distinct categories of "awakening."
Some will be awakened to "everlasting life." The quality of physical
life which they will enjoy is "everlasting life." This means that

physically they will enjoy what is later in the Greek Scriptures to be called "immortality" of the body.

On the other hand, some others will awaken as well, but not to the same quality of existence. Their existence will be in a condition of "disgrace" and "everlasting contempt." That means their bodies will merely be resurrected to normal human life, like a sick person who dies being brought back to his previous corrupt physical life. Not only that, their awakening (resurrection) to "*disgrace*" and "*contempt*" will be for an "everlasting" existence. Now we all must realize that the only way you can have everlasting "shame" and "contempt" is if you have "*everlasting*" *EXISTENCE* in mortal bodies.

Isaiah 33:14

Sinners in Zion are terrified;
Trembling has seized the godless.
Who among us can live with the ***consuming fire***?
Who among us can live with ***continual burning***?

This is actually a prophetic vision which Isaiah saw. Its setting in context will be the time when Israel will see her King in His beauty (verse 17). In contrast to the wicked, the righteous will "dwell on the heights" (see verses 15 and 16). To "*dwell on the heights*" with their Messiah will no doubt be in the Kingdom glory. In contrast, the wicked are "*to dwell with the consuming fire*" and "*continual burnings.*" This must be an existence just as certain as the other. However, it will be an existence or "*dwelling*" as described with "consuming fire" and "continual burning." This dwelling will no doubt be in Sheol until their appointed time for the Judgment to which they are reserved.

Isaiah 66:24

The primary reason this passage should be quoted is that the language from it is quoted or repeated again in the Greek Scriptures and from the mouth of the Lord Jesus Christ. It constitutes the terminology for future eternal punishment of the wicked. What Isaiah is inspired to say in this context has to do with the destruction of the wicked who revolt against the coming reign of the Messiah. This will take place just prior to Messiah's reign when all His enemies will be destroyed. Jesus Christ was proclaiming His coming Kingdom and in turn He uses this same language as in this Isaiah passage—

> Then they [mankind] will go forth [out of Jerusalem] and look on the corpses of the men who have transgressed against Me [God-Messiah]. *For their worm will not die and their fire will not be quenched*; and they shall be an abhorrence to all mankind.

This appears to be the physical *bodies* of those who revolted in the final phase of that climactic period we commonly call "the Great Tribulation." At that time the Messiah will trample the armies which come to fight against Israel and Jerusalem.

It must be kept in mind, however, that the application of these words made by our Lord Jesus Christ in the Gospel account (Mark 9:43–48) may be an altogether different proposition. We shall see when we come to the subject of Hell in the Greek Scriptures that Christ also applies these very same words to an altogether different period *after* the Kingdom reign, and after the final Judgment wherein the wicked are cast into the Lake of Fire itself.

Solomon on Ultimate Judgment

In the book of Ecclesiastes Solomon makes reference twice to the fact that all men will ultimately come to judgment for everything they have done. This includes all acts done whether known or in secret and whether good or evil.

> **God will judge both the righteous man and the wicked man.** Ecc. 3:17.

> *The conclusion, when all has been heard, is: fear God and keep His commandments, because this applies to*

*every person. **For God will bring every act to judgment,** everything which is hidden, whether it is good or evil.* Ecc. 12:13 and 14.

The fact that there is to be an ultimate judgment of mankind by God carries with it several very positive deductions. Every person will obviously have to be in existence. Even though all mankind experience physical death throughout the centuries, yet somehow all mankind will consciously be in existence in order for this judgment to proceed. Consequently we deduce that though people die physically, that does not end their conscious existence. In addition, later revelation comes in the Hebrew Scriptures that all mankind will experience the physical resurrection of their bodies (see Daniel 12:2). Thus it is, with mankind's souls rejoined with their resurrected mortal bodies they will experience this ultimate Judgment.

Of course, this revelation by Solomon is eventually complemented by the revelation in the book of Revelation of that ultimate Judgment—Rev. 20:11–15.

This Concludes Our Survey of the Revelation from the Hebrew Scriptures on the subject of Sheol

I am quite sure that much more could have been said about each of the passages and that there is much more information to be found. *But I am also quite sure that this collection will **refute** the stupidity of the accusation that "very little is said in the Old Testament about Sheol and the punishment of the wicked."* Likewise, it positively refutes the conclusion that Sheol is just another word for "grave" and that there is no conscious punishment for the lost after physical death.

CHAPTER ELEVEN

SUMMARY AND CONCLUSION

⸙

INTRODUCTION

As an introduction to this *Summary and Conclusion*, I would like to quote some words from one who, as I stated before, is regarded as having done the "definitive work" on this issue of Hell and the everlasting punishment of the lost. His work was 500 pages long. It is certainly a definitive work in cataloging what everybody else says about Hell. However, he spent only five pages on "Sheol of the Old Testament," and then concluded that the Old Testament says very little about the subject. Not only throughout his book—but also on the subject of Sheol in those five pages—most quotes are what *others say* the Old Testament says and NOT what the Old Testament *actually says*. In quoting some of these people, he actually gives *his own conclusion* as well—

- "The Old Testament 'contains little information, . . .'"
- "The scarcity of Old Testament material."
- "Old Testament references to life after death are 'few and rather obscure.'"
- "Man is not an eternal soul trapped in a crude body."
- "Nowhere in the OT is the abode of the dead regarded as a place of punishment or torment."
- "The New International Version usually translates *sheol* by grave, . . . This supports the conditionalists [his position], . . ."

180

- "The state of the deceased cannot be called 'life' in any meaningful sense."
- "'gravedom' [is] a suitable translation."
- "Sheol . . . is not a place of punishment."

All these statements are taken from *The Fire That Consumes* by E.W. Fudge, pages 77, 81 and 85 (said by some to be a definitive work on the subject of Hell from a "Conditionalist's" perspective). I say again, he certainly gave a definitive work, but it was most certainly NOT on the subject of what the BIBLE says about Sheol. Over against his conclusions concerning the Old Testament, **I place all of this** *Section Two*, which is specifically taken from the pages of the Hebrew Scriptures. You be the judge!

If you have read all the material to which I have drawn your attention, you will realize that I am endeavoring to allow the Bible to speak for itself. It speaks with a clarity, definition and *overwhelming volume* that one cannot escape. The pages of my study in this section equal about 50 pages compared to Fudge's five. When I read Mr. Fudge's book, I couldn't help but smile in some amazement—not because it was not well written and well researched, but because it becomes very obvious that, in all the supreme diligence of his investigation, he virtually forgot to investigate the Bible very carefully for himself! His research was indeed magnificent. He must have read a whole library of literature about Hell as researched by others. However, reading all the commentaries about the subject is not at all the same as studying the subject directly from the Scriptures. Most certainly his conclusions were not derived from what the Bible actually reveals!

SUMMARY of FACTS ABOUT SHEOL
Derived from the Hebrew Scriptures

I.

Sheol Should Never be Confused with the Grave.

1. The normal word for *grave* in the Hebrew Scriptures is <u>*queber*</u>—not *Sheol.*

2. There are many *graves* in the Hebrew Scriptures. Therefore, *queber* is often used in the <u>plural</u> approx. 29 times, whereas there is only <u>ONE</u> Sheol in the Hebrew Scriptures. Sheol is <u>never</u> used in the plural.

3. Men dug *graves* in the Hebrew Scriptures, whereas <u>no one ever dug a *Sheol*</u> because that was an understood impossibility.

4. Many men "had *graves*" in the Hebrew Scriptures, but no one ever "<u>had a *Sheol*</u>."

5. Men's bodies are laid out in their *graves.* No person's physical body was ever <u>laid out in *Sheol*</u>.

6. It is normally never stated that <u>a body goes to *Sheol*</u>. Bodies going into a *queber* is stated about 37 times.

7. In fact, in only one instance in the Bible did anyone's body ever go down into *Sheol*—<u>and that was alive</u>. The only thing ever said to be in *Sheol* were "*spirits* of the dead." On the other hand, *quebers* are for bodies.

8. Man was never said to <u>put someone into *Sheol*</u>. On the other hand, men are said to place people in a *queber* about 33 times.

9. Men are said to possess *graves*, but no one was ever said <u>to</u> possess *Sheol*.

10. Men often *touched and prepared graves*, but no one ever did so with *Sheol*.

11. Normally, dead bodies don't *talk* in their *graves*! In fact, we are never told of one that did. On the other hand, we have several conversations recorded for us in the Scriptures of those spirits residing in *Sheol*.

12. If you still think something like "gravedom" would be a better translation, then you still have the problem of explaining why it is placed in "*the lower parts of the earth*" instead of being where all the *graves* are.

II.

The Greek Septuagint—the Jewish Translators of the Hebrew Scriptures into the Greek most Uniformly rendered Sheol as Hades

Nearly every one of the 65 occurrences of *Sheol* in the Hebrew Scriptures is translated and rendered as *Hades* in the *Greek* translation. *Hades* was already commonly understood in the Grecian world and culture as the abode of the spirits of the dead. This translation was made by Hebrew scholars approximately 200 years before Christ. There was no question in the minds of those translators about the meaning of *Sheol* and what was the appropriate way to translate into the Greek in order to understand the significance of its meaning. They were most certainly positioned far closer to the subject as understood in the Jewish religion and its proper renderings in the Greek language than any scholar or group of scholars in our modern age.

Consequently, in the Greek New Testament *Hades* was used, especially whenever there was a quote from the Hebrew Scriptures of *Sheol*. The definition of *Hades* was automatic in the Greek Lexicons because it was already understood in the Greek culture to have the very same reference to the abode of the disembodied spirits of the dead.

Furthermore, in the Greek Scriptures a clear distinction is made between the realm of the physically dead (in the graves) and the realm of *Hades*, which was the same as *Sheol* of the Hebrew Scriptures; *see* Rev. 1:18 and 20:13, 14.

III.

The Location of Sheol

There is no debate about the fact that *Sheol* is always *downward*. As we saw in many cases, it is understood as "downward" in the ultimate sense of the word; it is the absolute maximum depth.

1. Over 35 times it is simply "**down**" or "downward"—Job 7:9; 17:15–16; 33:24; Gen. 37:35; 44:29, 31; Num. 16:33; 1 Kings 2:6, 9; Psalm 28:1; 30:3; 39:9; 55:15, 23; 88:3–4; 143:7; Prov. 1:12; 5:5; Isa. 14:11, 15, 19; 38:18; 57:9; Ezek. 26:20; 31:14, 15, 16, 17, 18; 32:18, 24, 25, 27, 29, 30.

2. From the Hebrew *tagh-tee* or *tachti* (Strong # 8482), Sheol is in the "**lowest**" part of the earth—Deut. 32:22; Psalm 63:9; 86:13; 88:6; Ezek. 31:14, 16, 18; "**the nether world**"—(32:18); "**the lowest part of the earth**"—Ezek. 26:20; 32:24 and Isa. 44:23.

3. "**below**"—Prov. 15:24.

4. "**depths**"—Jonah 2:2; Psalm 86:13; Prov. 9:18.

5. "**beneath**"—Isa. 14:9; Ezek. 31:14, 16 and 18.

6. Coming up "**out of the earth**"—1 Sam. 28:13, 14.

7. **"recesses of the Pit"**—Isa. 14:15.

8. **"descend"**—Num. 16:30; Prov. 7:27; Isa. 5:14–16; Jonah 2:6.

9. **"roots of the mountains"**—Jonah 2:6.

10. **"deep darkness"**—Job 38:17.

11. The **ultimate depth**, in opposition to heaven—Job 11:8; Psalm 139:8 and Amos 9:2

If God wanted us to know that *Sheol* was a place for the "*disembodied spirits*" in "*the heart of the earth*," how else could He have told us?

IV.

Descriptive Terms of a Residence

1. **"Gather[ing]"** place for the dead, especially used for the righteous—see such passages as Gen. 49:29–33; 25:8, 17; 35:29; 37:35, etc.

2. **"House,"** as a residence—Job 17:13.

3. **"Chambers of death"**—Prov. 7:27.

4. **"Prison"** with **"prisoners"**—Isa. 14:17; 24:22; 1 Pet. 3:19, 20.

5. **"Gates"**—Isa. 38:10; Job 38:17, etc.

6. **"Bars"**—Jonah 2:6.

7. **"The Pit"** or **"the lowest Pit"**—Prov. 1:12; 30:3; Isa. 14:15; 38:10; Ezek. 31:16; Jonah 2:6, etc.

8. **"Stones of the Pit"**—Isa. 14:19.

9. **"Never full"** or **"satisfied"**—Prov. 27:20; 30:16; Isa. 5:14; Hab. 2:5.

10. **"Abaddon"** (destruction)—Job 28:22; 31:12; Ps. 88:11; Prov. 15:11; 27:20, etc.

11. **"Land of separation** [or solitary land]"—typology of the Day of Atonement—Lev. 16:22.

12. **"The land of darkness"**—Job 10:21, 22; 38:17; Psalm 88:6.

13. **"The lower parts of the earth"**—Ezek. 26:20; 32:24 and Isa. 44:23. (This is also in contrast to *"The Land of the Living."*)

14. **"Assembly"** (of the dead)—Prov. 21:16.

Now some false teachers might look at all these expressions and say, "These are just figures of speech like metaphors; we can't take them literally!" To which I would answer—JUST WHAT ARE THEY FIGURES OF? CAN THE REALITY BE ANY LESS THAN THE FIGURE?

V.

The Occupancy, **All that Die—Souls or Spirits of Mankind**

Though "bones may be scattered at the mouth of *Sheol*" (Psalm 141:7), yet it is only the souls or *"disembodied spirits"* of the dead which *"descend into Sheol."* The Hebrew word for soul is *nephesh,* which can have a wide variety of meanings depending on the context. One of its meanings, as understood by the Hebrew people because of clear Biblical usage, was the inner spiritual nature of man which departs his body at death and continues to exist in *Sheol.* Those who reject the existence of a *conscious* place of torment for the wicked will use only the definition which suits their philosophy. For instance, "soul is just life or animation," they say. And again some say "one ceases to exist when the breath (spirit) is taken away." This distortion amounts to a fool-osophy which in reality sends people right into Hell. But our Savior will address this false idea more thoroughly later. David of old spoke by inspiration—

"For You will not abandon My **soul** to *Sheol*, nor will You allow Your Holy One to undergo decay"—Psalm 16:10.

The best commentary on this passage is that of the inspired apostle Peter as recorded in the book of Acts. He not only segregated the location of the soul apart from the body, but he used Christ, Himself, as the primary example. Notice, please, Peter's quote of this passage as recorded in the Greek New Testament—

"Because Thou wilt not abandon my soul to Hades, nor allow Thy Holy One to undergo decay" (Acts 2:27).

Now in the passage from the Psalms which Peter is quoting, David was talking about his own personal *soul* not being abandoned in *Sheol*. In addition, David was inspired to say that the Messiah Himself would not see bodily corruption. However, the apostle Peter applied both principles to the one person, Christ—

"He [David] looked ahead and spoke of the resurrection of the Christ, that He [Christ] was neither abandoned to *Hades* [Sheol], nor did His [Christ's] flesh suffer decay" (Acts 2:31).

Thus, not only did Peter separate Christ's soul by the designation "*HE*," but Peter also placed Christ, as to His person, in *HADES*, the place of disembodied spirits of the dead, the Greek translation of the Hebrew word *Sheol*.

So, let there be no misunderstanding, when the Hebrew Scriptures talk of "*souls*" or "*spirits*" in Sheol, this means the spiritual persons apart from their bodies. Again David and others by inspiration said the following—

"O LORD, You have brought up my **soul** from Sheol; You have kept me alive, that I should not go down to the Pit"—Psalm 30:3.

"But God will redeem my **soul** from the power of Sheol, . . ." —Psalm 49:15.

"And You have delivered my **soul** from the depths of Sheol" —Psalm 86:13.

See also Job 33:18, 22, 28, 30 and Isa. 38:17.

"The departed [disembodied] **spirits** tremble under the waters and their inhabitants. Naked is Sheol before Him, . . ."—Job 26:5–6.

"But he does not know that the [disembodied] **spirits** are there, that her guests are in the depths of Sheol"—Prov. 9:18.

"A man who wanders from the way of understanding will rest in the **assembly** of the [disembodied] **spirits**"—Prov. 21:16.

"Sheol from beneath is excited over you to meet you when you come; It arouses for you the [disembodied] **spirits** of the dead, . . .'" Isa. 14:9.

Also, please remember *Samuel* was brought up and spoke *the truth*.

VI.

Living People Went Down to Sheol.

On one rare occasion, the earth opened up, and some went down alive into *Sheol*. This means they physically went down alive into *Sheol*. See Numbers 16:30–33. This was therefore both a bodily judgment and a spiritual judgment against those who rebelled against God's order at that time. Other writers, in later Jewish history, had hoped it would be possible for their wicked enemies to have the same judgment (see Psalm 55:15 and Prov. 1:12), but this was never again realized.

VII.

Classification of Souls—A. The Righteous

As we have seen, the righteous of past ages either are said to have anticipated going to *Sheol*, or else actually went into *Sheol*— Job, Abraham, Isaac, Jacob, Joseph, Samuel, Saul, Jonathan, David, David's son, etc., etc., etc.

There is never any indication that the righteous suffered any type of punishment in *Sheol*. In fact, Samuel felt *"disquieted"* by being "called up" to speak with King Saul. In Genesis there are clear indications that the righteous were "gathered" together after physical death. Other Scriptures might indicate that the righteous had special treatment. For instance, as it was said with envy even by a false prophet, who looked out upon the tents of Israel and spoke under the control of the Holy Spirit—*"Let me die the death of the upright, and let my end be like his"* (Num. 23:10). Psalm 73:24 states, *"You [God] will guide me with Your counsel, and afterwards receive me to glory."*

Though Sheol was considered a place of *"darkness"* (Job 10:21, 22, etc.), yet this did not prohibit the rich man in death from being able to observe the realm of the righteous in the account by our Lord Jesus Christ in Luke 16:19–31.

189

VIII.

The Righteous Expected Ultimate Deliverance

There are several indicators that the righteous looked forward to an ultimate deliverance from Sheol. This is first expressed by Job—

"Oh, that You would hide me in *Sheol,* that You would conceal me until Your wrath returns to You, that You would set a limit for me *and remember me!* " (Job 14:13).

"The LORD kills and makes alive; He brings down to Sheol *and raises up*" (1 Sam. 2:6).

"For *You will not abandon my soul to Sheol;...*" (Psalm 16:10).

"But God will *redeem my soul from the power of* Sheol, *for He will receive me*" (Psalm 49:15).

"The Spirit of the Lord God is upon Me, . . . to proclaim liberty to captives and freedom to prisoners; . . ." (Isa. 61:1).

"*Shall I ransom them from the power of Sheol? . . . O Sheol, where is your sting?*" (Hosea 13:14).

IX.

Classification of Souls—B. The Unrighteous

Many are the indicators that the wicked are especially destined for Sheol. Often these serve as *warnings* to the lost. It is therefore inconceivable that—for the un-righteous—*Sheol* will not be a place of suffering. Annihilation would, theoretically, be blissful to one who has numerous heinous crimes which he has committed for which he would only "cease to be." Let there be no doubt about it,

Summary And Conclusion

annihilation is the false gospel which the lost would relish, for then there would be little retribution for their wickedness.

> "They [the wicked] spend their days in prosperity, and suddenly they go down to *Sheol*" (Job 21:13).

> ". . . *Sheol* [consumes] those who have sinned" (Job 24:19).

> "The *wicked* will return to *Sheol, even all the nations who forget God*" (Psalm 9:17).

> ". . . Let the *wicked* be put to shame, let them be silent in *Sheol*" (Psalm 31:17).

> (The unrighteous) "As sheep they are appointed for *Sheol;* . . ." (Psalm 49:14).

> (The prostitute) ". . . Her steps take hold of Sheol" (Prov. 5:5).

> (The harlot) "Her house is the way to Sheol, . . ." (Prov. 7:27).

> "Therefore *Sheol* has enlarged its throat and opened its mouth without measure; and [the wicked of] Jerusalem's splendor, her multitude, her din of revelry and the jubilant within her, descend into it" (Isa. 5:14).

X.

Condition of Sheol—Suffering *for the Unrighteous*

As we first learned in the book of Job, Sheol has an alternate descriptive term used which is **Abaddon**. Abaddon appears to be a name like the word Sheol. It specifically means "**Destruction**." Now since Sheol and/or Abaddon is located in "*the heart of the earth*," this could not be speaking of the destruction of a physical body. We saw that on only one rare occasion did any live, physical bodies go there. Since the Scriptures also tell us that it is the "*spirits* of the dead" which go to Abaddon, then the act of destruction is upon the spirits of the dead. Likewise, since the Scripture indicates the dead are "*reserved*" (2 Pet. 2:4 and 9) for the Day of Judgment, then this *destruction* is actually a **continuous condition**, not a singular event of cessation of being. Remember also that the righteous dead are not said to be in *Abaddon*. This would certainly tell us that *Abaddon* is a section of Sheol reserved for the unrighteous. See the following—

> "Naked is *Sheol* before Him [God], and **Abaddon** [Destruction] has no covering" (Job 26:6).

> "But You, O God, will bring them [the unrighteous] down to **the Pit of destruction** [Abaddon]; . . ." (Psalm 55:23).

> "*Sheol* and **Abaddon** [Destruction] lie open before the LORD, . . ." (Prov. 15:11).

> ". . . It is You Who has kept my soul from **the Pit of Nothingness**, . . . [Lit., *Abaddon* or *Destruction*]" (Isa. 38:17).

> See also Job 28:22; 31:12; Psalm 88:12; Prov. 27:20 and Rev. 9:1-12.

Other descriptions of suffering in Sheol are indicated by the words "*consume* "—Psalm 49:14; Isa. 5:14–15 and Job 24:19; "*no activity, planning or wisdom*" such as those on earth—Ecc. 9:10; "*silence*"—Psalm 115:17; intense "*darkness*"—Job 10:21, 22 and Psalm 88:6; *abandonment* such as on the Day of Atonement—Lev. 16; *punishment* and *confinement* "*like prisoners in the dungeon*"—Isa. 24:21, 22; and finally "*fire*" is associated with Sheol at least four times—

> ". . .*fire that consumes* to Abaddon, . . ." (Job 31:12).

> "For a *fire* is kindled in My anger, and burns to the lowest part of *Sheol*, . . ." (Deut. 32:22).

". . . Jealousy is as severe as *Sheol*; its flashes are flashes of *fire*, the very *flame* of the LORD" (Song of Sol. 8:6).

". . . Who among us can live with the **consuming fire**? Who among us can live with **continual burning?** " (Isa. 33:14).

Therefore there should be no problem when Christ says that the rich man was in "*torment*" and "*in agony in this flame*" (Luke 16:23, 24). That understanding was not only depicted in the Hebrew Scriptures, which Christ knew most thoroughly, but it was also the belief of Orthodox Judaism at that time.

I should not leave this section until I comment on one of the infidel statements by those who endeavor to, as they say, "take the Hell out of Hell." To eradicate the possibility of there being a "fire" to punish the lost, they argue, "How can there be a fire in Hell and yet Hell be a place of darkness?" They smile as if to say, "you can't have both." But they don't realize that in reality they are presenting God with the problem, because it is God's Word that reveals and states both facts. And I am sure that God just smiles and says, "There is nothing impossible with Me!" I could also answer their paradox another way by observing what is common knowledge to miners. They quickly found out that the deeper they go into the earth, the DARKER it gets, and the HOTTER it gets. Miners who descend deep into the earth must have different types of protection or provision specially designed to prevent death because of the heat.

XI.

The Occupants Stirred up and Speak

Ezekiel 32:21—"The strong among the mighty ones shall *speak of him* [the king of Babylon] and his helpers from the midst of Sheol, . . ."

This is actually similar in nature to the account in Isaiah 14. The one difference is that the account in Isaiah 14:9–11 also has long range prophetic significance. Listen now to the speech of the ones in Sheol—

> Sheol from beneath is excited over you to meet you when you come; It arouses for you the spirits of the dead, all the leaders of the earth; It raises all the kings of the nations from their thrones. They will all respond and say to you, '*Even you have been made weak as we, you have become like us. Your pomp and the music of your harps have been brought down to Sheol; maggots are spread out as your bed beneath you and worms are your covering.*'

1 Sam. 28:3—"Now Samuel had died, and all Israel had lamented for him and *buried him* in Ramah, in his own city. *And Saul said* **'Bring up Samuel for me.'** (Verse 11.) *And Samuel said, . . .*" (Verses 16–19.)

Obviously King Saul did not go to Ramah and ask to have Samuel's body dug up out of his grave. A dead body cannot know anything or say anything. Besides, decomposition would have done a lot of damage by that time. Apparently, Saul—as well as most every other Israelite—thought there was another part of man, namely his *soul* or *spirit*, which was very much in existence and could communicate if God so allowed. Thus we have the words, "*I see a divine being coming up out of the earth*" (v. 13). Then we have Samuel's conversation with King Saul (verses 15, 16, 17, 18 and 19). It is a very intelligent conversation. It is most consistent, factual and prophetically accurate.

Isa. 14:16—"Those who see you [the king of Babylon, and beyond him, Lucifer] will gaze at you [apparently, they have non-material eyes], and consider you [apparently, they have nonmaterial brains] saying [apparently, they nonmaterial voice boxes], . . ." Since we have already considered this, I need say no more.

XII.

SUMMARY DEFINITION OF SHEOL

In light of the overwhelming abundance of evidence from the Hebrew Scriptures we should have no problem whatsoever in defining Sheol as—

The deep subterranean chamber

within the very lowest regions of the earth

with several different compartments or zones

which is the gathering place for the
disembodied spirits of the dead,

both the righteous and the unrighteous.

For the righteous, it is a place of comfort
awaiting their liberation;

whereas for the unrighteous, it is a place of suffering,

awaiting their eventual Judgment.

It is also a place for certain fallen angels and eventually,

for Satan himself.

In addition, **remember**, the Hebrew Scriptures also give us a glimpse of the *Lake of Fire* (Dan. 7:11, see Rev. 19:20) and the ultimate Judgment (Ecc. 12:13, 14, see Rev. 20:11–15).

This is the revelation concerning Hell (Sheol) which permeates throughout the Hebrew Scriptures. This view was thus inherited by the Lord Jesus Christ, John the Baptist, the apostles and the early Church as revealed in the Greek Scriptures. The saints in the early Church did not get their understanding of Hell from Greek mythology, but rather FROM THE HEBREW SCRIPTURES!

195

PART TWO

THE GREEK SCRIPTURES

CHAPTER TWELVE

HADES

"HADES"

A s stated at the beginning of this study, "*Hades*" is the Greek word used to translate the Hebrew word "*Sheol*." When Jewish scholars translated the Hebrew Scriptures into the Greek language they nearly uniformly used "Hades" as the translation of "Sheol." So *Hades* as found in the Greek Scriptures is the same as *Sheol* in the Hebrew Scriptures. It is to be understood that the New Testament will simply carry on the revelation concerning *Sheol* which was given in the Hebrew Scriptures. Several times the New Testament writers quoted passages from the Hebrew Scriptures concerning *Sheol,* using the Greek word *Hades.* Therefore, in the four Gospels, Acts, the Epistles and the book of Revelation, the "Hell" which existed in the Old Testament was referred to by the Greek designation, *Hades.*

Sheol or Hades will exist until the time of the final "Great White Throne Judgment" and the New Heavens and Earth. At that time Sheol/Hades will be terminated or, we can say, transferred over to where the ultimate disposition of the unjust will be. Concerning this place of the final disposition of the lost, another Greek word is used — *Gehenna.* At the conclusion of the "Great White Throne Judgment," the final disposition of the souls of the lost will be in "*Gehenna,*" which is also called "The Lake of Fire." Some Bible teachers prefer to speak of "*Gehenna*" as the real "Hell."

In our English Bibles all three of these words—Sheol, Hades and Gehenna—are simply translated "Hell." In so doing, the Bible reader does not always understand the difference between them in time and purpose. It is important that Bible readers differentiate these words so that they know which aspect of "Hell" is in view. The Hebrew *Sheol* and the Greek *Hades* are the same place. However, *Gehenna* only comes into view after the "Great White Throne Judgment." Throughout the ministry of Christ the words "Hades" and "Gehenna" are both used, but are not so distinguished in most English translations. Actually, this is unfortunate because He is talking about two different aspects of "Hell." Sheol/Hades is the temporary abode of the spirits of the dead. It exists from Adam until the final Judgment. Certain fallen angels and demons are also occupants in Sheol/Hades. At the final Judgment there will be the resurrection of the lost who will be cast, both bodies and souls (or spirits), into *Gehenna*. Therefore, when Christ talks about *Gehenna*, He often stresses both bodily suffering and suffering of the soul. I will trace the use of Gehenna in the Scriptures after we finish with *Hades*.

The "Fiery" Ministry of John the Baptist

When John the Baptist came preaching "*Prepare the way of the Lord*" (Matt.3:3 and Isa. 40:3), he also preached the impending judgment of God's wrath upon impenitent, self-righteous individuals. To those John said, "*Brood of vipers! Who warned you to flee the **wrath** to come?*" (Matt. 3:7 and Lk. 3:7).

Herein we must distinguish between this great judgment event, occurring at the beginning of the Messiah's reign, from that *ultimate Judgment* at the end of Messiah's reign, when the final doom of the wicked will be determined. John the Baptist and Christ talked about the immediate judgment event which introduces the Kingdom Age. The wicked of the earth, who oppose the Messiah and His reign, will be physically destroyed and their spirits cast into Hades at the time of His second coming.

John the Baptist explained that this judgment wrath at the coming of the Messiah would be like a harvest scene in the orchards, *"And even now the ax is laid to the root of the trees. Therefore every tree which does not bear good fruit is cut down and thrown into **the fire**"* (Matt. 3:10 and Lk. 3:9). This illustration is also repeated by Christ in Matt. 7:19. The "fire" in view by John the Baptist is the fire of Sheol/Hades.

In addition, John the Baptist gave the same scenario in a slightly different manner. He said that the Messiah would *"baptize with the Holy Spirit and with fire"* (Matt. 3:11 and Lk. 3:16). John immediately gave us a commentary upon this statement so his audience would know what was meant. He differentiated between the two elements of baptism by the following explanation: *"His* [the Messiah's] *winnowing fan is in His hand, and He will thoroughly clean out His threshing floor, and gather His wheat into the barn* [this has reference to the Holy Spirit baptism]; *but He will burn up the chaff with unquenchable fire* [this has reference to the fire baptism]" (Matt. 3:12 and Lk. 3:17). In this case the harvest scene is from the grain fields. His *"wheat"* represents the righteous belonging to Messiah, whereas the *"chaff"* represents the unrighteous. The *"wheat"* being *"gathered into the barn"* represents the righteous being gathered into the Kingdom by means of a Holy Spirit baptism. The *"chaff"* being *"burned up with unquenchable fire"* represents the unrighteous being gathered into *Hades,* which is the baptism of fire. In other words, no one will be allowed into the Kingdom reign of Messiah who is not regenerated. Now the word *Hades* is not used in this passage, but later we shall see Christ using that word, and equating with it the same *"unquenchable fire"* for the lost at that judgment which will take place at the beginning of the Kingdom. Again, I say this is the "fire" of Sheol/Hades.

It is important to remember the fact that this is the very same *"fire"* which was indicated as existing for the lost in Sheol in the Hebrew Scriptures—Job 31:12; Deut. 32:22; Song of Sol. 8:6 and Isa. 33:14. Christ, Himself, indicated that this "fire" still exists in "Hades" at the time of His account of the rich man and Lazarus (Luke 16:23, 24). The rich man was *"in Hades . . . in agony in this flame."* Consequently the *"unquenchable fire"* of Hades had been burning *for four thousand years* at the time of Christ. Also, we are to understand this "fire" has still been burning for the last two thousand years of the present Church Age. And in addition, this "fire" will continue to burn for another thousand years during the Messianic Kingdom reign. That means this fire will have been burning for some seven thousand years. After this, it is simply transferred to the Lake of Fire. "*Unquenchable* fire" means that it can never be put out.

Most importantly, the subjects in that fire also *still exist*. They are not consumed into nothingness throughout that time. No one ceases to exist! In other words, this is proof positive that this fire is not to be put out and the occupants are not annihilated. False teachers like to argue that "unquenchable fire" simply means "a fire that cannot be put out UNTIL the person is consumed." In their ideology they think God is just operating a powerful "crematorium." They like to think this fire is unquenchable in the sense it cannot be put out until that person is annihilated. They presume that once the person is consumed, the fire goes out because the person ceases to exist. Of course, we all know it does not take seven thousand years to consume a person, if that is what it means! Obviously that is not what the expression means. "Unquenchable fire" is fire that CAN NOT BE PUT OUT—PERIOD. As I said before, the final phase of Hell is where Sheol/Hades is cast into *Gehenna* or the "Lake of Fire" (Rev. 20:14, 15). In the "Lake of Fire" the ungodly will "be tormented day and night forever and forever" (Rev. 20:10). I will remind you that this is the Scriptural reason for the title of this book—*The Fire That Is Eternal*.

Back to the "baptisms." Actually, both these baptisms of which John spoke were prophesied in the Hebrew Scriptures as taking place at the coming of the Messiah to rule and reign on earth. For instance, Malachi said of the Messiah, "*He is coming, says the LORD of Hosts. But who can endure the day of His coming? And who shall stand when He appears? For He is like a refiner's fire. . . .*" "*And I will come near to you for judgment*; . . ." (Mal. 3:1, 2 and 5). Then again Malachi says, "*For behold, the day is coming, burning like an oven, and all the proud, yes, all who do wickedly will be stubble. And the day which is coming shall burn them up, . . .*" (Mal.

4:1). See also, Zeph. 1:14–18; Joel 2:30, 31; Isa. 2:10, 11; 24:1–6; 33:10–14; 34:8–10; 66:15, 16, etc., etc.

In examining these passages, along with the expressions used by John the Baptist and Christ, one will note that there are actually two aspects concerning this fiery judgment. There is a very physical "*fire*" which will characterize an outward, physical destruction upon the "armies" of the Antichrist forces from many nations which will oppose Christ. This will obviously be an outward physical fire of destruction. However, there is also a designated judgment upon all the unrighteous and unrepentant who will not be allowed to enter the Kingdom reign of Messiah, but will be disposed of into the "fire" of Hades.

The future great outpouring of the Holy Spirit was prophesied in such passages as Joel 2:28, 29, "*And it shall come about after this that I will pour out My Spirit on all flesh; and your sons and daughters shall prophesy, and your old men shall dream dreams, and your young men shall see visions. And even on the male and female servants I will pour out My Spirit in those days.*" This prophecy was not literally fulfilled at the time the apostle Peter quoted it in the second chapter of the book of Acts. Nevertheless, Peter used it to explain the presence of the Holy Spirit in the early church. Concerning this future outpouring of the Holy Spirit, see also: Isa. 11:6–8; 32:15–18; Ezek. 11:17–20; 36:24–30; 39:25–29, etc.

"Hades" under the Ministry of Jesus Christ

As Christ ministered the Gospel of the Kingdom throughout the land of Israel, He often spoke about the consequence of the rejection of that Kingdom at the time it would ultimately be established on the earth. He did not mince His words. To reject Him and the Father's Kingdom was not like voting for a different candidate in one of our modern elections. On the contrary, to reject this Kingdom was to reject God's Son and God's order, which would bring eternal consequences beginning in *Hades* itself. Though this word *Hades* may not always be used, there is no mistaking the circumstances.

Once when Christ was preaching, He observed the clear marvelous faith of a Roman centurion. Now it must be remembered that Christ came to present His Kingdom message first to the nation of Israel to whom the promises of God were initially made. However, many of Christ's own people were rejecting Him, whereas this Roman showed more faith than any of them. Therefore Christ said, Matt. 8:10–12—

> *Truly I say to you, I have not found such great faith with anyone in Israel. And I say to you, that many shall come from the east and west, and dine with Abraham, and Isaac, and Jacob in the Kingdom of Heaven; but the sons of the Kingdom shall be* **cast out** *into* **outer darkness;** *in* **that place** *there shall* <u>*BE*</u> **weeping and gnashing of teeth**.

I am emphasizing here, not only the description of "**that place**," but also the fact of the condition that it will "<u>BE</u>." In other words, this is not a simple death with a burial of the body in a grave on earth, where the physical person *ceases to BE*. On the contrary, these people are "*cast out*" of the Kingdom (no funeral procession) "INTO *outer darkness*" (no sweet garden of roses), in which "*place*" will "<u>BE</u> *weeping and gnashing of teeth*." This is clearly stating a future condition of existence! The words "gnashing of teeth" is an idiomatic expression designating torments.

In a similar manner, looking back at one of the cities in which He spent a great deal of time ministering, which had heard His message but had not repented, Christ said the following—Matt. 11:23 (same as Luke 10:15)—

> *And you Capernaum, will not be exalted to heaven as you think.* [Instead] *You shall be* **cast down** *to* **Hades**.

Though this particular city was popular in its day, it was soon to totally disappear. Even now archeologists debate its actual location. But, most importantly, the occupants of that city were exposed to a tremendous witness by the Savior, Himself, and therefore having rejected His witness, they stood condemned to Hades.

Though the word *Hades* is not used in the next passage, <u>Matt. 12:40</u>, yet it is a reference by Christ to the account in the book of Jonah where the word *Sheol* was used. When Christ made reference to it, we most certainly learn *where it is*, and in this case *who will go there*—

> *For as Jonah was three days and three nights in the belly of the great fish, so shall **the Son of Man be** three days and three nights **in the heart of the earth**.*

Obviously Christ was not talking about His body being laid in an empty tomb. Christ's physical body was itself emptied of His spiritual person. As Christ herein stated, "The Son of Man" will be in *"the heart of the earth."* That, of course, is another reference to Sheol/Hades where our Savior spent three days and nights during His substitutionary death for the sins of mankind.

In the 13th chapter of Matthew, Christ spoke in many parables concerning the Kingdom of God. Though the word *Hades* is not used, the description of Hades most surely is. Note the following passages:

<u>Matt. 13:30</u> *Allow both to grow together until the harvest; and at the time of harvest I will say to the reapers, 'First gather up the tares* [the unrighteous] *and bind them in bundles **to burn them*** [Hades]; *but gather the wheat* [the righteous] *into my barn* [the Kingdom]'.

<u>Matt. 13:40–42</u> *Therefore just as the tares are gathered up and burned with fire, so shall it be at the end of the age. The Son of Man will send forth His angels and they will gather out of His Kingdom all that offends, and those who commit lawlessness, and **will cast them into the furnace of fire; in that place** there **shall be weeping and gnashing of teeth**.*

Matt. 13:48–50 . . . *and they sat down, and gathered the good fish into containers, but the bad they threw away. So it will be at the end of the age. The angels will come forth, and take out the wicked from among the righteous, and will* **cast them into the furnace of fire**. *There* **shall be weeping and gnashing of teeth**.

At the time when Christ began to turn towards Jerusalem (Luke 13:22), His ministry seemed to increase in intensity and soberness. On this occasion He said—

Luke 13:5 . . . *but unless you repent you will all likewise* **perish**.

Luke 13:27, 28 *But He will say, 'I tell you I do not know you, where you are from. Depart from Me, all you workers of iniquity.' There will* **be weeping and gnashing of teeth**, *when you see Abraham* and Isaac and Jacob and all the prophets in the Kingdom of God, and yourselves thrust out.

In another parable comparing the Kingdom of Heaven to a marriage feast, Christ said the following concluding words—

Matt. 22:13 *Then the king said to His servants, 'bind him* [an unrighteous person] *hand and foot, and* **cast him into outer darkness; in that place** *there shall* **be weeping and gnashing of teeth**.'

In describing the judgment which will occur at His coming, Christ used the illustration of a wicked slave being confronted by his master—

Matt. 24:51 . . . *and shall cut him asunder and appoint him his portion with the hypocrites; there shall be* **weeping and gnashing of teeth**.

And again it is recorded in—

<u>Matt. 25:30</u> *And shall cast out the worthless slave **into outer darkness; in that place** there shall **be weeping and gnashing of teeth**.*

In Matthew 25 Christ specifically described the judgment which will take place at His coming to reign. He used the following language—

<u>Matt. 25:41 and 46</u> *Then He will also say to those on His left, 'Depart from Me, accursed ones, into **the eternal fire** which has been **prepared for the Devil and his angels**; . . . And these will go away **into eternal punishment**, but the righteous into eternal life.*

After reading passages like this, coming so many times from the lips of the Lord Jesus Christ, Himself, we should be very sobered. Christ explained the condition of Hades as being *"cast down"* to a *"PLACE"* with *"outer darkness,"* and yet a *"furnace of fire"* which is an *"eternal fire,"* where there is *"weeping and gnashing of teeth"* and *"eternal punishment."* In the face of language like this, one wonders how the modern Sadducees could possibly come out and still argue there is no such thing as eternal conscious punishment. I can only say that their manifested attitude is nothing more than blatant infidelity. Such a person simply does not believe Christ or the Scriptures! Such arguments as, "How could there be darkness and yet fire?" "How can spirits gnash their teeth?" And "How can you believe in a God Who enjoys torturing people forever?" are all nothing more than "smart-alecky" expressions of infidelity.

We shall see a little further ahead, that Hades is itself emptied into the final form of Hell, which is called Gehenna. Before we go there, let us look at two other passages specifically speaking of *"Hades"* by Christ.

<u>Matthew 16:18</u> . . . *I will build my church and the **gates of Hades** shall not prevail against it.*

You may remember that in the book of Job the expression "***gates of Sheol***" is first used (Job 17:15, 16 and 38:17). Isaiah repeats this (Isa. 38:10). And now the Lord Jesus uses the same expression in regards to *Hades* which is the same place. Sheol/Hades continues throughout the present Church Age and the Kingdom Age as well.

The implication of Christ's statement is that the true Church Christ is building is so constituted of "saved," "redeemed," "born again" or "regenerated" people who possess "eternal life" and "shall never perish" as to be impregnable by the forces of Satan and Hades. Mere professing Christendom, with all its gigantic, ornamented cathedrals and denominations, is man-made and has no such safeguards, to be sure. Not only can physical fire destroy all man's superficial religious ornamentation in spite of his "fire insurance" policies, but so also can Hades-Fire prevail against religious hypocrisy itself. There are no "fire insurance policies" to compensate for this fire, other than the prevention ahead of time of individual, genuine salvation.

When a person is "born again," he is instantly joined to only ONE Church, and that is "the Church which is Christ's body" (Eph. 1:22, 23). Christ is building no other. This Church is truly universal and therefore could never be "Roman Catholic," etc. In addition, the "gates of Hades" will not prevail against this Church.

The Rich Man and Lazarus

The last passage which we will take up and carefully explore under Christ's earthly ministry, concerning *Hades*, is the famous "rich man and Lazarus" story as recorded in <u>Luke 16:19–31</u>. If this account presents the positive truth, then the theories of the modern Sadducees totally collapse. Therefore, those false teachers who reject the face value of this account have generated some "fairytale" stories of their own "pagan origin" in order to eliminate the obvious truth found in this account.

At the very same time, everyone admits that this story bears a striking realism. That is a fact no one can deny. False teachers rush to point out that in the context where this story is found Christ gives other stories which are expressly labeled as "parables." Therefore, they argue that since this is another parable, one cannot believe the actual realism employed in this story. Then these teachers say that Christ only borrowed a popular pagan ideology about the afterlife to illustrate His point about selfish rich men. Of course this is totally uncharacteristic of Jesus Christ.

The truth of the matter is, when one looks at the larger context of this account, he will find that Christ gives many narratives, some of which are designated as "parables." However, each and every story, even those called "parables," bears a striking resemblance to the reality of life's experiences. Let us note each one in context.

In Luke 15:3–7 we read of the "parable" of the lost sheep. This is an account which is very true to life and which happened every day in men's experiences. There is nothing far-fetched about it.

In Luke 15:8–10 we hear the story of the poor woman who lost a coin and rejoiced to find it again. Again, this is obviously a story which is true to common everyday experiences. Everyone can relate to the emotions expressed in this account.

In Luke 15:11–32 we read a long account of the man who had two sons. The one son took his inheritance and left. He went out into the world and spent all his wealth very foolishly. However, he finally came to his senses and returned to his father's house. There is beautiful restoration. This is a remarkably clear story touching every heart because it has actually been experienced by many families even throughout the ages.

Next we come to Luke 16:1–9 which is the account given by Christ of the rich man's steward who was reported as having squandered the rich man's possessions. The story is amazingly true to life's experiences. Everyone knows this very situation has happened many times in any society in the experience of managers who must give an account of their responsibilities. There is not the faintest taint in the story of any exaggerations or abnormalities.

And now we come to the story of the rich man and Lazarus, and the modern Sadducees fully expect us to believe that Christ borrowed a corrupt pagan ideology about the afterlife in order to strike fear into the hearts of the selfish rich people! Of course, every honest person admits that Jesus Christ would never stoop to employ a fairytale of false, perverted, superstitious ideology given without qualifications, as if it were true, in order to portray what is true to life in God's reckoning. To think Christ would do that is to create "another Jesus" (2 Cor. 11:4).

Whether we think the story is a parable or an actual account really makes little or no difference; the story speaks for itself— *loud and clear*! There is a Hell (Hades)! And there is suffering in Hell (Hades)! As we saw earlier, Christ had already spoken about the ungodly being cast into Hades. Now, let us hear the Christ of the Bible—

*"There was a certain **rich** man. . . ."* (Luke 16:19). The Pharisees who apparently were in the audience would prick up their ears right away because many of them were "lovers of money" (verses 14 and 15). This rich man ". . . *was clothed in purple and fine linen and fared sumptuously everyday.*" The words Christ used are choice and arouse our imagination. One can just visualize the luxury in which some men lived. *"But there was a certain beggar named Lazarus, . . ."* (v. 20). Now before our minds is placed another person of just the opposite situation in life. In addition, if this is a parable, then it is even more intriguing because Christ never named a person in any of His other parables. I think we will discover the reason for the name at the end of the account. Therefore, the realism becomes even more intense.

Christ continued to describe this poor man as ". . . *full of sores, who was laid at his* [the rich man's] *gate, desiring to be fed with the crumbs which fell from the rich man's table. Moreover the dogs came and licked his sores"* (vs. 20, 21). Christ was really pressing an emotional button with these words, because this is extreme poverty, and right under the rich man's nose. Our hearts are immediately touched. And furthermore, it is positively repulsive to think of dogs licking the sores. Yet indeed, this is itself true to reality, for dogs are characterized by licking their own wounds and each others'. With these very descriptive words Christ has captured our attention and we are locked in suspense—what is going to happen between these two characters so boldly portrayed?

"So it was that the beggar died, . . ." (v. 22). That is to be expected under his circumstances. Our minds tend to fill in the blanks and tell us that probably some of the rich man's servants had to be sent to drag off the body, dumping it into an unmarked hole and filling it over. So much for the poor man. Now, I might interject, if the theories of our modern Sadducees are correct, then of course they would point out that the poor man was at last out of his misery and no longer existed, except for a carcass which only needed time to return to the dust. After all, they would point out, when the body ceased to function, the soul ceased as well. Indeed, if what the modern Sadducees believe is the TRUTH about the nature of man, then Christ went on to tell a blatant LIE! However, "Let God [Christ] be true, but every man [modern Sadducees] a liar. . . ." (Rom. 3:4).

Now Christ continued, ". . . *And* [the poor man] *was carried by the angels to Abraham's bosom."* Can you imagine this? Christ took it for granted that the poor man still existed! And why shouldn't He? As we have previously seen throughout the Hebrew Scriptures, there is the continued existence of the departed spirits of men plainly given. Not only does the poor man still exist, but the angels are assigned to deliver him to the place of comfort—in the "bosom" position with father Abraham. And why would not the angels be thus assigned? The Scriptures make it clear they do many services for the saints—see Hebrews 1:14. And why should he not be taken to be with Abraham? Abraham, himself, at death was taken to be with his fathers in the faith. All that Christ said so far is *perfectly consistent* with *the revealed Word of God* and has nothing whatsoever to do with Greek mythology or so-called Jewish fantasies.

". . . The rich man died also and was buried." Nothing unusual here. His death had to come some time as well. Even his wealth could not keep him continually healthy. He also had to die. And no doubt, fitting to his wealthy circumstances, he must have had a

tremendous funeral with many professional mourners to bemoan his decease. But now, the rest of the story—

*"And **BEING** in torments in Hades, . . ."* (v. 23). Now why should anyone reject this as being factual? After all, this is perfectly consistent with all that we have learned about Sheol from the Hebrew Scriptures. Though they *"buried"* the rich man's body, only God could determine what was done with his soul. Jesus Christ taught very clearly that man is a dichotomy, possessing an outward physical body, and an inward spiritual life. Now the story goes on to say, *". . . he lifted up his eyes* [obviously, nonmaterial eyes] *and saw Abraham afar off, and Lazarus in his bosom."* We must remember that Christ will describe the spiritual person, "the Inward Man," with the same terminology used for "the Outward Man." Immediately the man who was rich on earth was now in torment and all his money would not do him one bit of good.

"Then he cried and said, 'Father Abraham, have mercy on me, and send Lazarus that he may dip the tip of his finger in water and cool my tongue [remember, Christ describes the 'inner man' just like the 'outer man']*; for **I am tormented in this flame**'"* (v. 24). A lesson emerges immediately. While they were both alive the rich man apparently did nothing to lesson the sorrows of Lazarus; no doubt, he could have done so. He could have done a great deal to alleviate the poor man's miserable condition. Now that the situation is reversed, he seemingly demands assistance. However, he is not going to get it. Every person should think soberly about this lesson!

In addition, it is important to recognize that Christ did NOT describe the rich man as being roasted alive on some rack, like a baking animal, with his flesh popping and peeling off. That type of nonsense is for the religious exaggerators. This type of language is never used in the Scriptures. If that were the case, I am quite sure the rich man would be asking for a lot more than just a drop of water to cool his tongue. He was certainly in misery, but Christ did not picture him bound on some iron rotisserie as certain poets and other religious "racketeers" have imagined. So Christ did not follow fantasies.

"*But Abraham said, 'Son, remember that in your lifetime you received your good things, and likewise Lazarus evil things, but now he is comforted and you are tormented*'" (v. 25). This is precisely in accordance with God's justice! "'*And besides all this, between us and you is a great gulf fixed, so that those who want to pass from here to you cannot, nor can those from there pass to us*'" (v. 26). Again, this is not derived from some fable. It is perfectly in accord with what we learned from the Hebrew Scriptures on the subject of Sheol. The righteous were apparently in a place of rest and comfort. Remember, Samuel had said, "*Why have you discomfited me?*" On the other hand, the unrighteous were in a place of suffering.

"*Then he said, 'I beg you therefore, father, that you would send him to my father's house, for I have five brothers, that he may testify to them, lest they also come to this place of torment.' Abraham said to him, 'They have **Moses** and the **prophets**; let them hear them*'" (vs. 27–29). This is clear confirmation of the fact which we learned from the Hebrew Scriptures that there is *torment* in Sheol/Hades for the unrighteous. After all, what the rich man wanted was simply a warning for his brothers to not "come to this place of torment." And the answer, "*They have Moses and the prophets*," meant among other things that **Moses and the Prophets warned about Sheol as a place of torment**. Apparently the rich man, himself, did not take the warning and so now he asked for additional warning for his brothers.

"*And he said, 'No, father Abraham; but if one goes to them from the dead, they will repent*'" (v. 30). The rich man thought that if Lazarus, himself, were raised from the dead to warn them, surely, that miracle would convince anyone! Humanly speaking, the rich man is right. If Lazarus were raised from the dead, you would think it would convince even the most hardened person to repent. But would it??

"*But he* [Abraham] *said to him, 'If they do not hear Moses and the prophets, neither will they be persuaded though one rise from the dead*'" (v. 31). What an amazing conversation! What amazing

truth! And what is even more amazing is that Jesus Christ did give the ultimate evidence by *raising* "Lazarus" from the dead—see John 11:28–44. Yes, Christ knew what He would be doing in the near future. He did, in fact, bring back another man named Lazarus who had been dead for four days. And in fact, just as Abraham said, the leadership *still did not believe*—see John 11:46–53. Instead of repenting, they only purposed to kill the resurrected Lazarus as well as the Savior.

Therefore, the story of the rich man and Lazarus has its—

exact parallel in life,
exact parallel in the afterlife,
as exactly revealed in the Hebrew Scriptures,
and its **exact parallel in historical fulfillment**.

And yet, the modern Sadducees (false teachers and some weak Christians) today will stubbornly contend that this story by Christ is just the repetition of Jewish folklore or that Christ was simply using some sacred strands of Greek mythology, which had been fixed in the culture at that time, in order to illustrate His point. All I can say, and need to say in response to this, is that this is demonic logic, *criminal* and *blasphemous* to the Savior Who soberly gave the story. Let these same teachers please tell us how it is possible for the early Christian apostles to convert souls out of paganism, if their very own Leader, Whom they worship, was found to employ horrible pagan ideology, Himself.

Objections Answered to the "Rich Man and Lazarus" story being literal proof of a fiery Hell where the departed souls of the wicked suffer.

Obviously many cults and other religionists are going to attempt to destroy the face value of this account given by the Lord Jesus Christ, Himself. It never ceases to amaze me to see the devilish maneuvers that the false teachers are inspired to use in order to evade the truth! Because their efforts are so strenuous, I thought it might be good to list some of their arguments so that one might see the superficiality of them. I will give their objections and underneath, the answers.

1. *"This is a parable! It cannot be real! We must look for moral truths; we cannot take it literally!"*

Answer—Real names are used; Lazarus, Abraham and Moses. This is normally never done in any of Christ's parables. These are most certainly real people! As already demonstrated, it is perfectly consistent with the revealed Hebrew Scriptures. Even if it happened to be a parable, remember—parables are given to illustrate real truths—NOT LIES! The truth reflected by a parable can be no less than the substance of the story. There are as many varied and contradictory so-called "moral truths" that men invent about this story as there are those who oppose the literal interpretation of the passage. Indeed, none of the doubters seem to have the final say as to what the "moral truth" really is!

2. *"How can a person in Hell communicate with a person in Heaven?"*

Answer—Yes, this is a real objection which I have actually seen in print by a notable organization. The answer is, of course, that this is not communication between Heaven and Hell, but between two sections of Hades. Before the ascension of Christ out of Hell and His physical resurrection from the dead, there were two compartments in Hades, one for the righteous and one for the lost. At Christ's ascension from Hell and into Heaven, He emptied Hades of the righteous. Now they are in Heaven and the souls of the righteous who die since then go straight into Heaven.

3. *"Are we going to hold conversations with people in Hell? Are we going to watch people suffer in Hell? What kind of heaven would it be to watch people suffer?!"*

Answer—No! we are not going to be doing any of these things in heaven! This was obviously a different situation and it all took place in Hell, not heaven.

4.   *"Christ is merely using a Jewish concept, mentioned by Josephus the Jewish historian, to illustrate spiritual truths."*

Answer—Christ consistently exploded false Jewish concepts and mere human traditions which contradicted spiritual truth. By not doing so on this occasion, He is endorsing the concept. It is more accurate to observe that Josephus reflected an actual Biblical concept believed by the Orthodox Jewish people at the time of Christ.

5.   *"This cannot be literal because, according to the Bible, people do not get their rewards at death, but at their resurrection from the dead."*

Answer—This is not at all talking about receiving their final rewards. It only concerns itself with the state and condition of existence in Hades. The souls of the lost will be kept in Hades until the final resurrection and the Great White Throne Judgment.

6.   *"This can't be literal because the Bible says the dead 'sleep' and 'they know not anything'—Psalm 6:5; 115:17; 146:4; Ecc. 9:5, 10."*

Answer—All these passages, which are carefully chosen to be quoted over and over again by false teachers, are simply talking about the *physical cessation* of life consciousness at the point of physical death. They are NOT at all talking about the cessation of spiritual consciousness.

7.   *"Spirits don't have bodies, hands, eyes, ears, etc."*

Answer—What this objector should say is, Spirits don't have *physical* bodies, hands, eyes, ears, etc. However, they are described with the same terminology. In addition, there are many Scriptures which describe the conversations of the souls of the dead and even of the garments that they wear. Christ said the High Priest would see His glorious second coming 2000 years later. That means he would still have "eyes" to see with! You either believe it or you don't. I say again, in the Biblical revelation God describes the "inward man" with the same language used to describe the "outward man."

8. *"Spirits cannot burn because they are non-material beings."*

Answer—First of all, Christ did not say the rich man, as to his flesh and bones, was actually burning and disintegrating. The rich man said he was "tormented in this flame," which simply meant he was miserable in the midst of the flames of Hades. Secondly, it is a lie to think spirit beings cannot suffer in the midst of such flames. The Bible clearly reveals that the Devil and all his fallen angelic associates, who jointly stand in rebellion against God and are spirit creatures, are going to be cast into "the Lake of Fire [Gehenna] . . . [where] they will be tormented day and night *forever and ever"*— see Revelation 20:10.

9. *"This event that Christ is describing must be the time of their resurrection because they both are said to 'open their eyes.'"*

Answer—It could not be describing the time of their resurrection because the resurrection of the righteous takes place one thousand years before that of the unrighteous. In addition, there would be no need for the rich man to warn his brothers not to come there, because their resurrection is at the final Judgment, and the wicked dead are all expelled from Hades. Again, God uses the same language to describe the spiritual person as He does in describing their physical bodies.

10. *"The only time anyone will see Abraham is in the Kingdom on earth."*

Answer—It is true that the resurrected Abraham will be seen in the Messianic Kingdom. However, Samuel was seen ascending out of Sheol long before that Kingdom. The apostles saw Moses and Elijah appear with Christ long before the same Kingdom. And here, Abraham is seen in Hades long before the Kingdom. Therefore, this remains perfectly consistent.

11. *"Angels will only come and assist Christ at His coming to gather the elect together at His second coming. Therefore, they would not actually be assisting someone else before that time."*

Answer—This is a desperate and shallow attempt to eradicate the truth of this passage. It is a vain assumption. The Scripture never indicates that the angels *only* assist Christ at His second coming. They do a great variety of work in every age (Heb. 1:14).

12.   *"The rich man was actually only in the grave, not in some fiery Hell. He is only spoken of as suffering mental anguish. This is because the flame that is mentioned is that of the future Gehenna which will burn up the wicked."*
    Answer—This is a fancy fairy tale misrepresentation. It has no resemblance whatsoever to the story that Christ related. Christ was talking about Hades, not Gehenna. One must certainly have "mental anguish" which would cause this lie to be propagated.

13.   *"'Abraham's bosom' is simply the place of rest and comfort for Gentiles who have been saved and made 'children of Abraham' by their faith."*
    Answer—There is not one thread of evidence that Lazarus was a Gentile. Nor is there any evidence whatsoever that Christ was trying to illustrate the difference between the Jew and the Gentile in this account.

14.   *One says "The 'Great Gulf' is the difference between Jew and Gentile." Another says "It is the chasm between good and evil." Yet another says "Immorality is the gulf between the righteous and the unrighteous." Etc., etc., etc.*
    Answer—This most certainly illustrates the "Great Gulf" between truth and error! There seems to be no limit in exercising their imaginations in efforts to discredit the truth of this account by Jesus Christ. Why not just believe what Christ says are the actual facts of the case? What is really preventing people from believing what the text says? Have you been deceived to think it would make God some sort of a cruel monster to have people suffering for eternity?
    Just remember, the destiny of the lost is just as much Divine revelation from a Thrice-Holy God as is His amazing grace. Do not presume that you have more love for the lost than does the Lord Jesus Christ Who gave this revelation. Just remember, it is the tender and holy love of Christ which was manifest over and over again in the Gospel accounts for the lost. Hell is the consequence of the cold

indifference of the unregenerate towards that amazing Divine love of our gracious Savior.

Remaining References to Hades

The remaining uses of the word Hades in the New Testament can be covered quickly. Actually we have already read from the apostle Peter's message on the Day of Pentecost where he used the word for Hell twice. First, in quoting from David in Psalm 16:8–11, "*. . . For You will not leave my soul in **Hades**, nor will you allow Your Holy One to see corruption*" (Acts 2:27). Then Peter made a total application to Christ, "*He* [David], *foreseeing this, spoke concerning the resurrection of Christ, that **His soul** was not left in **Hades**, nor did **His flesh** see corruption*" (Acts 2:31). Of course, in this context Peter also used the word "*soul*" to describe the inward spiritual person of the Messiah.

In 1 Corinthians 15:55 the apostle Paul used the word Hades in quoting from Hosea 13:14, "*O death, where is your sting? O **Hades**, where is your victory?*"

In both these last quotations from the Hebrew Scriptures (that of Peter and Paul), *Hades* is the Greek translation of the Hebrew word *Sheol*. In some translations, like the New King James Version, the Greek *Hades* will be transliterated so that the Bible reader can easily recognize its particular use.

Finally, the word *Hades* is used four times in the book of Revelation.

In Rev.1:18 Christ describes Himself in the following manner— "*I am He Who lives, and was dead, and behold, I am alive forever-more. Amen. And I have the keys of **Hades** and of Death.*" You will note that in all these references from the book of Revelation, Hades and Death are clearly distinguished. Therefore, "***Hades***" concerns itself with the souls or spirits of the dead who are in residence there, whereas "*Death*" is concerned with the physical aspect of death, i.e., the bodies of the dead. Jesus Christ has the "keys" because He, in His substitutionary death, burial and resurrection, spiritually conquered Satan and liberated the saints in Sheol/Hades and also was the first to be bodily glorified. He positively guarantees the same for all believers.

In <u>Rev. 6:8</u> the fourth Seal is opened and a pale horse comes forth, "*And the name of him who sat on it was Death, and **Hades** followed with him.*" This has reference to multitudes dying in this future time of the Great Tribulation, and also to an unleashing of demonic occupants from Hades who will be described later in the Book.

In <u>Rev. 20:13, 14 and 15</u> we have the last two references to Hades. "*Death and **Hades** delivered up the dead who were in them. And they were judged, each according to his works. Then Death and **Hades** were cast into the Lake of Fire. This is the Second Death. And anyone not found written in the Book of Life was cast into the Lake of Fire.*" This will be the termination of Hades in the sense of a chamber in the lower parts of the earth. No one else will go into Hades. This event will take place at the end of the one thousand year reign of Messiah on this present earth (Rev.20:1–10). All Hades' human occupants (spirits) will have been rejoined with their bodies (in reference to Death) to stand before the Great White Throne Judgment (verses 11 and 12) and then be cast into the Lake of Fire.

Other references Applicable to Hades

<u>John 3:16</u> *For God so loved the world that He gave His only begotten Son, that whosoever believes in Him should not **perish** but have everlasting life.*

<u>John 8:23</u> *And He said to them, 'You are from **beneath**, I am from above.*

Here is a remarkable statement from the lips of the Lord Jesus Christ. It was demonstrated earlier that Christ had a duel origin. He received His fleshly nature from Mary which went all the way back through David and Abraham. However, His spiritual nature was eternal and was implanted in the womb of the virgin Mary by the Holy Spirit. Therefore, He was spiritually from God in Heaven above. Now He says to the wicked religious rulers—"You are from beneath!" As everyone recognizes, this has reference to the Satanic occupants of Sheol/*Hades* below. This is meaningless unless Hades is a real place like Heaven is a real place. Furthermore, it has occupants and its realm of "destruction" was designed for Satan. This was simply another way of saying they were of the Devil! The place for the Devil was "beneath" in "the heart of the earth."

John 10:28 *And I give unto them eternal life, and they shall never **perish**.*

Mark 8:36, 37 *For what will it profit a man if he gains the whole world, And **loses his own soul**? Or what shall a man give **in exchange for his soul**?*

These words are commonly repeated as we witness to the lost today. They are a very sober warning that nothing can be exchanged in place of a man's soul. When life is over with, all the pleasures and all the wealth of the world will not be worth the cost of damnation— losing one's soul. This is yet another passage which demonstrates the separate conscious existence of the soul apart from the body.

Mark 16:16 *He who believes and is baptized* [merged into Christ] *will be saved; but he who does not believe will be **condemned**.*

1 Peter 3:18–20 . . . *being put to death* [Christ] *in the flesh but made alive by the Spirit, by Whom also He went and preached to the **spirits in prison**, who formerly were disobedient, when once the Divine longsuffering waited in the days of Noah,* . . .

It is sufficient for the purpose of this study to simply establish that this is a record of disembodied "spirits" who were the "disobedient" in "the days of Noah," but had been confined in the *"prison"* of Hades for some 2500 years at the time Peter was writing.

As to how and when Christ did this is probably explained by the following Scriptures. In 2 Peter 2:5 we are told that Noah, himself, was a "proclaimer of righteousness," or as usually translated, "a preacher of righteousness." He was obviously doing this before the flood came, during the time of the construction of the ark. In Hebrews 11:7 we read that Noah inherited "the righteousness which is by faith." Of course, he would be proclaiming the same as he received. Now in 1 Peter we are also told that the "Spirit of Christ" was in the prophets as they foretold the things concerning "the suffering of Christ and the glory that should follow." This means that the Spirit of Christ was in men like Noah because he and others certainly acted as prophets proclaiming God's message. We can surely say, therefore, that "the Spirit of Christ" was in Noah, proclaiming a message of "righteousness by faith," during the time preceding the flood. Now it is most probable that this is exactly what Peter is saying here in 1 Peter 3:18–20: "by the Spirit of Christ [Who died for our sins and was resurrected] the Lord made proclamation to the spirits [now] in prison, who were disobedient, when God was exercising patience and kept waiting in the days of Noah." And then Peter proceeded to use the ark as a type of how we are saved today through Christ's suffering and death baptism.

References by the apostle Paul to Hades and Final Punishment

Acts 17:31 . . . because He [God] has **appointed a day** in which He will **judge** the world in righteousness by that Man Whom He has ordained. . . .

Romans 2:5–8 But because of your stubbornness and unrepentant heart you are storing up wrath for yourself in the **day of wrath** and revelation of the righteous judgment of

God, Who will render to every man according to his deeds: to those who by perseverance in doing good seek for glory and honor and immortality, eternal life; but to those who are selfishly ambitious and do not obey the truth, but obey unrighteousness, **wrath and indignation**."

1 Thessalonians 1:10 . . . *Who delivers us from the* **wrath** *to come.*

1 Thessalonians 5:9 *For God did not appoint us to* **wrath**, . . .

2 Thessalonians 1:7–9 . . . *and to you who are troubled rest with us when the Lord Jesus is revealed from heaven with His mighty angels, in flaming fire taking vengeance on those who do not obey the gospel of our Lord Jesus Christ. These shall* **be punished** *with* **everlasting destruction** *from the presence of the Lord and from the glory of His power.*

This is a very sober passage concerning the fate of those who reject the gospel of salvation in Christ. The "*destruction*" is not momentary "termination of existence," but is a continuous "condition of existence" as we have demonstrated earlier. W. E. Vine in his *Expository Dictionary of New Testament Words* said of this "destruction [it is] not the loss of being, but of well-being."

Ephesians 4:8–11 *Therefore He says: 'When He ascended on high, He led captivity captive, and gave gifts to men.' Now that 'He ascended,' what is it but that He also first descended into the* **lower parts of the earth**? *He Who descended is also the One Who ascended far above all the heavens, that He might fill all things. And He Himself gave* some to be . . . [gifts to men]. (See Psalm 68:18.)

The apostle Paul takes this quote of Psalm 68:18 from the Septuagint translation where it reads "*he gave gifts*." Thus the image behind the quote becomes the scene where King David and his warriors, after a wearisome "*three days and three nights*" (1

Sam. 30:12) pursuit, conquered the invading Amalekites, who had taken "*captive*" (1 Sam. 30:3) all their families. David "*recovered all*" and led the captivity back. Upon his return he distributed gifts of the spoil (1 Sam. 30:26–31) to all the communities where they dwelt. This is an amazing parallel to the redemptive work of Jesus Christ, Who descended into the "*lower parts of the earth*" (Hades itself), and after "*three days and three nights*" "*destroyed him who has the power of death*," recovered all the saints, and led "*captivity captive*" back to glory with Him. In turn, as the apostle Paul is saying, Christ has now distributed "*gifts*" to the *communities* of His presence on earth.

Yes, *Hades* was full of "*captives*" whom Jesus Christ liberated and took to heaven with Him. Consequently, now when a saint dies, he immediately goes into the Paradise of Heaven to await his glorified body.

> Philippians 2:9 and 10 *Therefore God also has highly exalted Him and given Him the name which is above every name, that at the name of Jesus every knee should bow, of those in heaven, and of those on earth,* **and of those under the earth**.

This reference to "those under the earth" is, of course, a reference to the lost in Sheol/Hades. They are the ones who remain in Hades after Christ's ascension into heaven with the righteous. Indeed, when Christ returns in great glory and reigns on earth even the lost in Hell will give recognition to His royalty and authority.

> 1 Timothy 6:9 *But those who desire to be rich fall into temptation and a snare, and into many and foolish and hurtful lusts which drown men in destruction and* **perdition**.

> Hebrews 6:1 and 2 . . . the elementary doctrine of . . . **Eternal Judgment**.

In this passage, the writer to the Hebrews (Paul) classifies the doctrine of "Eternal Judgment" as one of the foundational or fundamental doctrines of Christ and Christianity. Remember, that as the *fire* is "eternal," so the *Judgment* is also "eternal." Obviously, if a fire is to be extinguished then it can never be said to be "eternal." The text does not say "the *result* of the fire is eternal"! "Eternal life" is continuous existence in fellowship with God. "Eternal damnation" is continuous existence in separation from the life and fellowship with God.

CHAPTER THIRTEEN

GEHENNA

Origin of the Word "GEHENNA"

Having noted before, *Hades*, as a residence of disembodied spirits, will have its climax or termination at the final Judgment for the lost (Rev. 20:13–15). We also saw that as a result of this Judgment, the contents of "*death* (the physically resurrected dead) and *Hades* (the spirits of the dead)" will be cast into "the Lake of Fire." This Lake of Fire is the final form of Hell; it is called by the Greek word *Gehenna*. I noted before that some Bible teachers prefer to call this the real Hell. This final Judgment is often spoken of by the Lord Jesus Christ during His earthly ministry using this designation, *Gehenna*. Sometimes Christ simply spoke of that final "*Day of Judgment*." It is after that Day of Judgment that the lost will be cast into *Gehenna* or "the Lake of Fire."

Normally our Bibles do not make this distinction and render the word *Gehenna* as "Hell," the same as they render Sheol and Hades. Therefore the reader does not always get the distinctive meaning and time period involved. It would have been better to always render this word by the transliteration—*Gehenna*. We will endeavor to look at all these references to get an accurate assessment.

The Greek word *Gehenna* itself has a well-known and important origin. Though the derivation of the word has been repeated many times in reference works, I will give a concise history because it is an important illustration of the reality of Hell.

Gehenna (or *geenna*) is the Greek transliteration derived from the Hebrew *ge-ben-hinnom*, which means "*Valley of Ben (the son of) Hinnom*." This is a valley beginning on the southwest side of Jerusalem, continuing eastward beneath the south side of the city. It terminates when it runs into the Kidron Valley which heads southward on the east side of Jerusalem. Originally it served as a border marker between the tribes of Judah and Benjamin (Josh. 15:8; 18:6 and Neh. 11:30). However, it was in this valley that some of the very corrupt Canaanite pagan worship took place. In addition, the corrupt kings of Judah, Ahaz and Manasseh, began sacrificing their own children (along with the idolatrous heathen) in fire to the god Molech in this valley (see 2 Chron. 28:3; 2 Kings 21:6 and Jer. 32:35). In an act of reformation, King Josiah "defiled" the area (2 Kings 23:10) so that they could no longer make offerings there. Jeremiah prophesied a great slaughter of the people of Judah there (Jer. 7:31–33), even a catastrophe that would fill the valley with bodies (Jer. 19:1–13) because of these ungodly rituals. Some historians believe the area became a literal dumping ground for refuse; consequently, a perpetual rot and burning ensued. This valley was also called "Tophet" and "the Valley of Slaughter" (see Jer. 7:31, 32; 19:6, 11–13; Isa. 30:33 and 2 Kings 23:10).

Long after the Babylonian captivity and the restoration under Ezra and Nehemiah, certain apocalyptic Jewish writers began to call "Hell" by the name of this Valley of Hinnom—*Gehenna* in the Greek. This was indicating that it was a picture or figure of the final Hell. And so the word *Gehenna* was used and understood as a reference for Hell in the Jewish world at the time of Christ. Christ never changed or corrected this designation. In fact, it was used by the Lord Jesus Christ almost exclusively as describing the final state of the unrighteous as a result of the final Judgment. Consequently, we understand that the geographical Valley of Gehenna is but a figure, in the temporal earthly scene, of that final *Gehenna* of eternal fire. It is in this eternal fire wherein the unrighteous, who have been resurrected from the dead to stand before the Great White Throne Judgment, will then be cast "alive" into *Gehenna*, also called "The

Lake of Fire." This is the ultimate horror for both the fallen angelic creatures and for all those who reject the grace of God.

Christ Speaks of "Gehenna"

Twelve times the word is used by Christ in the Gospel records, and one time it is used by James in his letter, plus there are other mentions of this final Judgment which do not use that particular word.

Christ began to speak of this final *Gehenna* in the famous Sermon on the Mount.

> Matthew 5:22 *But I say to you that whoever is angry with his brother without a cause shall be in danger of the judgment* [local, civil judgment]. *And whoever says to his brother 'Raca!'* [empty, a word of contempt], *shall be in danger of the council* [national, civil judgment]. *But whoever says 'you fool,' shall be in danger of Gehenna* [the ultimate Judgment].

Some words in one society mean far worse than in another. This last action implies a malicious, wrongful slander of the man's heart, which Jews by some traditions equated with killing a person by stabbing words. Christ is saying that such a slander, if not repented of, will bring retribution in *Gehenna*. Christ is not prohibiting the proper use of the expression, for He used it rightfully Himself, but He is warning against its cruel, malicious use on an innocent person.

> Matthew 5:29, 30 *If your right eye causes you to sin, pluck it out and cast it from you; for it is more profitable for you that one of your members perish, than for your whole <u>body</u> to be cast into Gehenna. And if your right hand causes you to sin, cut it off and cast it from you; for it is more profitable for you that one of your members perish, than for your whole <u>body</u> to be cast into Gehenna.*

I remember the first time I read these words as a young Christian, asking myself the question, "Should I go and gouge out my eyes and cut off my hands?" I knew I certainly must not understand the passage, but I did not have nerve enough to gouge out my eyes and amputate my hands, anyway. In time, I diagnosed the passage and came to understand its deeper meaning. First of all, in the final analysis, most everyone realizes that your eye or your hand does not directly "cause" you to sin. Many Scriptures indicate inward, evil desires as the cause. Our eyes and hands simply respond to the wicked impulses concocted within our hearts. So, therefore, to cut off the source of evil feeding those impulses and cravings is like cutting off your hand or plucking out your eye. You may be tempted to think that you absolutely cannot do without that iniquity and the evil craving. However, Christ is indicating that it is better to go on in life without them than to have the burden of facing that wickedness at the Judgment.

Of course, one important thing to remember in passages connected with Gehenna is this fact that it also pertains to the (resurrected) "body" of the wicked being destroyed and not just the soul. In the final Gehenna it is both the body and the soul which are cast into this place of perpetual destruction.

Mark the 9th chapter gives many of the same statements as did Matthew 5:29, 30. It is important to list them because Mark adds other ingredients, such as "unquenchable fire" to that ultimate Judgment of *Gehenna*.

<u>Mark 9:43–48</u> *If your hand causes you to sin, cut it off. It is better for you to enter into life maimed, rather than having two hands, to go to* **Gehenna***, into* **the fire that shall never be quenched—where their worm does not die, and the fire is not quenched.** *And if your foot causes you to sin, cut it off. It is better for you to enter life lame, rather than having two feet, to be cast into* **Gehenna, into the fire that shall never be quenched—where their worm does not die,** *and the fire is not quenched. And if your eye causes you to sin, pluck it out. It is better for you to enter the Kingdom of God with one eye, rather than having two eyes, to be cast into* **Gehenna** <u>*fire*</u>**—where their worm does not die, and the fire is not quenched.**

The same is repeated in <u>Matthew 18:8 and 9</u>

If your hand or foot causes you to sin, cut it off and cast it from you. It is better for you to enter into life lame or maimed, rather than having two hands or two feet to be cast **into the everlasting fire***. And if your eye causes you to sin, pluck it out and cast it from you. It is better for you to enter into life with one eye, rather than having two eyes, to be cast into* **Gehenna fire***.*

There are two important aspects in these statements. First is the fact that this is *"everlasting fire"* or the *"fire that is not quenched."* Taken literally and at face value, this fire is NOT going to be extinguished! It is not like other fires, which finally consume themselves and are extinguished after all is burned up. Some have argued that the fire is "everlasting" only in the sense that the results are everlasting; i.e., it burns up a person forever. They are arguing that merely an immediate RESULT of the fire is "eternal" and not the fire itself. But that is actually not what the language says. If Christ wanted to say that the "effect" or "result" was eternal, He could have—but He did not. What is said is the "FIRE" is "everlasting" and shall "not be quenched." That means the contents for the purpose of the fire are still there as well.

As I stated before, a second important aspect of all these statements is the fact that in this particular judgment of *Gehenna*, the **body** is involved as well as the soul. This is also specifically stated again in the next passages which we will consider—

<u>Matthew 10:28</u> *And do not fear those who kill the* **body** *but cannot kill the* **soul***. But rather fear Him who is able to destroy both* **soul** *and* **body** *in* **Gehenna***.*

<u>Luke 12:4,5</u> *And I say to you, my friends, do not be afraid of those who kill the* **body***, and after that have no more that they can do. But I will show you Whom you should fear: Fear Him Who, after He has killed, has power to cast into* **Gehenna***; yes, I say to you, fear Him!*

It is interesting to read some of the maneuverings of those whose doctrine is destroyed by this passage. Those who believe that the soul and the body are inseparable also believe that at physical death both soul and body terminate their conscious existence. When the animated body is killed, of necessity the soul or life consciousness ceases as well, they say. However, in this passage we have another example where the *"inner"* and *"outer"* men do the opposite from each other. The "body" can be killed, but not the "soul." So then we have a *dead* "body," but a living *conscious* "soul." This factor cannot be reconciled with their doctrine. But, instead of admitting their error, they focus on the second part of Christ's statement. "Ah, ha!" they argue, "Now Christ says that 'souls' can be 'destroyed,' whereas the traditionalists who believe in Hell think souls exist forever!"

By this dodge the modern Sadducees are showing their ignorance. *"Destruction"* does not mean "cessation of being" when it comes to the judgment of Hell! I have already pointed out in this study that Sheol has a compartment called "DESTRUCTION" (Abaddon). That compartment existed from the beginning, was first spoken of in Job's day (Job 26:5, 6), and continues (Psalm 88:10; Prov. 2:18; 9:18; Isa.14:9; 26:14 and 19) right up through the Great Tribulation where it is last mentioned. In Rev. 9:11 we are told that "Destruction" or "Abaddon" has a "king" over it who must be a great satanic personage. Now this is a personal being, and he has many, many subjects EXISTING in "Destruction." In Job 26:5 and 6, etc., we discovered that "disembodied spirits" of the lost are some of the occupants of "Destruction" and are never annihilated. In Rev. 9:1–12 some of "Destruction's" spirit occupants (probably demons) are released out upon the earth to afflict mankind. Now all these **creatures** in "Destruction" obviously never *"ceased to be,"* and "Destruction" has existed for over 6000 years. As I said before, *"destruction"* in Hell is a **"condition of existence"** and not the "termination of existence."

A few other references that use the word Gehenna —

Matthew 23:15 and 33 *Woe to you, scribes and Pharisees, hypocrites! For you travel land and sea to win one proselyte,* *and when he is won, you make him twice as much a son of **Gehenna** as yourselves. Serpents, brood of vipers! How can you escape the condemnation of **Gehenna**?*

The last use of Gehenna was in a metaphorical sense by James, the Lord's half brother—

James 3:6 *The tongue is a fire, a world of iniquity. . .and sets on fire the course of nature; and is set on fire by **Gehenna.***

Other References to the Final Judgment

Matthew 8:29 And suddenly they cried out [demons from within two men] *saying, 'What have we to do with You, Jesus, You Son of God? Have You come here **to torment us before the time**?'*

I do not know the time when angels and demons will be judged, but most presume it will be just after that of the unrighteous. The important thing for us to remember is that their judgment will involve a "*torment*," as well as that of the unrighteous.

Matthew 10:15 (see also Mark 6:11) *Assuredly, I say to you, it will be more tolerable for the land of Sodom and Gomorrah in **the Day of Judgment** than for that city.*

Matthew 11: 22 and 24 (see also Luke 10:12–15) *But I say to you, it will be more tolerable for Tyre and Sidon in **the Day of Judgment** than for you. But I say to you that it will be more tolerable for the land of Sodom in **the Day of Judgment** than for you.*

Matthew 12:41 and 42 *The men of Nineveh will rise up in **the Judgment** with this generation and condemn it, because they repented at the preaching of Jonah; and indeed, a greater* than Jonah is here. The queen of the South will rise up in **the Judgment** with this generation and condemn it, . . .

John 5:24 *Most assuredly, I say to you, he who hears My word and believes in Him Who sent Me has everlasting life, and shall not come into **Judgment**, but has passed from death into life.*

Acts 17:31 *. . . because He has appointed a day on which He will **judge** the world in righteousness. . . .*

Romans 2:2 and 3 *But we know that the **Judgment** of God is according to truth against those who practice such things . . . that you shall escape the **Judgment** of God?*

Romans 2:6, 8 (and 16) *Who will **render to each** one according to his deeds . . . But to those who are self-seeking and do not obey the truth, but obey unrighteousness—**indignation and wrath**. In the day when God will **judge** the secrets of men by Jesus Christ, according to my gospel.*

Hebrews 6:2 and 8 *The doctrine of . . . **Eternal Judgment** . . . . whose end* [those who reject the Son of God] *is to **be burned**.*

Hebrews 9:29 *. . . but after this **the Judgment**.*

Hebrews 10:27 and 29 *. . . but a certain **fearful expectation** of Judgment, and fiery indignation which shall devour the adversaries. Of how much **worse punishment**, do you suppose, will he be thought worthy who has trampled the Son of God under foot, and counted the blood of the covenant by which he was sanctified a common thing, and insulted the Spirit of grace?*

Hebrews 10:39 *But we are not of those who draw back to **Perdition**, . . .*

<u>2 Peter 2:9</u> *The Lord knows how . . . to reserve the unjust under **punishment** for **the Day of Judgment**.*

<u>2 Peter 2:17</u> *. . . for whom is reserved the **blackness of darkness forever**.*

<u>2 Peter 3:7</u> *. . . until the **Day of Judgment** and **perdition** of ungodly men.*

<u>Jude 6</u> (see also <u>2 Pet. 2:4</u>) *And the angels who did not keep their proper domain, but left their own abode, He has **reserved in everlasting chains under darkness*** [this is the present Sheol/Hades section for the fallen angels] *for the **Judgment of the Great Day*** [this is the judgment for the wicked angels after which they will be cast into the Lake of Fire].

<u>Jude 7</u> *As Sodom and Gomorrah, and the cities around them, in like manner to these* [the fallen angels above], *committing sexual immorality and going after strange* [or different] *flesh, are set forth as an example, of undergoing the **vengeance** of **eternal fire*** [literal trans.].

This particular verse (Jude 7) has been terribly misused by those who reject the doctrine of eternal conscious punishment in Hell, i.e., the ultimate fire of Gehenna. In fact, on the very day I was typing this verse into this study I received an e-mail from a teacher who opposes eternal suffering in Hell. He had a "sugar-stick;" it was a twisted use of this passage. He referred to it several times saying "Sodom and Gomorrah suffered 'the punishment of eternal fire' according to Jude 7. But was the fire itself eternal—never-ending? Is it still burning? Of course not." This an example of what others of the same persuasion have done.

Of course, Jude 7 says no such thing! What it actually says is that "Sodom and Gomorrah, and the cities around them . . . are set forth as an *example* of undergoing the vengeance of eternal fire." The *"eternal fire"* in view in this last part of the sentence is not the fire that consumed Sodom and Gomorrah, which fire had ceased long

ago, but the future "Gehenna fire which shall never be quenched."
Jude was very careful to NOT say that the fire which fell on Sodom
and Gomorrah was "eternal." Obvious to all is the fact that at the
southern end of the Dead Sea is one of the (if not, <u>the</u>) largest potash
industries in the world. The fire that fell from heaven and destroyed
those notorious cities came after they had been warned by God
through the use of earlier destructive armies (Gen. 14) which had
marched through that land. So it is that the destruction of Sodom and
Gomorrah serves as a warning to similar wickedness which is now
being practiced in the world.

Just compare Jude's description with that of the apostle Peter
and you will get the exact sense of Jude 7. Peter said (2 Pet. 2:6),
"And turning the cities of Sodom and Gomorrah into ashes, con-
demned them to destruction, **making them an example to those who**
afterward would live ungodly.*"* The example, Peter explained, is
that those who in the future will live ungodly are *"reserved under*
punishment for the Day of Judgment" (verse 9). Now this is exactly
what Jude is saying concerning Sodom and Gomorrah—they *"**are**
set forth as an example, **of undergoing the vengeance of eternal**
fire.*"* Peter and Jude are saying the very same thing!

The final "fire" is, indeed, an "eternal fire" which will last *"day*
and night, forever and forever" (Rev. 20:10, 14, 15). Admittedly,
the fire on Sodom and Gomorrah, though it serves as an example
of God bringing judgment, was not in that category; it did not burn
"day and night, forever and forever."

<u>Jude 13</u> . . . *to whom is reserved the* **blackness of dark-**
ness *forever*.

<u>Jude 23</u> *But others* [those who are repentant] *save with fear,*
pulling them out of ***the fire*** [a figure of speech, as if they had
nearly fallen into Hell].

"TARTARUS"

One last word which has been translated *Hell* in most of our English Bibles is the Greek verb *tartaroo* which basically means to incarcerate, but was used in the Greek world as another place in the subterranean for the punishment of the dead. It is used only one time and has reference to an abode for fallen angels—

2 Peter 2:4 *For if God did not spare angels when they sinned, but cast them into* **Tartarus** *and committed them to* **pits of darkness**, *reserved for Judgment*; ...

These angels are intelligent spirit creatures who were perverted in their actions back in the days of Noah (Jude 6; Gen. 6:1–4 and Job 1:6, 7). They have existed in *Tartarus* now for about the last 4500 years, plus they will be there for another 1000 years during the reign of Christ before their assigned final Judgment. They were obviously not annihilated. And furthermore, Peter is stressing their predicament as a warning to the false prophets who have arisen during this present Church Age—

2 Peter 2:1–4 *... just as there will be false teachers among you, who will secretly introduce destructive heresies, even denying the Lord Who bought* [paid the price for] *them, bringing swift destruction upon themselves. And many will follow their pernicious ways, and because of them the way of truth will be maligned; and in their greed they will exploit you with false words;* **their Judgment from long ago is not idle, and their destruction is not asleep**—*For if God spared not the angels.* . . .

In other words Peter is saying that what happened to the fallen angels is going to happen to these false teachers and all their followers. So here again is proof positive of *conscious existence* of the lost in a subterranean *Hell* to await the day of their Judgment. Just as angels are conscious, intelligent spirit beings awaiting their Judgment, so also are the disembodied spirits of the unrighteous.

CHAPTER FOURTEEN

The Book of REVELATION

The Book of Revelation

The book of Revelation is the last book in the cannon of Scripture. It reveals the final consummation of the history of the ages. In a similar manner it brings to a final conclusion this subject of *The Fire That Is Eternal*. I have traced *Sheol/Hades*, *Gehenna* and *Tartarus* up to this point. In addition I have discussed the Scriptural revelation concerning the spiritual nature of man. This subject of the spirits of the dead also comes to a consummation in the book of Revelation, primarily with the saints in Heaven.

I have already given some references from Revelation where the word *Hades* was used, and where the *Lake of Fire* (Gehenna) is mentioned. I have also written partially about the existence of the souls of the dead in Heaven from Revelation chapter six. Now, however, we are just going to go through the book of Revelation and observe all the various facets of these issues in the simple subject order in which they come. The book of Revelation will bring to a conclusion our exploration of "the doctrine of eternal judgment" (Hebrews 6:2).

"In The Spirit On The Lord's Day"

The book of Revelation is unique in regard to this whole subject, because the whole setting of Revelation is from John's perspective in *Heaven,* itself. Every scene throughout the book is viewed from John's position in Heaven. How did John get there? Was he physically there? Or was he spiritually there?

The book starts out with John on the Island of Patmos (Rev. 1:9). This is where John was physically present at the time he received a special vision or revelation. Then the tenth verse tells us that John *"was in the Spirit on the Lord's Day."* Everyone knows that this is a radically *different state of being.* This is actually another amazing statement from the Word of God. There has been a lot of debate about different aspects of exactly what it means. I not only want to know what it means, but I also want to understand how it relates to the whole issue of man's spiritual nature.

First, let us dismiss the traditional assumption that this is talking about John getting a vision on SUNDAY. This may be a cozy belief for traditional "Sunday go to Church" observers, yet nowhere in the Bible does it even hint that the first day of the week, i.e., Sunday, is called "the Lord's Day." Nor in this context is there even a remote idea that this reference is to a specific day of the week. However, the whole context of the book of Revelation falls right in the middle of the *"great and terrible **Day of the Lord"*** as often expounded upon throughout all the Scriptures.

Consequently, several conservative scholars explain this "Day" as having reference to the future time period identified many times in the Bible as "The Day of the Lord." For instance, John Walvoord in his commentary, *The Revelation of Jesus Christ*, page 42, states that this word in Rev. 1:10 is in the adjective form—*the Lord's*. In the Hebrew there is no adjective form for "Lord," and consequently the noun is always used. The Greek expression "is therefore the equivalent to the Old Testament expression 'the Day of the Lord.'" Walvoord goes on to say, "On the basis of the evidence, the interpretation is therefore preferred that John was projected forward to the future Day of the Lord." See, as well, *The Expanded Vines*

Expository Dictionary of New Testament Words under "judgment," where the word "day" (Greek, *hemera*) is also used with the adjective form before it. "Man's *day*" (1 Cor. 4:3) is properly understood as "man's judgment" and is so rendered in most translations. Similarly, W. E. Vine explains that "the Lord's Day" (Rev. 1:10) should be understood as a "period of Divine judgment," i.e., "the Day of the Lord's judgments."

Consequently, whatever is revealed to John, as he is supernaturally placed "in the Spirit," is to be interpreted as taking place in that future specific time period of "the Lord's judgments," and/or "the Day of the Lord."

What does it mean that John "*was in the Spirit*?" We read earlier where the apostle Paul had a similar experience concerning receiving "revelations" wherein he was transported into "the third Heaven." Paul told us that he did not know whether his body was present or not (2 Cor. 12:1–4). The prophet Ezekiel was also transported by the Spirit of God in visions. In his case it sometimes involved a bodily transport—Ezekiel 2:12–15. Sometimes this was a "vision" (8:3; 11:1, 24, 25) which may have involved his body. On other occasions it appears to be strictly a vision—37:1; 40:2, 3 and 43:5.

Surely we can conclude two things. First of all, this revelation which John received involved his *spiritual nature*. The text actually does not say that John was physically transported as was once the case of the prophet Ezekiel and possibly the apostle Paul. Secondly, throughout the book of Revelation, John's spiritual being is spoken of as having the same properties as a physical being. There was *sight* (many references), *hearing* (many references), *weeping* (5:4), *taking and eating* (10:9, 10), *measuring* (11:1), *standing* (13:1), *writing* (14:13), *being carried into a wilderness* (17:3), *being in amazement* (17:6, 7), *fell at His feet* (19:10), etc., etc. All these factors demonstrate conclusively the existence of a separate spiritual nature which is in nearly all parts and respects described the very same way as a person's physical body would be.

Revelation 5:13 "Under The Earth"

*And **every created thing** which is **in heaven** and on **the earth** and **under the earth** and **on the sea**, and all things in them, heard I saying, . . .*

All acknowledge that the book of Revelation will use a lot of figurative language. All that language is, however, a figure of real things, events and existing beings. Here in this passage it is clear that there are "created" beings not only in heaven, and not only on the earth and in the sea, but also **UNDER THE EARTH**. That can only be a reference to the realm of the disembodied spirits of the dead, and of fallen angelic beings and demonic creatures imprisoned in Hell. There were descriptions in both the Hebrew Scriptures and the Greek Scriptures of Sheol/Hades as being in the "lowest parts of the earth," "in the depths of the earth," "the lowest Pit," "in the heart of the earth," etc., etc. And now here in Revelation the fact is stated simply as "*under the earth*." All these descriptions are demonstrating the maximum location in opposition to that of Heaven. In addition, it is "*created*" beings which are "under the earth." What God "created" on the inside of man (i.e., the spiritual nature) is therefore positively understood in this context of Rev. 5:13.

The Souls of Those in Heaven

Revelation 6:9–11 We have already read about the "*souls*" of those under the altar in Heaven. These are "*the souls of those who had been slain for the Word of God and for the testimony which they held.*" They were given robes and told to "*rest*" awhile longer until the remaining of their brethren will have been "*killed as they were, was completed.*" So here we have disembodied spirits of the saints in Heaven. However, this is not the only group of saints which is mentioned in the book of Revelation. These had apparently died because of their testimony in the battle against the antichrist forces. These are understood as disembodied spirits of the believers who are awaiting the resurrection of their bodies. Another scene is in Revelation chapter seven—

> Revelation 7:9–17 *After these things I looked and behold,* **a great multitude**, *which no man could number, from every nation and all tribes and peoples and tongues, standing before the throne and before the Lamb,* **clothed** *in white robes, and palm branches in their hands; and* **they cry out** *with a loud voice, saying, 'Salvation to our God Who sits on the throne, and to the Lamb'. . . . And one of the elders answered and said to me, 'These who are clothed in white robes, who are they, and from where have they come?' And I said to him, 'My lord, you know.' And he said to me, 'These are the ones who have come out of Great Tribulation, and they have washed their robes and made them white in the blood of the Lamb. For this reason, they are before the throne of God; and they serve Him day and night in His temple; and He Who sits on the throne shall spread His tabernacle over them. They shall hunger no more, neither thirst anymore; neither shall the sun beat down on them, nor any heat; for the Lamb in the center of the throne shall be their shepherd, and shall guide them to springs of the water of life; and God shall wipe every tear from their eyes.'*

This "great multitude" is seen in heaven after the "*sealing of the servants of God,*" the "144,000" who will evangelize the earth— Rev. 7:1–8. That would mean that this multitude in heaven are the martyred fruit of their ministry and service. The promise given is that they will suffer no longer. This is further evidence of disembodied spirits of the dead; in these cases, they are in Heaven.

> Revelation 14:13 *Then I heard a voice from Heaven saying to me, 'Write, Blessed are the* **dead** *who die in the Lord from now on.' 'Yes,' says the Spirit, 'that they may* **rest from their labors**, *and their works follow them.'*

Here is the word of comfort to those who suffered death under the hand of the administration of the Antichrist. As the other passages indicate, along with this one, these saints are in Heaven. They are in a state of "rest" and their "works" will be remembered.

Revelation 15:2–4 *And I saw something like a sea of glass mingled with fire, and those who have the victory over the Beast, over his image and over his mark and over the number of his name standing on the sea of glass, having harps of God. They sing the song of Moses, the servant of God, and the song of the Lamb, saying:*
  'Great and marvelous are Your works, Lord God Almighty!
  Just and true are Your ways, O King of saints!
  Who shall not fear You, O Lord, and glorify Your name?
  For You alone are holy. For all nations shall come
    and worship before You.
  For Your judgments have been manifested.'

This is actually the fourth group of saints who are pictured in Heaven as a result of their victory over Satan and their consequent persecution unto death. Though figurative language has been employed, there is no mistaking the reality it represents. When a saint is put to death because of his battle with the antichrist forces, there is the disembodied spirit of each saint who goes into Heaven to be comforted until the time of the resurrection of his body. These scenes therefore present the time period where their spirits are awaiting their future bodily resurrection.

Revelation 19:7–9 *Let us be glad and rejoice and give Him glory, for the marriage of the Lamb has come, and His wife has made herself ready. And to her was granted to be arrayed in fine linen, clean and bright, for the fine linen is the righteous acts of the saints. Then he said to me, 'Write: Blessed are those who are called to the marriage supper of the Lamb!'*

It is generally agreed by expositors that these are saints in Heaven. Unfortunately, many conservative Bible teachers think these represent the Church of Jesus Christ of this present age. This is actually not the case. In all consistency, these are the *same* saints of whom we have been reading all along in the book of Revelation. They have been collecting in Heaven as martyrs for Christ their Savior. These saints are not only made ready for the wedding feast, but that feast is not said to take place in Heaven—it is awaiting the coming of Messiah to reign on earth.

The great wedding feast in view is the one prophesied which takes place at the beginning of the millennial reign of the Messiah— see Psalm 45:1–17; Matt. 22:1–14; 25:1–13 and Luke 14:15–24. After these saints will have received their resurrection bodies, they in concert with the saints on earth will be celebrating that great event as spoken of by Christ in the Gospel accounts.

> Revelation 20:4 *And I saw thrones, and they sat upon them, and judgment was committed to them. Then I saw the **souls** of those who had been beheaded for their witness to Jesus and for the Word of God, who had not worshiped the Beast or his image, and had not received his mark on their foreheads or on their hands. And they **lived** and reigned with Christ for a thousand years. . . . This is the first **resurrection.***

This is the final time these saints are mentioned. At this future time it is obvious there will be the resurrection of their bodies—that is what the text says. However, all the previous texts indicate very clearly that these "souls" were in existence after their physical death and prior to their resurrection. The previous Scriptures tell us they exist in Heaven, that they are singing and praising God and awaiting this glorious event of the resurrection of their bodies. This beautiful truth cannot be circumvented.

"The Bottomless Pit" (Abyss)

First I will quote the texts where this description of "the Bottomless Pit" or "Abyss" is used. Then I will explore the meaning of the word and its application to the general subject before us. The word is used seven times in the book of Revelation.

<u>Revelation 9:1, 2 and 11</u> *And the fifth angel sounded: and I saw a Star fall from Heaven to the earth. To him was given the key to the **Bottomless Pit**. And he opened the **Bottomless Pit** . . . .* [And creatures like locusts came out of the Pit to afflict men on the earth.] *And they have a **king** over them, the angel of the **Bottomless Pit**; his name in Hebrew is **Abaddon**, and in the Greek he has the name **Apollyon**.*

<u>Revelation 11:7 and 17:8</u> *. . . the Beast out of the **Bottomless Pit** will make war against them* [the Two Witnesses], *and overcome them, and kill them. The beast that you saw was, and is not, and will ascend out of the **Bottomless Pit** and go into perdition.*

<u>Revelation 20:1–3</u> *Then I saw an angel coming down from Heaven, having the key to the **Bottomless Pit** and a great chain in his hand. He laid hold of the dragon, that serpent of old, who is the Devil and Satan, and bound him for a thousand years; and he cast him into the **Bottomless Pit**, and shut him up, and set a seal on him, so that he should deceive the nations no more till the thousand years were finished. But after these things he must be released for a little while.*

<u>Revelation 20:7</u> *Now when the thousand years have expired, Satan will be released from his **prison*** [the Bottomless Pit], . . .

The meaning of the Word "Abyss"
And its Association with the Fire of Hades

The words or word in our English Bibles, usually rendered "Bottomless Pit" or "Abyss," is translated from the Greek word *Abussos*. The Greek *a*, here carries the meaning of *extreme* or *intensive*, and **bussos** means *depth*. Combined, it means *an immeasurable* *depth* or *bottomless*. Hence we have the English translation as either "the Abyss" or "the Bottomless Pit."

This word is used seven times in the book of Revelation, as descriptive of that lowest region beneath the earth which is the reservoir or holding chamber, in this case, of demonic creatures and eventually of Satan, himself. Satan will be confined there for the designated period of the 1000 year reign of Christ on earth. In this regard we must remember the words of the Lord Jesus Christ as recorded in Matthew 25:41. There Christ was speaking of the judgment which will take place at the time of His second coming. This judgment synchronizes with the judgment mentioned here in Revelation 20:1–6. In the Matthew account the wicked will be placed in *"the eternal fire which has been **prepared for the Devil and his angels**."* In the Revelation account "the Devil" is confined in *Abussos* (or Bottomless Pit), which therefore means it is the same place "prepared" for him in Matthew 25:41. Consequently, we are to understand that this place Christ called *"the eternal fire"* or *"Hades"* (see the section on Hades) was originally designed for Satan and his fallen angelic and demonic hosts and is herein called *Abussos*. When rebellious mankind follows Satan's deception, they too become occupants of the very same place which was originally designed for Satan and all his hosts.

Other Uses of Abussos

Surprisingly enough, this same word *Abussos* is used on two other occasions in the Greek New Testament; its use is very interesting. First, the writer of the Gospel of Luke applied it as recorded in Luke 8:31. In this context Christ was casting out demons who begged Him not to send them *"out into the Abyss (Abussos)."* Apparently they recognized the *Abyss* (or Bottomless Pit) as a place of confinement for them just as we read in the book of Revelation about the demons who were confined in *Abussos*. It seems that Christ acquiesced to their request by releasing them into a herd of swine. Yet, we read that the herd reacted violently and ran down a steep place only to be drowned in the sea. Now it just so happens that the sea is itself sometimes also called *"the Abyss"* in the Hebrew Scriptures. It meant a deep subterranean water supply or simply the depths of the ocean. Likewise, in the Greek translation of the Hebrew Scriptures this deep is called *Abussos*. It can be concluded, therefore, that the demons must have left the dead pigs and gone into an *Abyss* after all.

Secondly, the apostle Paul uses the word in <u>Romans 10:7</u>. In this case Paul is quoting from Deuteronomy 30:12 and 13 which speaks of the fact that God's Law was available to the children of Israel, so that they didn't have to go to Heaven to get it, neither did they have to go across the *sea* to get it. Paul is saying that "the righteousness of faith" is available in the same manner. Paul points out that one should never have to say "in his heart, 'Who will ascend into Heaven?' [to get the message], which would be like bringing Christ down from above, nor [should they say] 'Who will descend into the *Abyss* [*Abussos*]?' [to get the message], which would be like bringing up Christ from the dead."

Now it is noticeable that Paul in this parallel, rendered the word "sea," which was used in Deuteronomy, as *"Abussos"* instead. He undoubtedly did this because in the parallel he is likening it to Christ's ascension up from *Hades* itself. Thus, he uses the word *Abussos* as a synonym for Hades. In Christ's death He went into Sheol/Hades (Matt. 12:40 and Acts 2:31) or now, as we further understand—into the *"Bottomless Pit."* This may be shocking to our sensitivity, because most people recognize the "Bottomless Pit" as the residence of the demonic creatures. Nevertheless, there it is! Remember Paul made a similar contrast in Ephesians 4:9 and 10. There he said, "Now that He ascended, what does it mean but that He also first descended into the *Lower Parts* of the earth?" As we noted before in the Hebrew Scriptures, the expression "the lower part of the earth" was used in reference to *Sheol*.

The Final Use of Abussos

We saw in the Hebrew Scriptures that many times Sheol was referred to as *"the Pit."* There was also the terminology—*"the lowest*

Pit." And there was also the mention of "*Abaddon*," which meant the place of "destruction." The word "*Pit*" is apparently often used interchangeably with "*Sheol.*" "*The lowest Pit*" and "*Abaddon*" also refer to that particular chamber in Sheol for the unrighteous. Now, here in Revelation there is pictured before us a releasing of some of the demonic creatures from that chamber called "*the Bottomless Pit*" or the *Abussos* (the Abyss). The purpose of these demonic creatures is to afflict ungodly men on the earth. So it is, even in the last book of the Bible, there is confirmation to our conclusions derived from the earliest mention of this place in the book of Job (Abaddon, Job 26:6). Here it is a place of confinement for intelligent spirit creatures.

The contents of the *Abussos,* in the chapters of the book of Revelation as earlier listed, are most generally understood as *demonic creatures* who will afflict unregenerate mankind on earth. Their descriptions are a gruesome combination of animal-like and man-like beings. They are personages who have "a king over them" named *Apollyon* (Rev. 9:11). This probably has reference to Satan or some other super demonic creature.

The fact that in Revelation 11:7 and 17:8 the Beast is said to have ascended "out of the *Bottomless Pit*" is very interesting. The "Beast" is the final form of world government upon the earth. Generally speaking, prophetic Bible teachers have called this "the Revived Roman Empire" of the last days. It is composed of a ten nation confederacy which roughly follows the configuration of the old original Roman empire. It is directly headed by the Antichrist. This "Beast" will, in fact, not only "make war on the saints" (Rev. 13:7), but it will also "make war against Christ" (Rev. 19:20).

So what then does the text mean that the Beast "ascends out of the *Bottomless Pit*"? It means that the *source* of the motivating ideologies that this government will manifest is directly out of HELL. It is mediated to the minds and hearts of godless men through the agency of demons from the Pit or *Abussos.* Though it is a human government on earth, yet its ideology and spiritual motivation are from Satan and the demons of Hell. Just as false doctrine in the last days is from the spirit of demons (1 Tim. 4:1), so the last form of world government is also of demonic origin.

Revelation 14:9–11

Then a third angel followed them, saying with a loud voice, 'If anyone worships the Beast and his image, and receives his mark in his forehead or on his hand, he himself shall also drink of the wine of the wrath of God, which is poured out full strength into the cup of His indignation. He shall ***be tormented with fire and brimstone*** *in the presence of the holy angels and in the presence of the Lamb. And* ***the smoke of their torment*** *ascends* ***forever and ever;*** *and they* ***have no rest day or night,*** *who worship the Beast and his image, and whoever receives the mark of his name.'*

This is one of the strongest statements ever made in the Bible. Seeing that the Beast and his followers stand diametrically against God and His Christ, it is no wonder that God imposes the strictest of judgments against them. In this final period of great tribulation, the "everlasting gospel" has penetrated every nook and corner of the earth. God's warning has touched every ear. There are none without excuse. In addition, the blasphemous message of the Antichrist has made it very clear that he stands against Almighty God. There are no shades of gray in this confrontation.

Jesus Christ is the most compassionate person Who ever walked the face of the earth. No one has more love or consideration than He. Initially, these rebellious individuals are going to suffer fire and brimstone in His very presence and in the presence of the holy angels. Their "torment" is going to continue "day and night" "forever and ever." If you think that you, and a lot of other theological friends on this earth, have more compassion and love than Jesus Christ, then your compassion is perverted by the same Devil who inspired these men to worship the Beast and take his mark.

The apostle Peter had great compassion for Christ Who spoke of His impending suffering and death—"God forbid it, Lord! This shall never happen to You!" he said. And yet Christ immediately responded, "Get behind Me, Satan! You are a stumbling block to Me; for you are not setting your mind on God's interest, but man's"

(Matt. 16:22 and 23). What a shock it must have been for Peter to then realize that his soulish compassion was not in accordance with God's revelation and plan. Indeed, Peter's humanistic love was actually motivated by Satan. There is another old saying that epitomizes this reality. It has been said, "Truth given in *love* makes it easier to be received by the hearers, but love without *the Truth* is actually **not love**."

"THE LAKE OF FIRE"

<u>Revelation 19:20</u> *Then the Beast was captured, and with him the false prophet who worked signs in his presence, by which he deceived those who received the mark of the Beast and those who worshipped his image. These two were cast* **alive** *into* **the Lake of Fire** *burning with brimstone.*

<u>Revelation 20:10</u> *The Devil, who deceived them, was cast into* **the Lake of Fire** *and brimstone where the Beast and the false prophet are, and they will be* **tormented day and night forever and ever**.

<u>Revelation 20:13,14</u> *The sea gave up the dead who were in it, and* **Death** *and* **Hades** *delivered up the dead who were in them. And they were judged, each one according to his works. Then* **Death** *and* **Hades** *were cast into* **the Lake of Fire***. This is* **the Second Death**. *And anyone not found written in the Book of Life was cast into* **the Lake of Fire**.

<u>Revelation 21:8</u> *But the cowardly, unbelieving, abominable, murderers, sexually immoral, sorcerers, idolaters, and all liars shall have their part in* **the Lake of Fire** *and brimstone, which is* **the Second Death**.

<u>Revelation 22:11, 15</u> **He who is unjust***, let him* **be unjust** *still,* **He who is filthy***, let him* **be filthy still***;* **he who is righteous***, let him* **be righteous still***;* **he who is holy***, let him* **be**

***holy still**. But **outside are** dogs and sorcerers and sexually immoral and murderers and idolaters, and whoever loves and practices a lie.*

Some remarkable facts about the Lake of Fire are:

1. According to Revelation 19:20, the Lake of Fire exists for at least a thousand years prior to the final Great White Throne Judgment which takes place after the Millennial Reign of Christ (Rev. 20:7, 11–14). However, the only occupants of this Lake of Fire during the thousand years are the Beast and the False Prophet. So heinous was the rebellion of these two, that they are cast directly into this *Gehenna* without going before the final Judgment.

2. According to Revelation 19:20, these two individuals are cast "ALIVE" into the Lake of Fire. This is only the second time in Scripture that individuals went alive into a stage of Hell. As you may remember, in the rebellion of Korah, Dathan and Abiram (Numbers 16), the earth literally opened up and they and all who were associated with them fell down "alive" into Sheol or the Pit. That means they went into Sheol bodily, with their souls. The same is true in the case of the Beast and False Prophet. They are cast into the Lake of Fire "ALIVE." That means bodily.

3. Next, Satan himself is finally cast into the Lake of Fire where the Beast and False Prophet "**ARE**" (Rev. 20:10). In addition, "They will be tormented day and night forever and ever." In other words, their bodies and souls "are" in a state of perpetual destruction and torment along with Satan, himself. All the arguments of the modern Sadducees are to no avail in light of these Scriptures.

4. According to Revelation 20:13 and 14, both *"Death"* and *"Hades"* deliver up the dead, and both are then cast into the Lake of Fire. "Death" has reference to the physical bodies of the lost being resurrected, *but not glorified.* "Hades" has reference to the souls of the lost in Hades also being brought out. United with their resurrected bodies, the lost will stand before the Great White Throne Judgment.

Then the contents of "Death" and "Hades" (i.e., the lost) will be cast into the Lake of Fire to be punished "according to their works." They, therefore, receive the same fate and company as Satan, the Beast and the False Prophet. We shall see that there are degrees of punishment in this final Hell also called "*Gehenna*." This is the third and last time the Scriptures reveal the bodily deportment of mankind into the "nether world," in this case into *Gehenna*.

5. According to Revelation 21:8; 22:11 and 15, the lost will not change their moral or ethical inclinations. They will continue in their unified (body-soul) state of ungodliness. The one word that is stressed in this passage is simply —

"<u>BE</u>"
They will NOT "cease to be,"
but will continue to <u>BE</u> in their sins.

"THE SECOND DEATH"

The subject of "*The Second Death*" synchronizes with the subject spoken of by Christ under the designation of "Gehenna Fire," and also in Revelation by the designation of "The Lake of Fire." All three of these designations refer to the same thing—the final disposition of the lost after the Great White Throne Judgment of God. Gehenna Fire is the Lake of Fire. The lost are physically resurrected from the dead and united with their spirits, judged and cast into the Lake of Fire (or Gehenna). This condition of the lost is now called "The Second Death."

"The Second Death" is the direct antithesis of "the First Resurrection." In the Scriptures God promised a resurrection of both the righteous and the unrighteous. Read—

<u>Daniel 12:2</u> *And many of those who sleep in the dust of the earth will awake, these to **everlasting life**, but the others to **disgrace and everlasting abhorrence**.*

<u>John 5:28, 29</u> *Do not marvel at this; for the hour is coming in which all who are in the graves will hear His voice and come forth—those who have done good, to the **resurrection of life**, and those who have done evil, to the **resurrection of condemnation**.*

<u>Acts 24:15</u> *I have hope in God, which they themselves also accept, that there will be a resurrection of the dead, both of **the just** and **the unjust**.*

<u>Revelation 20:4–6</u> . . . *And they* [the saints] *lived* [the resurrection to life] *and reigned with Christ for a thousand years. But the rest of the dead* [the lost] *did not **live again*** [the resurrection to condemnation] *until the thousand years were finished. This is the **first resurrection*** [the righteous]. *Blessed and holy is he who has part in the first resurrection. Over such the **Second Death*** [i.e., the resurrection of condemnation] *has no power,* . . .

It is clear from these passages of Scripture that there are two resurrections of the dead. There is the resurrection of the righteous and the resurrection of the unrighteous. We also know from Paul's inspired explanation in 1 Corinthians 15 that the resurrection of the righteous will be in glorified, immortal bodies—bodies like that of our Lord Jesus Christ after His resurrection. On the other hand the resurrection of the unrighteous is just the opposite. It is described as *"in disgrace and abhorrence,"* and *"to condemnation."* Therefore, though the unrighteous are resurrected and are said to *"live again,"* it is to be understood that this is in the same corruptible bodies they had before. They are not resurrected into *"immortality,"* but rather into a state of everlasting *"mortality."* Therefore this is called "the Second Death."

<u>Revelation 2:11</u> . . *he who overcomes shall not be hurt by the **Second Death**.*

<u>Revelation 20:6</u> *Blessed and holy is he who has part in the first resurrection: over such the **Second Death** has no power.*

<u>Revelation 20:14</u> *Then death and Hades were cast into the Lake of Fire. This is the **Second Death**.*

<u>Revelation 21:8</u> *But the cowardly, unbelieving, abominable, murderers, sexually immoral, sorcerers, idolaters, and all liars shall have their part in The Lake of Fire which burns with fire and brimstone, which is the **Second Death**.*

"The Second Death" is a state or condition of existence for eternity. Daniel said *"everlasting abhorrence."* Christ said *"the fire that shall never be quenched—where the worm does not die, and the fire is not quenched,"* and *"into everlasting fire."* Jude said *"eternal fire"* and *"the blackness of darkness forever."*

CHAPTER FIFTEEN

SUMMARY and CONCLUDING OBSERVATIONS

❧

SUMMARY

From The Greek Scriptures

S imply stated, there are over 50 descriptive designations applied to the subject of the conscious existence of the lost in "Hell" given in the Greek Scriptures. These descriptive words and phrases are used over one hundred and fifty times throughout all the various individual manuscripts of the 27 books composing what has come to be called "The New Testament." This does not include the innumerable allusions to, and suggestions of, the final disposition of the unsaved in eternity. Regardless of the natural man's repugnance to these descriptions, they remain, very obviously, the exact words the Divine Holy Spirit has inspired and chosen to use. God's purpose is specifically for our comprehension so that there will be no false illusions about humankind's eternal destiny if one rejects the manifestations of God's grace and mercy. For any person who has chosen to ignore God's multiple manifestations of grace, especially in this Age of Grace—and has instead stubbornly chosen to follow Satan's seductive leadership—there remains:

1. Hades (11 times)
2. Gehenna (12 times)
3. Tartarus
4. Abussos (9 times)
5. Lake of Fire (5 times)
6. Second death (4 times)
7. Wrath (4 times)
8. Fire (5 times)
9. Unquenchable Fire (11 times)
10. Fire Never Quenched (5 times)
11. Furnace of Fire (2 times)
12. Eternal Fire (2 times)
13. Everlasting Fire
14. Fiery Indignation
15. Burn or Burned (2 times)
16. Weeping and Gnashing of Teeth (7 times)
17. Destroy
18. Destruction (7 times)
19. Everlasting Destruction
20. Perdition (3 times)
21. Judge (2 times)
22. The Judgment (9 times)
23. The Day of Judgment (5 times)
24. Eternal Judgment
25. Judgment of the Great Day
26. Condemned or Condemnation (2 times)
27. Resurrection of Condemnation
28. Prison (2 times)
29. Perish (3 times)
30. Punished
31. Punishment
32. Worse Punishment
33. Eternal Punishment
34. Sorer Punishment
35. Torments or Tormented (3 times)
36. Tormented in this Flame
37. Tormented Day and Night Forever

38. Tormented with Fire and Brimstone
39. Smoke of Their Torment Forever
40. Agony in this Flame
41. Damnation
42. Where the Worm Dies Not (3 times)
43. Indignation
44. Vengeance
45. No Rest Day nor Night
46. Darkness
47. Blackness of Darkness Forever (2 times)
48. Pits of Darkness
49. Outer Darkness (3 times)
50. Everlasting Chains of Darkness
51. Beneath
52. Under the Earth
53. In the Heart of the Earth
54. Lower Parts of the Earth

Furthermore, the Scriptures reveal that Jesus Christ the Son of God already went to "Hell" on mankind's behalf so that they "may not perish but have everlasting life" (John 3:16). I will give a more extensive study on this in Section Three. For now, note the following specific Scriptures in this regard—

1. Christ was "in *the heart of the earth* for three days and three nights"
    Matthew 12:40 (see also Jonah 2:2, *Sheol*).
2. Peter said Christ was in "*Hades/Sheol.*"
    Acts 2:31 (from Psalm 16:10)
3. Paul said Christ "descended into the *lower parts of the earth.*"
    Ephesians 4:9, 10
4. Again Paul indicated this was "*Abussos* (the bottomless pit)."
    Romans 10:6, 7
5. Christ liberated the souls of the righteous from *Hades/Sheol.*
    Ephesians 4:8 (from Psalm 68:18)

OBJECTIONS ANSWERED!

"Is not God a God of Love and Compassion?"

No doubt, the most common objections to the Biblical doctrine, as manifested in this particular study, of the eternal punishment of the lost are the continuous appeals to the Biblical aspects of God's revealed character of *"love," "mercy," "grace," "compassion"* and *"perfect goodness."* Objectors would generally argue that "the traditional teaching on 'Hellfire' is an embarrassment to the Christian Church." They would have us believe that it "contradicts the character of God as 'loving,' 'tender' and 'merciful'." They would say such things as "God would never torture people for eternity!" "How disgusting, the very idea of people writhing in torment for eternity!" "How could anyone else be happy knowing people were in such anguish?" "To send people to a place of eternal torment is to make God a sadist!" "No one preaches this traditional Hell anymore." "When was the last time you ever heard a sermon on Hell? — You probably can't remember." "This is not our concept of God today!" "My Bible says 'God is love'." In discussions of this subject, these types of statements have been repeated many times in many different ways.

I would like to answer them four (4) ways —

No. 1 For those of you who lean so heavily upon the "goodness," "mercy" and "kindness" of God in order to turn our emotions against the thoughts about eternal punishment, I would remind you of one very important fact which you apparently don't realize! Don't you know that the ONLY ONES going to Hell are the very ones who REJECT the "love," "grace," "kindness" and "goodness" of God???? Yes, in fact, that is the very reason, so clearly brought out in the Scriptures, that they are going to Hell! When people REJECT the multiplied demonstrations of God's kindness, goodness, mercy and grace, especially as manifested in the Savior Jesus Christ, what then is left for them? I will tell you what is left for them — everything that is just the opposite of God's kindness, mercy, love and grace!

255

The amazing thing about the Bible is that it is BALANCED! And the very same thing is true of God's character, as we shall see in a moment. If it is God's sovereign plan to bless those who accept His Divine mercy, grace, love and compassion with ETERNAL consequences, is it not perfectly consistent that the very same God will reward those who have cold contempt upon His mercy, grace, love and compassion with ETERNAL consequences as well? It is not our prerogative to determine what eternity holds in either case. It is our privilege to read the revelation and accept it.

No. 2   For those of you who emphasize this one aspect of God's character, I would like to RE-INTRODUCE you to the God Who is revealed in the Bible!

Yes, it does say one time in the Bible that "God is love" (1 John 4:8). But the very same Bible one time says *"For our God is a Consuming Fire"* (Hebrews 12:29). Now if this aspect of God's character does not suit your pleasure then just cut it out of your personal Bible, because that is the only way you are going to get rid of it!

Those of you who argue this way remind me of Thomas Jefferson. And though Tomas Jefferson was a highly respected person in our national history, a lot of things about Jesus Christ did not set well with him. He solved his problem by making his own copy of the New Testament. He just did not include all those passages which convicted his conscience or upset his estimation of what he thought Christ should be. Jefferson simply made his own New Testament by cutting out all those portions which did not suit his ideas about Christ and God. He cut and pasted up a Bible which was suitable to his philosophy. Now I have seen copies of Thomas Jefferson's New Testament offered for sale, but I have never even been tempted to buy one. I don't think it has ever been a best seller—just a novelty, at best. I am afraid that it leaves a whole lot out—so much so that it makes most people feel very suspicious. In fact, most scholars thought it was far more interesting to see what he left out, than it was to read what he left in. It is also an interesting fact to many that what Mr. Jefferson left in his New Testament actually became lifeless, mute and even daft when the basic contexts were all taken away. Of course, people who just emphasize this one aspect of God's character end up with what the apostle Paul calls "another Jesus" (2 Corinthians 11:4).

Mark Twain once said "It is not those things I don't understand in the Bible that cause me problems. It is the things I do understand!" That the doctrine of Hell in the Bible causes people problems is exactly what God intended! The solution to the problem is not to attempt to "take the Hell out of Hell," but to turn in repentance to the God of grace, mercy, love and compassion!

Again I say, for those of you who prefer to believe that God is nothing but a great big old "Santa Claus," let us walk through the Bible just once more.

* Shall we stop and stand with Noah on the mount in Ararat and realize that our whole globe was purged by a cataclysm of unbelievable proportions? A year has transpired since we heard the last mocking laughter of the filthy, violent earthlings; now there is nothing but a haunting silence. Not only all mankind on the face of the whole earth, but even everything that breathed lays inundated beneath us in the valleys and canyons of the watery abyss. Obviously this is but a temporal judgment from a loving God, Who warns those who in pride scorn His grace and love. In addition, He left the record of this inundation as a sober reminder to our own generation as it once again approaches the same moral depravity of Noah's day. The apostle Peter said—

> For this they willfully forget: . . . the world that then existed perished, being flooded with water. But the heavens and the earth which are now preserved by the same word, are reserved for FIRE until the day of Judgment and perdition of ungodly men (2 Pet. 3:5–7).

* Perhaps you are somewhat soulish like Abraham was when he bargained with God over the notorious cities of Sodom and Gomorrah. ". . . Shall not the Judge of all the earth do right?" Abraham asked (Gen. 18:25). Then, let us get up early in the morning and go out with Abraham, as he stands once again in the very spot

where he interceded on behalf of those cities and looked to see *"the smoke of the land which went up like the smoke of a furnace"* (Gen. 19:28). And as we look, let us remember the words of Jude wherein he says of Sodom and Gomorrah, ". . . [they] are set forth as an example, suffering the vengeance of eternal FIRE" (Jude 7). The TEMPORAL FIRE judgment on those cities is but the "example" of the "ETERNAL FIRE" on all rejecters of God's grace.

* Perhaps you would rather stand comfortably with the people of Israel at the foot of Mount Sinai to witness the giving of the most ethical and moral Law system of all time. Pharaoh of Egypt did not appreciate his meeting with the One Who said "I Am that I Am." But certainly Israel under such ideal conditions would appreciate the God in Whom they have come to trust. What an amazing surprise they were in for—the whole mountain quaked and was raked by thunder and lightning. It was engulfed in a fiery tempest, with the shocking blast of a supernatural trumpet. The great congregation screamed out for Moses to intercede and speak to them, but not for God to do so. (See Exo. 20:18–21; 24:17, 18; Deut. 4:24; 5:22–26 and 9:3.) Why is it that such a righteous and holy God would accompany Himself with such scenes of violence and terror? Is it not because of the consequence of man's pernicious will to violate the righteousness of God?

> See that you do not refuse Him Who speaks. For if they did not escape who refused Him Who spoke on earth, much more shall we not escape if we turn away from Him Who speaks from heaven, Whose voice then shook the earth; but now He has promised, saying, 'Yet once more I shake not only the earth, but also heaven' (Hebrews 12:25, 26).

* Perhaps we all need to stand silently along the side of the High Priest, Aaron, as he shockingly beheld the charred bodies of his two sons, Nadab and Abihu, being drug out of the Tabernacle. "Why, the only things those boys did was to 'offer strange fire' before the God of Israel," someone might whisper. I would suggest you keep your mouths shut, because that is what Aaron did! Furthermore,

he was told to not make any demonstration of frustration (see Lev. 10:1–7). Does this incident cause you to doubt God's goodness? If so, just be reminded that the only fire to be presented before the God Who resides over the mercy seat is the fire from off the altar, which represents the sacrifice of our Lord Jesus Christ on our behalf. Jesus Christ said, "I am the way, the truth, and the life; no man comes to the Father but by Me" (John 14:6). The fire which burned into the soul of our blessed substitute, paying the just penalty for our sins, is the only "fire" that can represent and preserve us in the presence of a holy God.

* Would you like to stand before the God of Daniel who beheld in vision —

...And the Ancient of Days was seated . . . His throne was a fiery flame, its wheels a burning fire; a fiery stream issued and came forth from before Him . . . and the books [of judgment] were opened (Daniel 7:9, 10).

* Or would you like to see what Isaiah saw —

The sinners of Zion are afraid; fearfulness has seized the hypocrites: 'Who among us shall dwell with the devouring fire? Who among us shall dwell with everlasting burnings?' (Isaiah 33:14).

* Do you expect the Thessalonian saints should stand with some of you modern preachers who have expressed hypocritical disgust —

. . . when the Lord Jesus is revealed from heaven with His mighty angels, in flaming fire taking vengeance on those who do not know God, and on those who do not obey the gospel of our Lord Jesus Christ. These shall be punished with everlasting destruction from the presence of the Lord and from the glory of His power, . . . (2 Thess. 1:7, 8).

259

* Lastly, just exactly what do you think should happen to all those who scoff and have contempt at the warnings of God?

> For if we [mankind] sin willfully after we have received the knowledge of the truth, there no longer remains a sacrifice for sins, but a certain fearful expectation of Judgment, and fiery indignation which will devour the adversaries. Anyone who has rejected Moses' Law dies without mercy . . . **Of how much worse punishment**, do you suppose, will he be thought worthy who has trampled the Son of God underfoot, counted the blood of the covenant by which he was sanctified a common thing, and insulted the Spirit of grace? (Hebrews 10:26–29.)

No. 3 As to the fact of who preaches the Biblical truths of Hellfire today and who does not, permit me to make this observation. It is very interesting that at the beginning of this very nation of ours, over three hundred years ago, the Puritans and Pilgrims, who took their religion seriously, laid a solid foundation of righteousness for our society. All historians admit they did not hesitate in the least to preach on Hell. In fact, all through the early days of this nation the evangelists and reformers were characterized by consistency on that subject. If there was going to be a revival, you can rest assured that Hellfire was on the preaching menu.

It was not until liberalism and modernism began to creep into the seminaries and respectable churches that the modern pulpiteers began to be squeamish about Hellfire. And why shouldn't they be? They were now tolerating all kinds of compromising immodesty, immorality and so called "liberation" of values. The great "sexual revolution" and "women's liberation" brought this nation to the condition of mind that it has allowed for the holocaust of some 45 million babies in the last 35 years. Do you think this nation will applaud the preacher who dares to stand up and preach on Hellfire? Do you think society and its preachers, who have now opened the doors for same sex marriage and toleration for the grossest homosexuality imaginable and sex trade in child pornography and molestation will come to hear someone preach on Hell? Do you think the apostle Paul lied when he spoke —

> But know this, that in the last days perilous times will come: for men will be lovers of themselves, . . . having a form of godliness, but denying its authority . . . For the time will come when they will not endure sound doctrine, but according to their own desires, . . . they will heap for themselves teachers to tickle their ears. (See 2 Timothy 3:1, 2, 5 and 4:3.)

Of course, everyone who reads the Bible knows that the very One who spoke on Hell more than any other, was none other than the Lord Jesus Christ, Himself. And we should add that the apostles followed closely behind. Can you find more consistent and reliable preachers than these?

No. 4   In reality, the Wrath of God is the perfect complement to the moral perfection of God. In addition, it is not at all accidental that the majority of those who choose to ignore the *wrath* of God also characteristically choose to ignore the *sinfulness* of man. Furthermore, it naturally follows that when one ignores the sinfulness of man, he will also characteristically ignore the *substitutionary sacrifice* of Jesus Christ. In fact, he will generate contempt for it. The modernistic churches of our society mock the very mention of the "blood of Christ." They have taken the word "blood" out of their song books and theological vocabulary.

When these modern theological artists paint the wrath of God in soft, delicate pastels, just watch how they paint the *sinfulness* of man in similar light hues. And not only that, but then watch their brush strokes as they turn to the Gospel of Christ and wash out, with "tints of contempt," the gravity of the substitutionary sacrifice of Jesus Christ for the sins of mankind. They proclaim, "such a barbaric necessity is unworthy of our idea of God."

These fools don't realize that their attack upon the wrath of God is an attack upon *the grace of God.* It is a positive reality that if we have no such thing as **"bad news,"** then we could never have any such thing as **"good news!"** The one does not exist without the other. To do away with the *wrath* of God is to do away with the *grace* of God. The amazing grace of God is the perfect complement to the righteous and just wrath of God. Make no mistake about it, *Extinction of Being* is the **best news** the unrepentant sinner ever heard. *Annihilation* at death is the false gospel of the lost. "Preach it, brother!" they would shout to you modern day Sadducees.

It has been properly stated that "the wrath of God is an expression of the justice of God." And again, "the wrath of God demonstrates the moral perfection of God." In this sense, proper wrath is but a manifestation of God's moral goodness. The absolute moral perfection of God demands His absolute justice and wrath. Those who choose to have contempt upon the values of God's moral perfection in this life will experience in the afterlife the Holy contempt of God upon their values of unholy sinfulness.

Amazing as it may seem, God's wrath was visited upon His own people in a large portion of the Hebrew Scriptures. Of the Israelites it is said by one translator, "Their carcasses littered the desert" (Heb. 3:17). Anyone who reads the story of the wanderings of the children of Israel in the desert will be amazed at the many times God disciplined them in great severity. Sometimes it was with fire, sometimes with plagues, sometimes with snakes, sometimes with the sword, etc., etc. And yet at the very same time, God's judgments were a cleansing process so that when Balaam came to curse Israel, the Holy Spirit put these words in his mouth—"*I find no fault in Israel*" (Num. 23:21). God called Israel "*My son*" (Exo. 4:22, 23). Therefore the principle upon which God chastened Israel is expressed in the Proverbs this way, "My son, do not despise the chastening of the Lord, nor detest His correction; for whom the Lord loves He corrects, just as the father the son in whom he delights" (Prov. 3:11, 12). The apostle Paul quotes this whole passage and applies it to believers today in the book of Hebrews (Heb. 12:5–11). In light of passages like these we can say that God's wrath accentuates the manifestation of God's love.

God's wrath could never be a display of "unrighteousness." The apostle Paul says, "If our unrighteousness demonstrates the righteousness of God, what shall we say? Is God unrighteous Who inflicts wrath? (I speak as a man.)" (Rom. 3:5).

Is it not a fact that our Savior, even the very Son of God, experienced the most horrible wrath of God, which wrath placed Him in Hellfire on our behalf? Do you not remember the lessons of the burnt sacrifices? Do you not believe the words of John the Baptist, "Behold the Lamb of God Who takes away the sins of the world" (John 1:29)? Just think—if there should be no wrath of God, then there would be no sacrifice of Christ. And this is the very design of Satan—to eliminate the substitutionary sacrifice of Christ. We will study the sacrifice of Christ in the last section of this book.

"Does not the Bible say 'The dead know not anything'?"

Probably the second most important attack upon the Biblical doctrine of eternal judgment in Hellfire is the constant repetition by these preachers of certain verses in the Bible which speak of man's termination being complete and final. More recently, Edward William Fudge in his works on Hell is a good example of this. These preachers will glibly quote many passages which actually are only speaking of man's *physical* and *temporal* demise under the judgment of God as if they are talking about man's complete ultimate spiritual demise as well. Such is clearly not the case.

For instance, as noted before, some will quote God's words to Adam in Genesis 3:19, *"Dust thou art and unto the dust shalt thou return,"* as if this should stand as God's full description of man. It is certainly a description of man's physical nature. However, even these preachers themselves know that God is not herein trying to tell us the whole nature of man; man is not merely "dust." An older minister I am thankful to have known (Maurice Johnson) has said, "Just ask one of them if they think God was only talking to '*dust*' when He spoke to Adam." Maybe these materialistic propagators of their "dust-ology" have forgotten that man stands as a reflection upon the person of God, Himself. Obviously, if God was just talking to "dust," and "dust" is the full nature of man who was formed "in the image of God," then you must have a *"dust-god,"* as well. Who wants to worship *"dust"*? Need I say more?

The book of Ecclesiastes provides a little successful hunting ground for those religious infidels looking for any verses of Scripture which seemingly define death as a total termination. And it is a fitting book for such adventuresome hunters of any evidence of *nothingness* after death. The book of Ecclesiastes is like a ranch which has a big sign over its entrance gateway stating **"Vanity of Vanity, all is Vanity"** (Ecc. 1:2). Consequently, any hunter adventuring onto this property is bound to find evidence of **"Vanity!"** You will find "Vanity" some thirty-six times in just 12 acres (chapters). One could hardly miss getting at least a few good examples. In addition, the writer of the book warns you ahead of time that the only view you are going to get of "Vanity" is from the perspective of what you can see **"Under The Sun"** (Ecc. 1:3). This expression is also used nearly thirty times on the same 12 acres. So just make sure, when you drive out onto this acreage to do your hunting, your vision is not clouded by some other kind of worthwhile inspirational insight.

It seems as if those who like to hunt on this property simply don't want to realize that Solomon apostatized in his later years and consequently came to view everything by the futility of his own human materialistic infidelity. God captures for us an inspired record of Solomon's humanistic thinking, which only led him into fruitless "Vanity." Thankfully, by the end of the book Solomon recaptured the actual and ultimate destiny—"But know that for all these God will bring you into *judgment*" (Ecc. 11:9 and 12:13).

Ecclesiastes 3:20 "*All go to one place: all are from the dust, and all return to dust.*" Some preachers actually quote this passage as if they are big game hunters posing before your camera. They boastfully quote this passage as if it has really proved their theology that all mankind only goes to one place after death and that is *to dust*. Of course, it should be humiliating to them when we enlarge the view on our cameras to capture the whole setting for this verse—3:18 and 19—

I said in my heart 'Concerning the estate of the sons of men, God tests them, that they may see that they themselves *are like animals.*' For what happens to the sons of men *also happens to animals*; one thing befalls them; as one dies *so dies the other.* Surely, they all have one breath; *man has no advantage over animals*, for all is <u>vanity</u>.

We have in the Bible an inspired record of some of the things Satan said. We also have in the Bible an inspired record of Solomon's apostate philosophy. Now in this case "vanity" becomes an ugly backdrop for such a magnificent "dust" trophy. Amazing as it may seem, these colorblind preachers often seem proud of these verses and so they would quote them as well. They actually think this reinforces their conclusion that *in death man has no preeminence over a beast.* It apparently never dawned on them that this comparison, if it stands as the total truth about man and death, would have to mean that the "**Son of Man**," Jesus Christ, Himself, died just like a beast as well.

Need we have any further refutation of this "vain" conclusion? Solomon properly called it "Vanity of Vanities."

<u>Ecclesiastes 9:5</u> "*For the living know that they will die, but the dead know not anything.*" "There, that should prove that when a man dies, he ceases to know anything!" these teachers will shout. Of course, once again, to quote the rest of the verse can be embarrassing! "AND THEY HAVE NO MORE REWARD, for the memory of them is forgotten." Even the most fanatical peddler of this false doctrine believes there are the future rewards for both the just and the unjust. This verse can be describing only man's physical awareness, not his eternal spiritual awareness.

<u>Ecclesiastes 5:15</u> As he [man] came from his mother's womb, naked shall he return, to go as he came; and he shall take nothing from his labor which he may carry away in his hand.

Obviously, this is speaking purely from the aspect of man's physical being. In that perspective, it is obviously perfectly true.

There is no contradiction whatsoever between this observation and the facts presented in this Bible study which pertain to the spiritual nature of man. Man is a dichotomy—as clearly taught by the Lord Jesus Christ, Himself.

> Ecclesiastes 9:10 . . . for there is no work or device or knowledge or wisdom in the grave [Sheol] where you are going.

Again, "work," "devices," "knowledge" and "wisdom" are active ingredients characterizing the tools of the human struggle in our inter-social relationships in the world in which we live. However, after our death this social struggle is over. All these ingredients, as active agents, are useless. The only thing the unsaved are going to learn after their physical death is the conscious reality of Hell. Consequently, by no stretch of the imagination is this passage saying that man, as to his nonmaterial spiritual being, is no longer in conscious existence after death.

Several times in Job, Psalms, Proverbs and Ecclesiastes the writers speak of man's total physical demise, including the functioning of his mental faculties at the point of death. Psalms 146:4 says that at death man's "thoughts perish." Psalm 115:17 says, "The dead praise not the Lord, neither any that go down into silence." No one disagrees with any of these passages. They are self-evident. There is no need to list each of them.

There are many such passages which speak of physical death from this perspective. At death man's physical brain ceases to function. Obviously, his thoughts perish along with his brain function. The dead are obviously no longer walking up to the Temple to praise the Lord. And yet propagandists will quote passages like this as if they were designed to tell us the whole story about man's existence. They want to make us think that the Bible says nothing else about the subject. They want to totally ignore all the other Biblical evidences before them.

The Watch Tower Society teachers will characteristically quote all the verses which speak of the humanity of Christ, as if that tells the whole story! They bury their heads in the sand, like the proverbial ostriches, when it comes to verses describing Christ's absolute and perfect Deity. I would no more trust these spiritually blind teachers to tell me the nature of death and the afterlife, than I would expect a physically blind person to be able to describe for me what a man looked like in a casket.

"Eternal punishment is not Eternal punishing!"

This is now a popular cliché among the many other expressions used in an attempt to discredit the Biblical doctrine of "eternal judgment" (Hebrews 6:2).

Some of the earlier theme songs which have been on the "Top Ten" list of the modern Sadducees have focused on death. They go like this: "Death is the opposite of Life," "Death is not Life in another place," "To Die is to stop living!," "The Devil is the first one to say, 'You will never Die'," "Where does 'Death' ever mean 'Go to Heaven'?" "Destruction means they no longer Exist," "Perish means to cease to be," etc., etc.

I had one man write to me recently and exclaim that since I "reject the normal meanings of 'death,' 'perish' and 'destruction,' I'd truly like you to define these words in which you assure us God wasn't meaning 'death,' 'perish' and 'destruction.'" This man further indicated he was frustrated because I seem to reject the "normal meaning" of words as used in the "human dictionaries" and the actual "Greek Scripture." In response, I sent this man a large segment of this Bible study. All these arguments have been fundamentally answered in that section wherein we discovered Christ's definition of death, which is "*a condition of existence apart from the life and fellowship of God.*"

We must remember that God's *revelation* on the subject does not normally come in man's dictionaries. The inspired apostle said, "*These things we also speak, NOT in WORDS which man's wisdom teaches but which the Holy Spirit teaches, comparing spiritual things with spiritual*" (1 Cor. 2:13).

By the way, it just so happens that the dictionary also uses the word "death" in a great variety of ways, one of which is "*the period of greatest intensity*, as of: 'the dead of night,' or 'the dead of winter'." (The American Heritage Dictionary, which was distributed to a large number of our public school systems.)

The latest song (cliché), that I have seen revived and sung again, which seems to be at the head of their "Top Ten" list, is one that attempts to qualify "eternal" by another route—"Eternal Punishment is Not Eternal Punishing." They argue that "eternal," "everlasting" and "forever and forever" do indeed mean just that. However, they say the punishment God decrees towards the lost *totally* destroys them so that its *effect* lasts forever, but not the act of punishing. In addition they say such things as, "The fire is unquenchable in that it cannot be put out until it has totally destroyed the lost." In answer to this I would point out the following:

1. We already saw that "Destruction" as a synonym for Sheol was first mentioned in the book of Job and has or will exist for some 5000 years with its occupants never disappearing. All continue to exist in "Destruction" the whole time. "Destruction," therefore, in this context could never possibly mean they "cease to exist." Rather, "Destruction" is a description of the *"condition of existence."*

2. The same is essentially true of the descriptions of the fire of Sheol/Hades. As described by John the Baptist and the Lord Jesus Christ, it is *"unquenchable fire."* We saw proof positive that the lost will experience this as a *"condition of existence"* and not a "termination of existence." This fire has or will have burned for over 5000 years, and will, in the final Judgment, be transferred to the Lake of Fire, which burns "day and night forever and forever" (Rev. 20:10).

3. Likewise, Daniel 12:2 speaks of the resurrection of the lost to a condition of *"shame and everlasting contempt."* The only way these conditions can exist for an *everlasting* duration is if the subjects upon whom these conditions are placed exist for an *everlasting* duration.

In the passage, this condition stands as the antithesis to "everlasting life," which is a known condition of existence of the righteous in fellowship with God. No one argues that this condition for the righteous does not exist for eternity! And likewise, no one argues that the righteous themselves do not exist for eternity! Both are positively indicated in the inspired statement. Why then should anyone even want to argue that the unrighteous cease to exist at their resurrection and Judgment, whereas their "shame and contempt" are everlasting? How could "shame and everlasting contempt" be a proper judgment from God if the unrighteous don't exist to experience it? They, in effect, could care less! In fact, the point of their death would be the happiest moment of their short lives. As I said before, *"extermination"* would be their one and only "gospel of good news."

4.   We likewise saw that "death," as spoken of by our Lord Jesus Christ and His apostles, is NOT the cessation of being, but rather the ***"quality of being."*** As far as Adam's fallen race is concerned, sin plunged them into a spiritual condition of "death" (separation from the life of God). In the process of time the same fallen race will experience the culmination of their earthly existence by physical death. In fact, every man's physical death is a process itself. What God literally said to Adam was "dying, you shall die" (Gen. 2:17). When Hades (spirits) and the grave (bodies) give up the unrighteous dead, they are finally resurrected in mortal bodies to be judged and receive their final sentencing in their total condition of "death," i.e., "the second death."

5.   Our Lord Jesus Christ repeatedly stated concerning those unsaved, who will be judged at His second coming, that they would be "cast into the furnace of fire." But he did not stop there. He carefully added, ***"In that place there will BE weeping and gnashing of teeth."*** Note that Christ did not say they would "cease to BE." Rather He said there would "BE [the existence of the lost] weeping and gnashing [their] teeth." Now we all know that non-existing people don't "weep and gnash their teeth"! See—Matthew 8:12; 13:40–42; 13:48–50; Luke 13:27, 28; Matthew 22:13 and 24:51, 52.

6.   Now, here is the passage from which this last theme song is taken—Matthew 25:46 *"And these will go away into **eternal***

*punishment, but the righteous into **eternal** life*." The theme song says "Eternal punishment is not Eternal punishing!" Obviously, this conclusion is not possible from this text for three important reasons—

First, the context tells us the method of the punishment is by "***eternal** fire*." Verse 41 says, "*Then He* [Christ] *will also say to those on His left hand, 'Depart from Me, you cursed, into **eternal** fire prepared for the devil and his angels.'*" The text does not say the "effects" of the fire are eternal, but rather the "*fire*" itself is "*eternal*." This simply means that the "fire" exists forever. In addition, this fire was primarily designed for Satan and his angelic conspirators. In Revelation 20:10 it is clearly stated that their "*torment*" continues "*day and night forever and ever*." Consequently, the "*eternal punishment*" of the lost in Matthew 25:46 is similarly understood to exist forever as well.

Second, remember these teachers say that the "punishment" is actually "***extinction of being***." That being the case, "extinction of being" is momentary. One second you *are* and the next second you *aren't*. When a person does not exist, then no punishment exists for him. In other words, the punishment ceases to exist as well. For the wicked to know ahead of time that "extinction of being" is their "punishment" would be the **happiest day of their lives**, because after their "extinction" they know there is "no punishment!" To say that the punishment of "extinction of being" is "*eternal*" becomes a joke—Who cares? The punishment on the victim is very temporary. And the victim is very temporary. "Extinction of being" in actuality becomes "**the great liberator**." By way of illustration, just imagine—Adolph Hitler was guilty for twelve years of the unimaginable torture and death of an estimated 50 million souls. He was horrified at being captured because he knew what prolonged vengeance would be taken upon him. He put a gun to his head and in an instant received what he thought was his eternal reward—"*extinction of being*." Yes, he thought he was escaping it all. Was he right? God forbid!

Many who espouse this ideology realize that the above scenario could not possibly be proper justice, so they say that after the resurrection and Judgment of the lost there will be a longer time of "punishment" fitting to their crimes—but not eternal. However, this admission demolishes their original position. In addition, it inevitably makes them the judge (rather than God) of how long they think the person should be punished.

Third, as I stated before, it has long been pointed out that the "eternal punishment" of the lost stands in opposition to the "eternal life" of the righteous. If "eternal life" for the righteous means their continued existence in fellowship with God, and it most certainly does, then "eternal punishment" for the lost must mean their continued existence in association with the Devil, and I would add—it most certainly does!

"'Eternal,' 'Everlasting' and 'Forever' do not mean 'Endless Duration'"

"There is nothing in the meaning of these words designed to convey the idea of endless duration." So states a prominent teacher whose religious organization strongly opposes the doctrine of "eternal punishment" in "Hellfire." Several others as well have long pointed out that the Hebrew and especially the Greek words translated in our Bibles as "eternal," "everlasting" and "forever" actually mean only "an age" or "a definite period of time." This argument is not nearly as strong as it once was due to the fact that most everyone who researches this finds that it is only partially true. A partial truth is great if you only base partial facts upon it. A partial truth becomes dangerous when one bases his total conclusion upon it. Indeed, the very teacher from whom I quoted above admitted later in his explanations that sometimes these words do, indeed, convey the idea of "endless duration," but only "in rare cases," he said. This admission actually destroys his basic argument. In addition, when one searches he finds a great number of cases where those Hebrew and Greek words mean exactly *"time of endless duration."* Nevertheless, I will briefly deal with this argument lest I be accused of omitting what some may think of as an important stone unturned.

271

This is much like the argument that the words "spirit" and "soul" only mean "wind" or "breath" and "animation." It is indeed true that these words often mean wind or breath or animation but, as I previously proved, everyone knows they very often absolutely do not mean merely "wind," "breath" or "animation." In a similar vein they argued that "death" and "destruction" mean "cessation of being," whereas the Scriptures qualify them as often meaning "a condition of existence." Thus, the whole problem boils down to allowing the Scriptures to define words in Scriptural context, not biased pretext. The Sadducees, both of olden times and modern, were masters of narrow materialistic concepts. Jesus Christ blew this procedure wide open by His definitions of "death," "the inward man" and "everlasting life" or "immortality."

Olam The Hebrew word *olam* is taken from the basic word meaning "hidden." It is especially used in the sense of "hidden time," or "a long period of time," or "endless duration." It is used well over 400 times according to *Young's Concordance*, *W.E. Vine's Dictionary of New Testament Words* and the *New American Standard Concordance*. Throughout the Old Testament it simply expresses "the perpetuity of time." Usually it would mean "a long duration of time" or "forever." This can be divided roughly into three categories: (1) *of time past*, ancient time, long ago, of old or even time before creation; (2) *of time future*, and this is always defined by the nature of the thing discussed, as in all the days of one's life, as long as one lives, as long as a condition or promise exists, or even from now on, forever, unending; (3) *of eternity*, especially as an expression of the nature of God, Himself, or of the attributes of God, or as expressing God's eternal decrees, or an unending, eternal purpose. (It might be added that a few times it seems to be used of "the world.") This is taken from *The Brown-Driver-Briggs Hebrew and English Lexicon*, *Gesenius Hebrew-Chalde Lexicon To The Old Testament* and *Vine's Complete Expository Dictionary of Old Testament Words*. In the *New American Standard Concordance* it is rendered "eternal" or "everlasting" 125 times and "forever" 201 times. This means that over three quarters of the time the word is used, it has in view "endless duration."

Now if I just picked out a definition from number (2), and said it only means "as long as a man lives" or something like that, you would judge me to be dishonest in my representation. That is precisely what certain ones do. They will cite cases where the word simply means an indefinite period of time, sometimes what amounts to a relatively short period of time, or just for the rest of one's life. Yet at the very same time they will admit that when used describing God, an attribute of God, or certain decrees of God, it does indeed mean "endless time — eternal."

So when it comes to a passage like Daniel 12:2, "*And many of those who sleep in the dust of the earth shall awake, some to **everlasting** [or eternal] life, some to shame and **everlasting** [or eternal] contempt,*" these modern Sadducees find themselves "in a bind." On the one hand, they cannot deny that the "*eternal life*" for the righteous means exactly that—"endless duration of time." On the other hand, they find positively unacceptable the fact that the fate of "*eternal contempt*" for the unrighteous is described by the exact same word signifying its time duration. Of course, that remains their problem. The Scriptures are clear and remain unchangeably the same.

When the Jewish scholars translated the Hebrew Scriptures into the Greek language, i.e., the Septuagint, they rendered the Hebrew word *olam* by the Greek word *aion* approximately 250 times, and also by the word *aionios* nearly 100 times.

Aion The Greek word *aion* literally means "age;" however, it was commonly used in the Greek world to stand in "contrast to that which came to an end." Therefore it can carry the meaning of "an age," "a time of indefinite duration," "perpetuity of time," "eternal" and "time of endless duration." It is also used several times in the sense of that which is pertaining to "the world." Unfortunately, in the King James Version it was rendered "world" far too many times. This brought a lot of actual confusion. The word is used some 91 times (depending on which Greek text is used). In the *New American Standard Translation* the word *aion* is rendered as a form of "eternal" or "forever" some 49 times, "age" about 32 times, and "world" only 8 times. Like the Hebrew word *olam*, it is also used of past time. At least 5 times this word has reference to eternal punishment of the wicked—2 Peter 2:17; Jude 13; Revelation 14:11; 19:3 and 20:10.

Aionios   This is the adjectival form of the word *aion*. Literally, therefore, it means "that which pertains to an age." However, in both Greek usage and in the New Testament it nearly always has reference to unlimited duration of time, as "eternal," "everlasting" or "forever." It is used some 70 times in the Greek text. It has clear reference to "eternal life" or "eternal salvation" over 50 times. No one disputes that this has reference to "time of endless duration and/or eternal." It, likewise, refers to aspects of Deity, the gospel, covenant, God's glory, honor and kingdom 8 times. It also has clear reference to "eternal fire," "eternal punishment," "eternal damnation" or "eternal judgment" 7 times. There is absolutely nothing in the context of these final references, as we have seen in this study, to limit this duration to a mere speck of time.

Aidios   This final word in the Greek New Testament is *aidios*. It means "everlasting" or "eternal." It is used only twice: Rom. 1:20 "even His [God's] *eternal* power and Divine nature," and Jude 6 "And [fallen] angels. . .He has kept in *eternal* bonds under darkness for the Judgment of the Great Day."

All the previous material is referenced by—*A Greek Lexicon Of The New Testament, by Walter Baurer, edited by Arndt and Gingrich; Thayer's Greek-English Lexicon of the New Testament; The Expanded Vine's Expository Dictionary of New Testament Words* and *The New American Standard Concordance and Dictionary*.

In light of these undisputed facts demonstrated here, the claims of certain false teachers that "eternal," "everlasting" and "forever" in the Bible (such as the NASB, NRSV or the NKJV) do not mean "time of endless duration" are seriously "found wanting," and deserve to be trashed.

DEGREES OF PUNISHMENT IN HELL

One of the most astonishing passages I have ever read in the Gospel accounts, which truth is given twice, is that found in <u>Matthew 10:14 and 15</u>, and <u>Matthew 11:23 and 24</u>. The Lord Jesus Christ is addressing the apostles in the first account and then He is addressing the multitude in the second account after the disciples left to go out preaching the gospel of the Kingdom of God. He states the following:

> *And whosoever will not receive you nor hear your words, when you depart from that house or city, shake off the dust from your feet. Assuredly, I say to you, it will be **more tolerable** for the land of Sodom and Gomorrah in the Day of Judgment than for that city. And you, Capernaum, who are exalted to heaven, will be brought down to Hades; for if the mighty works which were done in you had been done in Sodom, it would have remained until this day. But I say to you that it shall be **more tolerable** for the land of Sodom in the Day of Judgment than for you.*

These are, truly, two of the most surprising passages in the Gospel accounts. The words of Christ totally realign our thinking about this subject of judgment—especially from God's perspective. On the one hand, we can think of no more despicable iniquity than the perversions which existed in those two notorious cities of Sodom and Gomorrah. Indeed, God, after long patience and warning, expressed His wrath upon them, and the consequent judgment of indignation caused the cities to become monuments of ashes at the far end of the lowest spot on the face of the earth—the Dead Sea. Thus God spelled out His just decree and holy wrath upon that type of iniquity.

Yet now, on the other hand, Christ indicates that there will be more allowance for Sodom and Gomorrah in the Day of Judgment than for other cities, who had no such social iniquity, but which had rejected the preaching of the gospel at that particular time by the ministers of Christ, no doubt with the supporting miraculous evidences. That reveals to us that God hates self-righteous social

275

hypocrisy, and judges that those who have rejected more evidences of truth given to them as being more responsible; therefore they will receive the greater condemnation.

Christ said "it would be more tolerable" for those two cities. What did he mean by this? The Greek word *anektoteros* simply means "to bear with, to endure or tolerable." Our understanding is that in the final Judgment God will give more *allowance* or *toleration* in the dispensing of punishment for the inhabitants of Sodom and Gomorrah than for the inhabitants of some of those cities who heard and witnessed the gospel presentation of that age, and yet firmly rejected it. This is amazing! However, it is telling us that in the Judgment God will have explored all the factual evidences and existing conditions of the times and weighed them in careful consideration in light of the truth that they had before pronouncing judgment. In other words, His judgment will most certainly be a perfect and equitable judgment.

In addition, it substantiates the fact that in the final Judgment there will be degrees of punishment meted out; not all in Hell will receive the same degree of punishment.

A similar statement is made by Christ as He continues speaking in the same passage, Matthew 11:21–22

> *Woe to you, Chorazin! Woe to you, Bethsaida! For if the mighty works which were done in you had been done in Tyre and Sidon, they would have repented long ago in sackcloth and ashes. But I say to you, it will be **more tolerable** for Tyre and Sidon in the Day of Judgment than for you.*

On another occasion Christ gave a parable to illustrate the administration of degrees of punishment for the lost. This is recorded for us in Luke 12:42–48. I will only quote the last part, verses 46–48.

> *The master of that servant will come on a day when he is not looking for him, and at an hour when he is not aware; and will cut him in two and appoint his portion with the unbelievers. And that servant who knew his master's will,*

*and did not prepare himself or do according to his will, **shall be beaten with many stripes**. But he who did not know, yet committed things deserving of stripes, **shall be beaten with few**. For everyone to whom much is given, from him much will be required; and to whom much has been committed, of him they will ask the more.*

Another passage is <u>Luke 20:45–47</u>.

*Then, in the hearing of all the people, He said to His disciples, 'Beware of the scribes, who desire to go around in long robes, love greetings in the market places, the best seats in the synagogues, and the best places at feasts, who devour widows' houses, and for a pretense make long prayers. **These will receive greater condemnation.**'*

Of course, this can just as well be a description of the modern day Roman Catholic or certain Protestant clergymen. It is certainly evidence of God's hatred of religious hypocrisy.

Another passage is <u>Romans 2:5 and 6</u>.

*But in accordance with your hardness and your impenitent heart you are treasuring up for yourself wrath in the day of wrath and revelation of the righteous judgment of God, **Who 'will render to each one according to his deeds.'***

It is clear from this passage that in the final Judgment God will dispense punishment in accordance with the deeds of each and every individual. This means that though all the lost will go to the same destination, yet each will suffer in accordance with his own wickedness.

The last passage which I will use to illustrate this principle is <u>Rev. 20:12 and 13</u>.

*And I saw the dead, small and great, standing before God, and books were opened. And another book was opened, which is the Book of Life. And the dead were judged **according to their works**, by the things which were written in the books. The sea gave up the dead who were in it, and Death and Hades delivered up the dead who were in them. And they were judged, **each one according to his works**.*

In conclusion, it becomes evident from this type of judgment, where there are degrees of punishment clearly indicated, that there must be some type of prolonged period of suffering. If the termination of existence was the judgment for everyone, then they would all receive the very same judgment, which would never be based on the nature of their crimes. As I have stated from the very beginning of this study, the final disposition of the lost is like a final prison sentencing; it is based on the nature of each one's iniquity. Everyone who goes to Hell goes for the very same reason, which is the rejection of the grace and mercy of God as variously manifested to them in their different ages and circumstances. However, everyone does not experience the same intensity of suffering in Hell; that suffering is based upon the deeds in their sinful lives.

Actually the very same principle is true of those made righteous. They all are redeemed for the very same reason: their repentance and acceptance of the gospel of the grace and mercy of God. However, their final rewards, or lack of rewards, will be based upon their own service, or lack thereof, to Christ and to God (see 1 Corinthians 3:10-15).

IN THE END—

*"Righteousness and justice are the foundation of Your throne;
Mercy and Truth go before Your face"
Psalm 89:14.*

SECTION THREE

THE SUFFERINGS OF JESUS CHRIST EVEN TO THE DEPTH OF HELL

BY
RUSSELL ROSS and JACK LANGFORD

First presented as a much smaller edition in June of 1977,
re-edited and enlarged by Jack Langford in October of 2006,
finally incorporated into the present book—
The Fire That Is Eternal,
in September of 2013.

CHAPTER SIXTEEN

INTRODUCTION And PRELIMINARY THOUGHTS ON THE CROSS WORK OF CHRIST

By Jack W. Langford

INTRODUCTION

In the spring of 1977 Russell Ross first approached me for the purpose of assisting him in dealing with a problem. There was strong opposition by a certain brother against our occasional public statements on the sufferings of Christ, beyond the cross, during the three days and nights in Hell. At the time I had only casually assumed this position to be true, based on a few Scriptures which I knew. On the other hand, Russell Ross had done more extensive research with a larger body of Scriptural evidences, to the effect of demonstrating the doctrinal accuracy of our position on the subject. I appreciated very much Russell's ground breaking work. After doing more thorough study myself, I added several other Scriptural evidences which I found were strongly supportive of this truth. Our combined study was the basis of our presentation to those who may have doubted or challenged our teaching on the subject at that time.

Since then, and from time to time, different individuals have asked me about this subject. Sad to say, I had long put off typing up this work in a final form. Therefore, I have recently edited these earlier notes, first typed up in 1977, and added to them this larger introduction and comments about the cross work of Christ.

I believe this is also timely due to the continued public interest in the death of Christ which was prompted by the Mel Gibson movie, *The Passion of Christ.* People may be shocked by the violence of a Roman scourging and crucifixion, but this was only the outward manifestation of a far worse form of suffering which Christ endured that no earthling can imagine, nor could any film crew ever recreate. The Bible clearly indicates that when Christ died for our sins, He went into Hell for three days and nights bearing the penalty for sin under the condemnation and wrath of Almighty God. This last statement is probably going to shock a lot of people. They certainly should demand Scriptural proof for this assertion.

Many others may think that this is not an important subject to them. However, the vital importance of this subject to every Christian is illustrated for us in Romans the sixth chapter. Here the apostle Paul, by divine inspiration, tells us that every believer "baptized into Christ" was, first of all, "baptized into Christ's death." Now, my dear Christian brother and sister, no matter what you may believe about the sufferings of Christ, it is nevertheless a Biblical fact that our baptism into Christ's suffering death was *a three day baptism!* Our Savior was immersed into the state of *death for three days and three nights,* and in God's reckoning, *so were we!* When the court of heaven was satisfied with the judgment Christ bore against our sins, only then was Christ released from that DEATH. Then He ascended from Hell, and was gloriously resurrected from the dead. *The purpose of this study is to explore this three day death baptism of Christ from a careful Biblical perspective. We are going to allow numerous passages of Scripture to illuminate that dark and mysterious corridor of existence so that we might have a deeper appreciation for the price of our redemption.*

I hope that all who read this study will be noble Berians (Acts 17:11) and "prove all things" (1 Thess. 5:21). I most certainly believe that in reading this material all believers will strongly enhance their appreciation of the Gospel of Christ.

THE APOSTLES' CREED

Though many of the major denominations of Christendom will in some way, shape or form repeat the so-called "Apostles' Creed" during their Sunday morning services, yet the statement in that creed that Christ "descended into Hell" is understood by very few of the people. Perhaps only a very few people have asked themselves the question — what does it mean that Christ "descended into Hell"? The Apostles' Creed continues to be used today as a cardinal summarization of the Christian faith. Tradition has it that this statement of faith somehow derived from the apostles, themselves — hence it is called "The Apostles' Creed." It actually derived as a result of some of the early Roman Catholic "church councils" in an attempt to make a formal statement of their Christian faith. Eventually it came to be used throughout Protestantism as well. It stands as an affirmation of the most widely accepted creedal statements of the basic tenets of Christianity. It also bears the evidence of early polemical statements which repudiate the major heretical errors. In many churches throughout the world today this will be read or even repeated by the congregations during solemn Sunday morning services.

I believe in God, the Father Almighty, Creator of heaven and earth; and in Jesus Christ, His only Son, our Lord, who was conceived by the Holy Spirit, born of the virgin Mary, suffered under Pontius Pilate, was crucified, died and was buried. **He descended into Hell***; the third day He rose again from the dead; He ascended into heaven, and is seated at the right hand of God, the Father Almighty; from thence He shall come to judge the living and the dead. I believe in the Holy Spirit, the holy catholic church, the communion of saints, the forgiveness of sins, the resurrection of the body, and everlasting life. Amen.*

Right in the middle of this statement is the theme of this present Bible study, *"He* [Christ] *descended into Hell."* Men have written eloquently of all the other facets of this creed, virtually filling thousands of religious libraries with innumerable volumes of expositions.

However, this central statement has remained almost hidden through the centuries as if it were a theologically forbidden area. No one seemed to dare elaborate upon the statement. It has remained, as it were, in a "no-man's-land" of sober silence—a veritable "haunted house" which no one enters.

Unfortunately, even a certain few modern Pentecostal "prophets," who do take notice, would distort and pervert their analysis of the person of Jesus Christ so grotesquely as to make many Christians want to recoil from the subject entirely. These religious theatrical performers fit right into Satan's scheme very well. They go so far as to picture the Devil chasing Christ in Hell with a pitchfork, and Christ needing to be "born again" in order to get out of Hell. They take advantage of their "secret insight" so as to draw more attention to their own agenda of religious enchantment. A lot of people are entertained by these perversions. Let me assure you at the outset in this Biblical study, we will not be characterized by such carnival theatrics in theology.

Not only is this statement about descending into Hell emanating from the heart of the Apostles' Creed, it also emanates from the heart of the Gospel of Jesus Christ as revealed in the Scriptures. How could any minister of Christ ignore it?

A FUNDAMENTAL DIVERSION

That Christ, at the time of His death, descended into Hell is not challenged by any Bible believer. The Scriptures say very plainly that Christ's soul was in Hades after His death, Acts 2:27 and 31. However, the dignified liberals in Christendom will not even talk about it. Some conservatives will approach it with mixed caution on rare occasions. Most "fundamentalists" will often regulate Christ's presence in Hell to the section at that time called "Paradise." This is taken from the fact that Jesus Christ taught in Luke 16:19–31 that there were two different sections in Hell. In one section was the place of suffering where the wicked were confined. The other section was called "Paradise" where the righteous souls at that time were residing. Between the two sections was a "great gulf" which could not be crossed. "After all," these teachers usually argue, "did not Christ say to the thief on the cross, *'Today shalt thou be with Me in Paradise'*" (Luke 23:43)? To them, that settles it! If the thief was with Christ in Paradise, then it naturally follows that Christ was in the Paradise section of Hell after He died. They will, therefore, in careless confidence refuse to examine any further study of the many Scriptural evidences which speak candidly on this subject. Some careful Bible teachers have acknowledged that those many other Scriptural evidences do in fact complete the story accurately and correct this hasty conclusion. Every teacher of the Bible realizes that quite often one's first impression of a situation may very well be in error.

In response to this rather hasty conclusion, we give a preliminary word of sober caution by pointing out that Christ is Divine. That means, that among other Divine qualities, He is said to be "omnipresent." He can certainly be in more than one place at a time. For instance, just the night before His death He told His apostles (John 14) that He was leaving this earth and going to be with His Father in heaven. However, they were not to be troubled because, at the *very same time*, Christ said, "I am *coming to you*" (v. 18), and "I [will be] *in you*" (v. 20), and *"I will **manifest** Myself to you"* (v. 21), and "My Father and I will come and ***abide with*** you" (v. 23). Now we would ask, how could Christ possibly *"abide with"* the disciples here on earth if He plainly told them He was leaving this earthly residence and going into heaven? Do we choose which truth to believe and discard the rest? Do we conclude that since He is said to be residing in heaven that He, therefore, could not also be on earth? Of course not! Both these facts are true and one does not cancel out the other. Nor do we dare disregard one and believe the other. Christ is Divine and He can be in both places at once. Heaven will be His actual residence, and yet through the agency of the Holy Spirit, and He being omnipresent, He will also just as surely be ***"in"*** and ***"with"*** His disciples here on earth.

Is anyone going to be so callous as to argue that since Christ said He would be "in" and "with" His disciples here on earth that He is actually not in heaven?

Again, Christ said, "Where two or three are gathered together in My name, there am I *in the midst* of them" (Matt. 18:20). We could ask, how could Christ be "*in the midst* of them" here on earth and yet at the very same time be at the right hand of the Father in heaven? Is it appropriate to carelessly discard one revelation and choose the other? The answer is similar to that above. The apostle Paul would express the same phenomenon in these words, "We are seated with Christ in heavenly places" (Eph. 2:6). Now we might ask, concerning our own selves, how we could be in two places at once in the reckoning of God. How could we be on earth and yet also be seated with Christ in the heavenly places? Do we pick which fact we want to believe? Obviously, from these Scriptures we realize there is, as to the believer, a physical or actual location on earth, and yet there is a real but spiritual location understood in such texts. As to Christ's situation, though Christ is actually residing in Heaven, yet spiritually and in reality, He is in His brethren on earth. And conversely, though we are actually on earth, yet in the reckoning of God, we are really and spiritually seated "with" Christ in glory.

Now the important question is—is it possible that the very same thing might well be true of the thief on the cross? Could he be comforted with Christ in Paradise while at the very same time Christ was suffering in Hellfire?? Of course it can be—**if the Scriptures so reveal!** The actual question is, "Do the Scriptures give convincing evidence that Christ suffered for three days and nights, under the judgment of God, in the pains of Hellfire?" If the Scriptures do give convincing evidence, then we should realize that Christ could be "with" and "in" the thief spiritually while the repentant thief was in Paradise, and yet Christ could actually, as these other Scriptures testify, be suffering the wrath of God in the section of torment in Hell. Another older minister has stated this in an excellent manner by the following illustration, "Noah and his family were safe *in the ark*, and yet the ark was suffering the billows of God's wrath against the world of that day. Christ is our antitypical *ark* (1 Pet. 3:18–22). We can be safe *in* and *with* Him, *yet He was suffering the billows of God's wrath against sin which we deserve!*"

Are you willing to look at the evidence? I will guarantee that there is an abundance of evidence—which you probably never even realized was in the Bible—to the effect that Christ suffered for our sins in Hellfire for three days and nights.

Before we go to these many evidences, let us first review the truths about the cross work of Christ. In doing this, we will erase many of the abysmal perversions of this simple and important truth which Satan has instigated. This will also, in fact, better prepare us for our journey into another region after the cross.

1. The Spectacle of The Cross

Preachers and theologians have often expounded with vivid details concerning the physical sufferings of Jesus Christ in the Roman crucifixion. No doubt, the actual event of crucifying a man was meant to be a very cruel spectacle and a most sober warning to the populace looking on. It was a death designed for spectators so as to warn them of the consequence of rebellion against the Roman authority.

We have even sometimes read accounts by those in the medical profession explaining the technicalities of death by crucifixion. By all accounts, it was a most agonizing scene. One time I witnessed a woman scream out in uncontrollable anguish as she sat in the midst of a large audience watching a semi-professional pageantry reenacting the scene of the crucifixion of Christ being nailed to the cross. The actors were good. The scenery was very well done. The timing and sound of the hammer blows driving the huge spikes into the wrists and feet sent shock waves into the heart of this lady. She screamed out and would not stop and had to be escorted out of the auditorium. The whole audience seemed locked into the realization of how dreadful was the suffering of Christ in this form of death.

No doubt God, Himself, allowed this form of outward punishment and suffering for His own Son in order for Him to be a spectacle to be seen before the whole world. Christ Himself had said, "*'And I, if I be lifted up from the earth, will draw all men unto Me.'* This he said, signifying by what death He would die" (John 12:32).

This aspect of the death of Christ was exactly what God allowed to be presented before the eyes of the world. It vividly portrayed in an outward manner the gospel of Christ in His substitutionary death for the sins of all mankind. The gospel could not be explained in more vivid form than as stated by the apostle Paul, "But we preach Christ crucified, . . ." (1 Cor. 1:23). Again Paul told the proud Corinthians, "For I determined not to know anything among you except Jesus Christ and Him crucified" (1 Cor. 2:2). And again, Paul would say to the Galatian believers "before whose eyes Jesus Christ was clearly portrayed among you as crucified" (Gal. 3:1).

However, it is actually in the explanation about the spiritual reality of what God was doing in Christ's death which brings understanding to the heart of the sin-laden person, in order for him to fully realize the salvation God has provided. Each person must realize that Christ died because of and for the penalty of his own sins. In this sense we put Him there. The sinner's reciprocal response of repentance of heart and trusting in Christ brings the personal experience of the remission of sins by God's grace. How glorious is the moment of cleansing by the realization and acceptance of God's redemptive plan through the substitutionary death, burial and resurrection of Jesus Christ (1 Cor. 15:1–4). By the cross work of Christ, the whole doctrine of salvation by Christ paying the penalty for sin is *epitomized*.

However, it is only by the glorious resurrection of Christ from the dead that the application of the gospel to the repentant sinner is to be *realized*. *"For if Christ be not raised, you are yet in your sins"* (1 Cor. 15:17). In between these two very important events, and out of sight of any human eye, is a period of three days and three nights. If we do not have the resurrection of Christ from the dead, preceded by the three days and nights in Hell, *we have no gospel*! (See 1 Cor. 15:2–4 and 14.)

2. The Irony Of The Cross

The Scriptures reveal that the betrayal, trial and crucifixion of Christ was seemingly Satan's hour of VICTORY! What is meant by this? Simply, the fact that Satan was responsible for inspiring men to reject and mutilate the Son of God. Satan, as the archenemy of God, thought that he could destroy this One Whom God has sent to redeem us and bring peace on earth. Thus Satan, himself, could gain the inheritance of the Son of God (please see Luke 20:14). Therefore, as one follows the passion story through the gospel accounts, he will notice Satan's active part.

Satan initially "entered into Judas" to move him to go to the religious leaders to bargain for the betrayal of Christ (Luke 22:3). Again, Satan moved upon Judas "to betray" Christ the night of the last supper (John 13:27). Christ warned the disciples at that last supper that shortly "The ruler of this world is coming, and he has nothing in Me" (John 14:30). To the religious rulers Christ would say, "But this is your hour and the power of darkness" (Luke 22:53). The "power of darkness" is "the power of Satan" (Acts 26:18 and 2 Cor. 4:4). Yes, the horrible rejection, trial, mutilation, humiliation and crucifixion were all at the instigation of Satan. Satan, himself, is the avid enemy of, and in mortal combat with, the Lord Jesus Christ. Though he is awesome in wisdom and power, yet he must also be the ultimate unbeliever in what God has purposed and predicted in the Scriptures.

Now, ironic as it may seem, though Satan inspired the cross, yet the death of Christ on the cross also spelled out the utter and total defeat of Satan.

Long before, in the Hebrew Scriptures Satan was initially portrayed as the Serpent which would strike the heel of "the seed of the woman" (Genesis 3:15). This meant that Lucifer would instigate the death of the Divine Son of God Who had been miraculously born of the virgin Mary. Yet at the very same time "He," the seed of the woman, would "crush the head of the serpent." As explained by Paul, "through death, He [Christ] would destroy him who had the power of death—that is, the Devil" (Heb. 2:14). It has been said by another that, at the climax of the ministry of Christ, He would allow Satan to use his strongest weapon against Him—death! And yet, marvel of marvels, it was through His substitutionary death that Christ bore the penalty for sin, and thus robbed the Devil of any effectiveness of his greatest weapon. "The sting of death was sin" (1 Cor. 15:56), and Christ took upon Himself the sinners' death and bore it all. Christ in His death took the "sting" (the guilt and penalty of sin) away. Now, the sinner only needs to take a look of faith at Christ as the antitypical "brazen serpent and live forever" (John 3:14, 15). Thus the cross, though actually inspired by Satan, has become the very vehicle through which we proclaim the gospel of the grace of God.

From a different perspective we see another amazing fact which demonstrates a further irony of the cross. Amazing as it may seem— *Christ did not actually die by crucifixion!*

Now this may sound like a contradiction to all that has been said thus far and to what many other Scriptures say. However, sometimes the Scriptures give what first appears to us to be a contradiction yet, in light of all that God has designed, is not a contradiction at all. The very nature of Christ, Himself, seems to be a contradiction. He is presented as truly man, and yet other revelation speaks of Him as Divine. Cults often accept only one aspect of truth and reject the other. Actually both are true. Jesus of Nazareth is the Divine Man.

As to Christ's death, a careful reading of the gospels will prove that Christ died just like He was conceived and born—*miraculously*. Christ had a miraculous entrance into this world by the supernatural conception and the virgin birth and, as we shall see, He also had a miraculous exit out of this world. Yes, Christ had said long before the cross, *"No man can take My life from Me, but I lay it down of Myself. I have power to lay it down, and I have power to take it again"* (John 10:18). Now this statement means that actually men could not kill Jesus Christ. The only way Jesus Christ could die was by His own Divine power and choice.

Christ demonstrated this fact when the crowd led by Judas came to apprehend Him (John 18:3–8). As recorded in the Gospel of John, Christ asked them who they were looking for, and they answered, "Jesus of Nazareth." Then Christ said the simple words, "I am *He*." Notice that the *"He"* is added in most translations to normally complete the thought. However, the singular words or word "I am" is, literally in Hebrew, the holy Name of the Deity, "Yahweh." When Christ uttered this word, it was with power. We are told that when Christ uttered this word—"they went backward and fell to the ground." They might as well have tried to harness the power of the sun itself as to be able to take this Jesus Who was, in fact, "Yahweh" (I Am), the Divine Son of God. However, when Jesus repeated the same word the second time, He withheld the power, and instead voluntarily yielded Himself to them. This is an amazing demonstration of the fact that nothing would or could ever happen to Him without His permission and/or design. He alone would have total control of His Divine life, and His Divine death.

The Roman crucifixion was designed to last more than one day, sometimes up to three days or even longer. Christ was actually on the cross for only about six hours before He was reported to be dead. When the report came to Pontius Pilate that Christ was dead, he did not believe it! He called for a centurion to deny or confirm the report. This is recorded for us in that gospel which most theologians say was designed for the Roman ear—Mark 15:43–45. It was indeed amazing that Christ was already dead. The Roman executioners were professionals at their job. They knew how to keep a man alive, and how to bring his death. The religious rulers had requested an early death for those being crucified on this occasion because of the approaching High Day of Passover. To hasten the deaths of those being crucified that day, the executioners broke their legs. The Scriptures say that when they came to break the legs of Jesus, they were surprised when *"they saw that He was already dead"* (John 19:33).

It can be said that, most certainly, Christ died prematurely! No, Christ did not die by suffocation, or a heart attack, or by excruciating pain. Matthew tells us that Jesus Christ *"yielded up His spirit"* (Matt. 27:50). Christ's life was not taken from Him, though those who crucified Him were guilty of it. Nor did Christ die by the spear which was thrust into His side. This was done only as the guarantee for the Romans that He was already dead. In fulfillment of His earlier statement (John 10:18), when Christ "yielded up His spirit," He had power to do something no other man could ever do. He literally *"gave Himself* for our sins" (Gal. 1:4). This death is the most unusual death which has ever occurred on planet earth. This death was just as amazing as His birth. Christ alone gave up His life in a death that He alone could experience. No one else ever died like this, either before or after. Christ, of His own voluntary will and power, *yielded up His spirit*, bearing upon His soul the penalty for all the sins of all mankind, for all the ages. So, I say again, Christ died just like He was born—*miraculously*.

This aspect of the *supernatural* death of Christ is very important, because it demonstrates that the mere physical punishment that Christ bore, no matter how severe it was, was not and could never be the real punishment that brought to Christ the great agony of soul that He alone could experience. Many men have died by equal or worse agony of body. Even the two thieves, who had to suffer the crude breaking of their legs to bring about their suffocation from being suspended only by the nails in their hands, seemingly had a worse physical death. No, the physical punishment Christ bore was awful, but it was not the real agony He was facing! No other human being on earth could ever face what Christ was facing! The burden He bore and the horror of His suffering was *supernatural* and *inexplicable*. We shall see in this study that Christ's suffering and death began long before the cross, existed on the cross and continued long after the cross for three days and nights in agony. Christ went to Hell with our sins upon Him—in separation from God—as we shall see as we travel through this study.

3. The Confusion Of The Cross

Satan had been frustrated by the subtitutional death of Christ for our sins, and by the amazing resurrection of Christ, and was thus despoiled of his ultimate plan in the death of Christ. Yet still, in all his craftiness, we shall see him bring more confusion toward the redemptive plan of God.

In his cruel wisdom he does everything in his power to distract men from the actual truth of the gospel of Christ. One of his more subtle ways of doing this is to bring about a sensual carnal devotion to Christ's death which is entirely physical and superficial. Many times the Roman Catholic sculptors and artists have gruesomely portrayed a battered form of Christ on a cross for the singular purpose of drawing sensual religious sympathy and devotion. In fact they have many times plunged into a depraved, morbid preoccupation with the mere physical aspects of Christ's death, and rejected entirely the direct spiritual benefits of Christ's substitutionary death obtained by faith without religious works of any kind. They actually theorize that by focusing entirely on the outward physical aspects of Christ's suffering, they can somehow enter into some dramatic religious discipline of self-atonement for their own sins.

In certain Roman Catholic countries, fanatical devotees will torture their own bodies as they suppose Christ was tortured on the cross. Their imitation of the outward crucifixion could never atone for anything because they already deserved eternal Hell. Yet crowds of religious devotees will literally swoon in the streets as these tortured bodies pass by. This is a damnable lie and a disgusting, superficial and Satanic preoccupation with the mere physical aspect of the crucifixion.

In recent Roman Catholic articles, the authors have loudly proclaimed the new Hollywood movie production of "The Passion of Christ" as a "*Roman Catholic* masterpiece." This could be, and probably is, a masterpiece of subtle distraction. I have seen a supposed life-size statue of the crucified Christ with the toes on the feet of the image nearly worn off by the innumerable pilgrims who pass by, kissing the statue on its feet. I have stood back and shaken my head in disgust at the unbelief propagated by this form of religious idolatry.

Actually the four Gospels contain only a few words in telling us of Christ's beating and crucifixion. They purposely do not dwell upon, nor do they describe in any detail concerning the various aspects of the physical scourging or the crucifixion of Jesus Christ.

Most certainly, Hollywood could never make a movie of what really happened in Christ's death for the simple reason that the vast majority of the time of Christ's death was *out of sight*, for three days and three nights, *within the lower regions in the bowels of the earth*. There were no earthly spectators to gaze upon this horrible scene. There were no cameras down there. There were no stage hands and actors available for that aspect of Christ's suffering. This study is going to explore what the Scriptures actually reveal as to the totality and reality of Christ's substitutionary death for mankind in Hell.

Sad to say, another method of confusion that Satan has instigated is in the opposite direction. He has also moved upon men's carnal sentimentality to cause them to reject any indication that Christ was to suffer beyond the cross in Hellfire. Such a thought, to the natural man, as Christ suffering in the fires of Hell itself, is so repulsive as to be automatically discounted in contempt. Some will rise up in (self) righteous indignation against any hint that their precious, sinless Savior would have to descend into the awful pollution of Hellfire. These sentimental people forget all about the fact that Christ died with the load of the world's sin placed upon Him. In fact, it was not the physical punishment which separated Christ from His heavenly Father, but rather the sins of all mankind which brought about the death separation between the Father and the Son. Obviously no one could see the sins of the world being placed upon Christ. This was a spiritual transaction beyond the sight of man and even beyond his capability of comprehension. *Even the sun hid its light and shrouded the place in darkness.*

Consequently, *Christ died a spiritual death of separation from Almighty God.* The guilt and penalty for sins could never be mere physical death. The sins of the world are not physical; they are spiritual. The essential and primary death Christ died was **spiritual!** Christ died as to His *inward spiritual nature* being in separation from His Heavenly Father, bearing the guilt and penalty of sin—all the sins of the world. Christ bore in His *soul* the guilt and penalty of sin. That is why He initially cried out "now is My *soul* troubled" when He even contemplated His death (John 12:27). And that is why "His *soul* was not left in Hell" (Acts 2:27). His flesh did not go to Hell—His *soul* did—bearing the sins of the world. Christ's death was a total death involving His outward man, His physical body, and His inward man, His spiritual soul. At the point of death His physical person was left hanging on the tree. However, His soul, bearing the world's cesspool of filth, was plunged into the depths of Hell. As we shall see in a moment, Christ did not die as a "saint."

He died the "sinners'" death. "He made Him . . . to be SIN, for us, . . ." (2 Cor. 5:21).

4. The Idolatry Of The Cross

I said before that Christ did not actually die by crucifixion, though He did die in the act of being crucified. In addition, those who crucified him, both the religious rulers and the Roman government, were guilty of murdering the Son of God. He died on the cross—but He died miraculously.

Now I am going to say something else that may astonish you even more. It is quite possible Christ did not die on a "CROSS." Notice my words carefully. *Christ died upon what has come to be called a* "cross." However, it has long been known by careful Bible teachers and lexical scholars that the actual Greek word which is translated in most of our modern Bibles as "cross" is ***stauros,*** and its normal meaning is NOT a cross! As the great lexical scholar, W.E. Vine, has said, "Both the noun and the verb *stauroo, to be fastened to a stake or pale*, are originally to be <u>distinguished from</u> *the ecclesiastical form of a two-beamed cross*" (*The Expanded Vines Expository Dictionary of New Testament Words*, pg. 248). All lexicons agree that the basic meaning of the Greek word *stauros* was simply *a stake, pole or plank of wood, such as is set upright in the ground.* (See also Appendix #162 of *Bullinger's Companion Bible.* It was not until the middle of the third century after Christ's death that the modern form of the cross began to be used.)

The English word "cross" is actually taken from the Latin translation of *stauros* which was "*crux.*" Most expositors of the word derivation will tell us that the Roman "crux" had about four versions, the earliest being the simple upright pole or stake called the *"crux-simplex."* This actually corresponds to the Greek word *stauros.* The other versions were called *"crux-commissia,"* the shape of a T, then the *"crux-immissa,"* with the top piece of wood lowered slightly. This is the one which came to be adopted to stand for the emblem of Christianity. There was also one in the shape of an X. This was called the *"crux-decussata."* However, the *early and normal* method of (Roman) "crucifixion involved elevating the condemned upon a pole, some form of frame or scaffolding, or a natural tree, thus exposing him to public view or derision" (*Evangelical Dictionary of Theology*).

Alexander Hislop, in his famous book, *The Two Babylons*, which was devoted to the subject of the Babylonian paganism brought over into early Roman Catholicism, has a section on the origin of the use of the "Sign of the Cross" (Pages 197–205). He gives many illustrations of the pagan origin of the use of the symbol of a "cross." He explained that "The cross is looked upon as the grand charm, as the great refuge in every season of danger, in every hour of temptation as the infallible preservative from all the powers of darkness. The cross is adored with all the homage due only to the Most High" (pg. 197).

It has been noted by several writers of history that during the middle ages there were enough relics of the supposed cross upon which Christ died, scattered throughout the churches of Christendom, that several large houses could have been built with them. Today, in our very own world, we will see impressive crosses on most church buildings. In addition, there are beautiful crosses of every size and metallic substance adorning parts of the body, most clerical garments and most devout homes in the world of Christendom. This is all a very sickening form of idolatry, and a clear perversion of the tree beam upon which our Savior died. Technically, some scholars believe there is only a very slight chance that Christ died upon the modern form of the cross.

According to the Bible, the *stauros* upon which Christ died was actually a horrible, filthy thing. This is true, not merely because the gore and blood of the victim was splattered upon it, but also because all the sins of the world were affixed to it in the person of Christ. In Galatians 3:13 the apostle Paul quoted from Deut. 21:22, 23 to demonstrate the *"accursed"* nature of the person so affixed to a tree or wooden beam. According to ancient Jewish custom the pole or beam upon which a man died was *"accursed"* along with the man who died upon it. Therefore the pole was also to be disposed of or buried (Moses Maimonides). In Ezra 6:11 the decree was made by king Darius that assistance was to be given to the people of Israel in rebuilding their land. Any man who refused to assist Israel was to have a beam taken from his house and erected for him to be hanged upon. In addition, his house would itself become a "refuse heap." This might serve to demonstrate the contempt which should be placed upon the object upon which our Savior died. It most certainly was not to be an object of veneration or worship.

The *stauros* upon which Christ died was also referred to in the Greek as an *xulon,* which simply means a tree or timber. And so it is called a "tree" several times—Acts 5:30; 10:39; 13:29; 1 Pet. 2:24 and Gal. 3:13. Combining the simple, roughhewn, single tree timber (*xulon*) with the upright pole (*stauros*), we can conclude that there was nothing in the object itself to make it a fit article for veneration or even decorative adoration. And yet, one can see in the Vatican, for instance, such splendid crosses—gold plated, radiating spectacular light—with other articles of veneration and ornamentation.

The modern readers of the Word of God have to live with several words in our Bibles of ecclesiastical origin. During the translation of the very popular King James Version, behind the scenes there was a very strong opposition by the Puritans to the use of such clerical words as "church," "bishop" and "Easter," none of which had any actual relationship with the Greek word being translated. The English word "church" had reference to "the Lord's house" (the building) and was an English derivation of the Greek word *kurios* (Lord). The actual Greek word being translated was *ekklesia* and should be translated as "congregation" or "assembly." The word "bishop" was a clerical title and should have been translated simply as an "overseer." "Easter" had derivation from the Babylonian goddess *Ishtar.* The feast in view was simply the "Passover," and that is how it should have been translated. As to the word "cross," we simply have to live with it, and think of it in the context of the whole Biblical revelation. But, by no stretch of the imagination are we to idolize it! Most people simply don't realize that this English word "cross" (from Latin, *crux*) is actually never used in the original Word of God.

In closing, let us look upon—

5. *The Bronze Serpent on the Pole*

In John the third chapter the words of Christ are recorded, *"And as Moses lifted up the serpent in the wilderness, even so must the Son of man be lifted up, that whoever believes in Him should not perish but have everlasting life"* (John 3:14, 15). Not only was Christ giving the plan of salvation, but He was also using an object lesson of supreme significance as it relates to the explanation of that salvation process. In addition, almost as a side attraction, He was even giving us a view of the *"stauros"* upon which He was hung. When we go back and read the initial account in Numbers 21: 4–9, we learn that Moses had a bronze (or copper) serpent made which was suspended upon a *"pole."* Everyone who had been bitten by the poisonous snakes could come and merely look upon that bronze serpent and be instantly healed of the deadly snake bites.

And so the typology of this event, as given by Christ Himself, becomes one of the foremost objects in the Hebrew Scriptures prefiguring the death of Christ and an object lesson concerning God's salvation plan. Amazing as it may seem, the bronze serpent prefigures Jesus Christ, Himself, as "He became *sin* for us." We should look very carefully, therefore, at the whole of this story and we will see amazing things.

Normally the serpent would be emblematic of Satan. Satan was specifically called "that old *serpent,* the Devil and Satan" (Rev. 12:9). Satan used the *serpent* in the garden to deceive the woman. Satan was the origin of *sin and rebellion*. But now that Christ became *"sin"* in His death (2 Cor. 5:21) He, Himself, was prefigured by a *"serpent."* The pole upon which the bronze serpent was hung prefigures the pole or wooden tree beam upon which Christ was hung. The mere "look" at that bronze serpent hung on the pole prefigures the mere look of "faith" in Christ by lost sinners. The resulted physical healing from the deadly snakebite infection prefigures the eternal spiritual redemption those have who look in faith to the antitypical bronze serpent (Christ) hanging upon a pole.

Seeing the importance that Christ gave to it, let us rehearse the story even more carefully and slowly. Israel rebelled against God at this stage in their wilderness journey. As a consequence God sent fiery serpents among them which bit them. The poison which infected their bodies brought thousands to the point of death. This typifies what happened to the whole human family. As a consequence of Adam's sin and rebellion, the whole human family received a corrupt fallen nature which was destined for death. Mankind, as it were, was bitten by that Satanic serpent, the Devil. The poison of sin, which brings death, has entered into mankind's constitution, even eternal death (Rom. 7:17, 18 and 20). Satan's poison of sin in our beings brings corruption and death. What could save the Jewish people from that physical death, and what will save mankind from such a cruel eternal death, both spiritually and physically??

To erect the bronze serpent and hang it upon a pole to be viewed by the people of Israel brought physical deliverance to the Israelites. And what did God provide for all mankind? First of all, when Christ came to earth the Scripture says that He took upon Himself the "likeness of sinful flesh" (Rom. 8:3). Notice, it is careful to not say Christ "had sinful flesh." He was simply made like mankind. We can rest assured that Christ was "Holy, harmless, undefiled and separate from sinners" as to His own personal being—Hebrews 7:26. He never sinned. He was absolutely sinless. However, when Christ died upon the cross, all the sins of the whole world were transferred upon Him and He became "sin." Therefore, He died as it were, in the form of a serpent. Thus when Christ died, He essentially was a "sin offering" (see Rom. 8:3, NASB and NIV). *SIN* was judged and damned in the person of our sin-bearer. When sin was judged, man's fallen sin-nature was judged. This death and judgment is credited to the repentant person when he believes in Christ (Rom. 6:6). In fact, at Christ's death the whole *WORLD* of lost sinners was judged (John 12:31). When the world was judged the "prince of this world," *SATAN*, was judged (John 16:11). When Satan and sin were judged, the potential was to release the believer from the bondage of *DEATH*, which comes as a result of sin (see 1 Cor. 15:55–56 and 2 Tim. 1:10). Hallelujah!! Praise be to the Lord!

"Nehustan"

What startling and beautiful simplicity. Yet Satan would want to destroy this simplicity entirely. Amazing as it may seem, the bronze serpent on the pole became an object of idolatry among the Israelites in their later history! This is the same as what happened to the "cross" of Christianity. When King Hezekiah began to rule over Israel, the very first thing he did was to have the bronze serpent broken in pieces so that the "sons of Israel" could no longer "burn incense to it" (2 Kings 18:1–4). Hezekiah called it "Nehustan" (that piece of bronze). And this same exact thing is what should have happened to most of the crosses in Christendom!

This precise same trail leading up to idolatry was followed in Christendom. Instead of receiving by faith the everlasting benefits of Christ's substitutionary death in the place of the sinner, crosses were created—similar to the pagan crosses of long antiquity—and idolized in different ways. Instead of worshipping the Savior Who died upon the cross, the cross was religiously adored and even worshipped—what brazen idolatry!

It is of supreme importance in this study is to remember that Christ died as the antitypical serpent, bearing upon Himself the sins of all mankind of all the ages. Furthermore, He was not delivered from that death till three days and three nights had transpired after the time of His being "cursed" of God in our place.

CHAPTER SEVENTEEN

THE SUFFERINGS OF JESUS CHRIST EVEN TO THE DEPTH OF HELL

By Russell Ross, edited and enlarged by Jack Langford

T here are many dozens of verses in the Bible which state that our sins were paid for by the work of Jesus Christ in dying for our sins on the cross. It was on the cross that Christ's blood was shed and where He died. However, not one of these dozens of verses states that Christ's suffering for sins *began* on the cross or was *concluded* on the cross. It should be understood that all the sufferings for sins and the atonement accomplished for mankind is often only summarized by the cross work of Jesus Christ. This is what mankind could see with their own physical eyes. Yet there is much more to the sufferings and death of Christ which is entirely beyond the sight of mortal man. The Scriptures are very explicit in this revelation. Let us now step into that realm.

The Sufferings of Christ Prior to the Cross

When we speak of Christ's suffering before the cross, we are not talking about all the human suffering Christ did in His lifetime. All should well understand that Christ suffered in the garden of

Gethsemane when He contemplated what was shortly to occur. The Bible says, "And being in *agony* He prayed more earnestly. And His sweat became like great drops of blood falling down to the ground" (Luke 22:44). We can only groan in our own spirits as we try to measure the depth of His pain in this preliminary hour of suffering. There is no other one on the face of this earth who has sweat as it were "great drops of blood." The only explanation is that the inner pain of soul that Christ bore is beyond our comprehension.

And yet, this was not the beginning of His sacrificial sorrow. Christendom inherited a tradition from some of the early so-called "fathers," to the effect that the whole week before Christ died should be called "Passion Week." This has become in religion a ritual observance of something which was actually factual in Christ's experience. These teachers saw and observed that on the Sunday beginning this week Christ actually began His soul-suffering in contemplation of His death.

At the time of Christ's "Triumphal Entry" into Jerusalem, when crowds of people were shouting His praises in anticipation of the Kingdom, Jesus stopped and cried out, *"Now is My soul troubled, and what shall I say? 'Father, save Me from this hour'? But for this purpose I came to this hour . . . And I, if I am lifted up from the earth, will draw all men to Myself"* (John 12:27, 32). A statement like this at the time of great celebration in anticipation of the Messiah's Kingdom seems totally out of place and confusing, to say the least. Yet it clearly happened. However, this confusion is explained when we remember that in the Jewish reckoning this was the tenth day of Nisan (or Abib). This is the specific day upon which the lambs were to be selected and set aside for the Passover sacrifice four days later (Exo. 12:2). Therefore, this was also the day in which Christ knew, deep inside His soul, that in reality He, as the antitypical Passover Lamb, was marked for death just as surely as all those Passover lambs. Therefore, though His cry to the Father would seem contradictory to the crowds around Him, who knew nothing of His inner suffering of soul, yet Christ as "the Lamb of God" was actually marked and selected for death! Christ knew how quickly men could change their minds under pressure. Yes, from that moment on, Christ bore in His conscious being the realization that He had now

302

actually been selected and set aside for examination for the next several days until the time came for His sacrifice.

The Sufferings of Christ in Preparation for the Cross

Did Christ *suffer* during the long hours of the investigative judgments? Of course He did! The harassments, humiliations and brutal beatings all took place prior to His being hung on the cross. Christ suffered before the High Priest Annas and before his son-in-law Caiphas, who was the High Priest officiating at this time. Christ suffered mockery and a beating before Caiphas (Matt. 26:67; Lk. 22:63–65). Pontius Pilate sent Christ to Herod's judgment hall where He became the entertainment of the officials by further mockery and humiliation (Lk. 23:11). Christ was then sent back to Pilate. Pilate finally had Him brutally scourged, beaten, mocked and paraded before the people as a public spectacle (Matt. 27:26–31).

No doubt the Scriptures spare us from the actual details of the sufferings of Jesus Christ during these repeated mockings and beatings. This all took place prior to His being sent to Calvary. The prophet Isaiah describes this brutal mauling of Jesus Christ in no uncertain language: ". . . many were astonished at You, so His visage was marred more than any man, and His form more than the sons of Men" (Isa. 52:14). Again Isaiah said by inspiration, "He has no form nor comeliness; and when we see Him, there is no beauty that we should desire Him, . . . and we hid as it were our faces from Him" (Isa. 53:2 and 3).

We are furthermore told in Isaiah 53:5 and 7 such things as, "With His stripes we are healed," and "He was oppressed, and He was afflicted, yet He opened not His mouth: He is brought as a lamb to the slaughter, and as a sheep before his shearers is dumb, so He opened not His mouth." These prophesied sufferings of Christ as The Lamb of God took place as He silently stood before His accusers, prior to His being nailed to the tree.

We can conclude from these passages that all Christ's sufferings for the sins of the world were from the moment He voluntarily yielded Himself to God for that purpose. This initially began as he was selected as the antitypical Passover Lamb, intensified in the garden of Gethsemane, continued through the investigative judgments, and culminated, as far as the punishment man could administer, at His death on the cross. But it did not stop there, either!

The Real Sufferings of Christ are not Understood by the Natural Man

The apostle Peter, in his own personal soulishness, was repulsed by the idea that Christ would even have to suffer, and Christ rebuked him for his human reasoning (Matt. 16:21–23). Christ had told the apostles that He must go to Jerusalem and "suffer many things of the elders and chief priests and scribes and be killed and raised again the third day." When Peter said "Not so, Lord," the Lord Jesus Christ rebuked him severely, and said ". . . you are not setting your mind on the things of God, but of man."

Many people are also utterly shocked and even repulsed when they are told that there was much more to Christ's suffering than just the physical punishment, and that Christ was actually cursed of God and damned in our place. Such is a contradiction to the thoughts of the natural man. Yet the Bible clearly states in no uncertain words that Christ was "made a curse for us: for it is written; 'Cursed is everyone who hangs on a tree'" (Gal. 3:13), and "For he who is hanged is accursed of God" (Deut. 21:23). In addition, John 5:24 says, "Verily, verily I say unto you, he who hears My word, and believes in Him Who sent Me has everlasting life, and shall not come into judgment, . . ." Here the word "judgment" (in the K.J.V. it is translated *condemnation*) is in opposition to "everlasting life" and obviously means the "condemnation of Hell" (as used in Matt. 23:33) in separation from God. The only reason penitent souls can escape such condemnation is precisely because Christ was literally *con-damned* in our place.

The reason Christ was damned is because He was bearing the sin penalty of all the world upon His soul. The superficial religious

304

world, which views Christ as a mere martyr for a good cause, is utterly repulsed by the idea expressed in the Word of God that Christ actually *"became sin for us"* (2 Cor. 5:21). This is the very reason He was "God-forsaken" in His substitutionary death (Matt. 27:46). For four thousand years men had laid their hands upon the heads of sacrificial lambs and confessed their sins—transferring their sins, and the guilt and penalty of their sins, to the lambs. Now when the "Lamb of God" was selected, the sins of all the world and of all the ages were transferred to Christ. He thus "became sin," though He, Himself, knew no sin. He bore the sins of all mankind. As the contaminated "Scapegoat" (which we shall study again later), he bore the filth of all mankind into the wilderness of damnation. No doubt, the reason the natural mind is repulsed by such revelations is because men themselves do not want to face up to the reality of how awful their own sins are in the sight of a Holy and Righteous God. Nor does Satan want mankind to realize the gracious reality of what God did for us through Christ.

The Sinners' Death

Let us never forget that the substitutionary death of Christ was essentially not the death of a martyr. Christ was certainly a martyr. However, primarily Christ died the sinners' death! Christ died in total separation from Almighty God—"God-forsaken." He died as the sinners' substitute and as a Hell-deserving "sinner" in total separation from God, His Father. We say this in holy sanctity.

The Psalmist of old had stated, "Precious in the sight of the Lord is the death of His saints" (Ps. 116:15). Such was not the case in the death of Jesus Christ. There is the sense in which Christ did not die as one precious to God, nor did He die as a saint. Christ died as one "accursed of God," as one contaminated with the sins of the world upon Him—the sinners' death—"God forsaken!" And furthermore, Christ was not *liberated* from that death until three days and three nights had transpired.

Superficial religionists will often dabble in the outward temporal sufferings of Jesus Christ. As we said earlier, the Roman Catholic

Church is noted for its morbid art depicting the physical sufferings and crucifixion of Jesus. This is done because the Devil has inspired them to convey the idea to people that if they suffer as did Jesus Christ, they can somehow gain a foothold in heaven by appeasing God. In so doing, the religious world misses the Divine revelation that it was the spiritual sufferings of Christ which broke His heart, and caused the real anguish of His soul. This was the real basis for our redemption as He took the sinners' place.

The outward, physical woundings that Christ bore in His flesh were only the signs or symbols of the real inward wounding of His soul when He became God-forsaken and took upon Himself the sins of all mankind and died in separation from God. Who can contemplate or understand the fact that one who was totally righteous and without sin has now taken to His sinless bosom all the sins and vile filth of mankind? How incomprehensible! It is totally beyond our ability to conceive how such a Holy One could *voluntarily* become so defiled!

Remember, when Christ first cried out at His triumphal entry into Jerusalem "Now is My *soul* troubled," that is when His *soul* torment began in anticipation of all that He was to suffer, both physically and spiritually. No one could see His *soul*. His inward person was spiritual and eternal. This anguish of *soul* intensified in the garden of Gethsemane. The main outward evidence was the incomprehensible "sweat as it were of great drops of blood." That same anguish of *soul* continued right through the several trials and beatings and mockery. It culminated, as far as what man could detect, when His body was taken down from the cross. However, the apostle Peter made it unmistakably clear that Christ's "*soul* was not left in Hell" (Acts 2:27), and "the *pains* of death were not loosened" until Christ was raised from the dead (Acts 2:24). Consequently Christ's "*soul-suffering*" had continued until the time of His resurrection from the dead.

Christ said while He was here on earth, "Fear not those who kill the body, but are not able to kill the *soul*. But rather fear Him Who is able to destroy both *soul* and body in *Hell*" (Matt. 10:28). Christ suffered death as to His body, but more than that, He suffered death even to His *soul* in separation from God. I do not believe for one instant that the spiritual separation from God ceased the moment Christ expired physically. Such conclusions do not come forth from the Word of God.

Was the sin-satisfying death of Christ limited to and completed upon the cross of Calvary? Why the three days and three nights following Christ's death? Was He in the heart of the earth? Was there the continuation of Christ's suffering in the regions of Hell? Did the three days and three nights have nothing to do with His substitutionary work of redemption for the sins of mankind? What does God's Word reveal further on this subject?

We should never base our conclusions to these questions on man's soulish sentimentalities. Our conclusions can only and should only be based on the startling revelations that come from the Word of God!

Jonah as a Type of Christ

One foremost Biblical reason why we may know that the substitutionary work of Jesus Christ was not limited to the cross of Calvary is in the story of Jonah. Jonah 1:17 speaks of how the prophet was "in the belly of the fish three days and three nights." In chapter 2, verses 2–6, Jonah prayed thusly unto God from within the fish's belly:

> *I cried out to the LORD because of my AFFLICTION,*
>   *and He answered me.*
> *Out of the BELLY OF SHEOL I cried,*
>   *and You heard my voice.*
> *For YOU CAST ME into the deep,*
>   *into the heart of the seas,*
>   *and the floods surrounded me;*
> *ALL YOUR BILLOWS and YOUR WAVES*
>   *passed over me.*
> *Then I said, 'I HAVE BEEN CAST OUT OF YOUR SIGHT;*
>   *yet I will look again toward Your holy temple.'*
> *The waters surrounded me, even to My soul;*

the deep closed around me;
weeds were wrapped around my head.
I WENT DOWN TO THE MOORINGS OF THE MOUNTAINS;
THE EARTH WITH ITS BARS
CLOSED BEHIND ME FOREVER;
Yet You have brought up my life from **THE PIT**,
O Lord, my God.

Jonah obviously was not in a place of comfort or bliss, but rather in a place of agony and suffering for those three days and nights. Jonah's three days of agony and suffering spoke of the three days and three nights that the Lord Jesus Christ would be in the heart of the earth, according to Matthew 12:40—"For as Jonah was three days and three nights in the fish's belly; *so shall* the Son of Man be three days and three nights in the heart of the earth." Who would be so foolish as to think that Jonah was a type of the Lord Jesus Christ only by the *time* duration he spent in the fish's belly? A close look at the passage will reveal that the Holy Spirit of inspiration was moving Jonah to express the sufferings of a man in the very pit of Hell (*Sheol*). Since Jonah, himself (physically), was not actually in Hell we must understand this passage to be like many other prophesies before it—namely, it has a twofold application. First, it has an application to Jonah who was under the disciplinary hand of God while physically in the fish's belly. Yet as a prophecy, there is obviously more of a direct application to Jesus Christ in His sufferings and death, Who was likewise under the disciplinary hand of God as our substitute.

Psalm 22 is one good example of what we are saying. It is also on the subject of the sufferings of Christ. David said by inspiration, "My God, my God, why hast Thou forsaken me?" He goes on to say, ". . . and all my bones are out of joint; . . . my tongue cleaveth to my jaws; . . . They pierced my hands and my feet; . . . they part my garments among them, and cast lots for my vesture" (verses 1, 14–17). On the one hand we do not doubt that David had experiences of despair and persecution, but on the other hand, David was not "Godforsaken" in the sense intended in the Psalm, nor did any of these other things ever happen to him. Instead, by inspiration of the Spirit, these are the actual words of Jesus Christ while hanging on the cross. The remainder of the Psalm cites many details about what actually happened to Christ while He was a spectacle before men in His physical sufferings. This is a prophetic prayer of David wherein the Holy Spirit of inspiration caused David to impersonate the Son of God in His suffering. In reality, this is the prayer of Jesus Christ, uttered centuries in advance, through the Spirit of prophecy.

Now the same is precisely true of the prophet Jonah. The words of Jonah in his prayer to God out of the fish's belly are motivated by the Spirit of Christ Who was in him—see 1 Pet. 1:11 and 2 Pet. 1:21. The apostle Peter said, "The Spirit of Christ was in the prophets, testifying beforehand the sufferings of Christ and the glory that should follow." Did the Spirit of Christ in David "testify of the sufferings of Christ?" Of course He did! Did the Spirit of Christ in Jonah "testify of the sufferings of Christ?" Of course He did! Thus, the words of Jonah are primarily the words of God's dear Son, Who was totally God-forsaken and sent into the lowest regions of the earth—Hell, itself.

Jonah's agony in the fish's belly for three days and three nights was no doubt very frightening. Though men could and did cast Jonah overboard (and that was all that they could do), yet this was the beginning of God's way of disciplining Jonah. At the very same time, Jonah had told the crew to throw him overboard in order to save their own lives. In that sense, Jonah was a substitute for them. Jonah thus was typical of the Lord Jesus Christ, Who was a substitute for all mankind. Jonah was therefore a substitute, yet under the disciplinary hand of God for three days and nights because of his disobedience. Jonah's agony came, therefore, because God brought this unique form of suffering upon him.

I have actually seen the study of one writer, rebelling against the fact of Christ's suffering in Hell. He makes Jonah's experience almost a pleasure cruise, thus marvelously sparing him from death. Of course, to arrive at such an interpretation, he had to virtually rewrite the story. Needless to say, there is no divine inspiration for his Remanufactured Per-Version of the story.

In the inspired account, Jonah's prayer then transcended his own predicament and we see One suffering in another realm altogether. Though Jonah went down into the depths of the ocean, yet in his prayer the One he was impersonating was placed in *"Sheol,"* the Hebrew word for Hell. Mingled with the prayer of Jonah is that of another Who sinks below the mountains and into the very heart of the earth. This One cries out as if from a prison house, "The earth with her *bars* was about Me," and this prison was in the *"belly of Sheol."* Thus He cries out in agony to God. This is the cry of Jesus Christ, Himself. As Jonah was cast out from the presence of God, so it was that Christ was cast out from the presence of God into the lower regions in the earth.

By way of a careful review of this testimony, we must note four important truths which are revealed in this passage from Jonah (chapter 2):

1. **First** of all, Jonah's prayer is motivated by the fact that he, himself, was under the disciplinary hand of God.
   a. Verse 3, "For You [God] cast me into the deep."
   b. Verse 3, "All Your [God's] billows. . . ."
   c. Verse 3, "and Your [God's] waves passed over me.
   d. Verse 4, "I have been cast out of Your [God's] sight."

2. **Second**, Jonah's prayer is based upon his suffering affliction under this discipline of God.
   a. Verse 2, "I cried out to the Lord because of my affliction."
   b. Verse 2, "Out of the belly of Sheol I cried."
   c. Verse 4, "I have been cast out of Your sight."
   d. Verse 7, "While I was fainting away."

3. **Third**, Jonah's prayer was physically situated from within the fish's belly in the great depths of the ocean.
   a. Verse 1, "From the stomach of the fish."
   b. Verse 3, "[from] the heart of the seas."
   c. Verse 5, "The deep closed around me."

d. Verse 6, "I went down to the moorings of the mountains."

4. **Fourth,** Jonah's prayer was spiritually situated from within Hell, itself.
    a. Verse 2, "Out of the belly of **Sheol** I cried."
    b. Verse 6, "[from] the moorings [bottom or roots] of the mountains."
    c. Verse 6, "The earth with its **bars** closed behind me forever."
    d. Verse 6, ". . . from the **PIT** [a synonym for Sheol]."

Because Jonah was obviously crying out as a man within Hell itself, some very capable teachers have taken the position that Jonah actually died in the fish's belly, and his *spirit* went into Hell from whence he cried out. Then after three days and nights Jonah's *spirit* was once again joined to his body and he was resurrected from the dead and vomited out of the fish upon dry land. I do not know that I could disprove this. However, if we but remember that Jonah is like the earlier inspired psalmist who impersonated the Lord, then we can understand that Jonah was miraculously preserved in the fish for the three days and nights until he was vomited out. This prayer of Jonah was followed by God speaking to the fish so that it cast out the prophet.

We must remember, however, that Christ was subjected to the wrath of God, not because He personally had been disobedient as was Jonah, but because He had voluntarily taken upon Himself the guilt and penalty for the sins of mankind. Thus, as Jonah was vomited out of the fish's belly, so Christ could not be contained in the lower regions of the earth. When God was satisfied by the sufferings of Christ, Hell had to discharge Him, and He was gloriously raised from the dead. He did not see corruption as was further typified by Jonah.

The prophet Jonah introduces us to—

The Shadow of Christ in the Psalms

In Jonah's prayer out of the midst of Sheol (Hell), he quoted from the book of Psalms (42:7). Jonah's experience was reminiscent of much that was written in the Psalms about suffering, especially suffering from and even within the horrors of Hell, itself. Some commentaries will list many references to the Psalms from this ordeal of Jonah. Most of them are allusions to similar circumstances which are expressed by the inspired Psalmist. One primary statement in the book of Psalms concerning Jesus Christ is Psalm 40:7 which says, "*. . . In the volume of the book it is written of Me.*" And this whole section (verses 6–8) is quoted by the apostle Paul in the book of Hebrews (10:5–7). Thus it is that in the Psalms we have an overwhelming number of references to the Lord Jesus Christ, especially in the realm of His rejection, betrayal and sufferings—and even references to His suffering the wrath of God in Sheol.

Jonah (Jonah 2:3) quoted the last part of verse seven of Psalm 42, "*All Your waves and billows have gone over me.*" To Jonah this was descriptive of the wrath of God under which he was suffering. And remember that Jonah was speaking from the perspective of being in Sheol. However, in Psalm 42 these words are also prophetic of our Lord Jesus Christ. Psalm 42 starts off with verses 1–3:

> *As the deer pants for the water brooks,*
> *so pants My soul for You, O God.*
> *My soul thirsts for God, for the living God.*
> *When shall I come and appear before God?*
> *My tears have been My food day and night,*
> *While they continually say to Me,*
> **'Where is your God?'**

The spectators at the crucifixion scene kept mocking Christ— "*He trusts in God; let Him deliver Him now, if He takes pleasure in Him*" (Matt. 27:43). We shall see that when Christ died, the "billows" of

312

God's wrath poured over His soul as He was plunged into Sheol bearing the weight of the sins of the world. Jesus Christ was most certainly not in a state of bliss and enjoyment for the three days and nights after His death on the cross. Rather, there was the pain and agony of suffering the "billows of God's wrath" against Himself. Note that Psalm 40:2 says *"He also brought Me up out of a horrible pit, out of the miry clay."* This was certainly true of Christ.

Psalm 69

That Psalm 69 speaks prophetically of Jesus Christ in His suffering, there is no mistaking. "They gave me gall . . . and vinegar to drink" (v. 21) is stated by all four Gospels (Matt. 27:34, 48; Mk. 15:23, 36; Lk. 23:36; Jn. 19:29). That he was "smitten" by God (v. 26) is also stated in Isa. 53:4. Verse 9 is quoted in John 2:17. Another part of this verse is quoted in Rom. 15:3. That Christ was "estranged from His brothers" (v. 8) is fulfilled in John 7:5.

In this amazing Psalm of David, he prays that he may be delivered from going into that "Pit" of separation from God.

> *Save Me, O God! For the waters have come up to My neck.*
> *I sink in deep mire, where there is no standing;*
> *I have come into deep waters, where the floods overflow Me.*
> *I am weary with My crying; My throat is dry;*
> *My eyes fail while I wait for My God.*
> *Those who hate Me without a cause*
> *are more than the hairs of My head; . . .* (Ps. 69:1-4).

> *Deliver Me out of the mire, and let Me not sink;*
> *Let Me be delivered from those who hate Me,*
>   *and out of the deep waters.*
> *Let not the flood water overflow Me,*
>   *nor the deep swallow Me up;*
> *And let not the **Pit** shut its mouth on Me.* (Ps. 69:14, 15).

It is obvious from this Psalm of David that to slip off into the state of death, described as "deep mire," and a "Pit" and the "deep waters," would be a horrible thing. (See also Psalm 40:2; Psalm 86:13 and Psalm 116:3) This could not be describing a new tomb which was just hewn out of rock (Matt. 27:60). It would certainly not be a place of bliss and contentment!

And now let us look very carefully at this next Psalm to understand more about this "Pit."

Psalm 88

One of the most explicit Psalms concerning the suffering of Jesus Christ in Hell is this particular Psalm. If one can read this Psalm and understand no more about Jesus Christ's sufferings than His being nailed to the cross, then we believe you are resisting the teaching of the Holy Spirit of inspiration.

O Lord, God of my salvation,
*   I have cried out day and night before You.*
Let My prayer come before You;
*   incline Your ear to My cry.*
For My soul is full of troubles,
*   and My life draws near to **Sheol**.*
*I am counted with those who go down to the **Pit**;*
I am like a man who has no strength,
*   adrift among the **dead**,*
Like the slain who lie in the grave,
*   whom You remember no more,*
And who are cut off from Your hand. (Verses 1–5)

*You have laid Me **in the lowest Pit**,*
*   in darkness, in the depths.*
***Your wrath lies heavy upon Me**,*
***You have afflicted Me with all Your waves**. Selah*
You have put away My acquaintances far from Me;
You have made Me an abomination to them;
I am shut up, and I cannot get out;
My eye wastes away because of affliction. (Verses 6–9a)

LORD, I have called daily upon You;
I have stretched out My hands to You.
Will you work wonders for the dead?
*Shall the **dead** arise and praise You?* Selah.
[literally, in Hebrew, *raphah*, **disembodied spirits**;
and so it is properly translated, *departed spirits*,
    in the NASB]
Shall Your lovingkindness be declared in the grave?
Or Your faithfulness in the place of destruction?
Shall Your wonders be known in the dark?
Or Your righteousness in the land of forgetfulness?
    (Verses 9b–12)

But to You I have cried out, O LORD,
And in the morning My prayer comes before You.
LORD, why do You cast off My soul?
Why do You hide Your face from Me?
I have been afflicted and ready to die from My youth;
I suffer Your terrors; I am distraught.
Your fierce wrath has gone over Me;
Your terrors have cut Me off.
They came around Me all day long like water;
They engulfed Me altogether.
Loved one and friend You have put far from Me,
And My acquaintances into darkness. (Verses 13–18)

Like Jonah's prayer from the fish's belly, this prayer as well impersonates the words and experience of the Divine Son of God in Sheol under the wrath of God. Notice again the word "dead" as found in verse 10. This word for the dead is entirely different. It is used only 8 times in the Hebrew Scriptures and always in reference to disembodied spirits of the dead (Job 26:5, 6; Ps. 88:10; Prov. 2:18; 9:18; 21:16; Isa. 14:9; 26:14 and 19). Four (4) of those times it specifically mentions *Sheol*. It is the Hebrew word *raphah* (raw-faw) and is taken from the word *rash* which means "feeble, weak, flaccid, or to tremble." It means "ghosts, shades, or disembodied spirits residing in Sheol" (see *Gesenius Hebrew Lexicon, NASB Hebrew Dictionary*, or *Strong #7496*).

Therefore, when the Psalm says "I am counted with those who go down to the Pit," (v. 4) it means Sheol or Hell. Likewise, when it describes this as the "lowest Pit" (v. 6), it means the abode of the spirits of the unrighteous. When it says "Your wrath lies heavy upon Me" (v. 7), it means the one being spoken of is suffering the judgment of God in condemnation. When it speaks of God's "fierce wrath . . . like water; they engulfed Me altogether" (vs.16, 17), it is speaking of Christ's baptismal judgment in death when He was plunged into the wrath of God for our sins (Matt. 20:22; Mk. 10:38; Lk. 12:50 and Rom. 6:3).

Can we accept these words for what they teach and believe them regardless of what natural repulsion our human reasoning may conjure up?

Psalm 18

The pangs [cords] *of death encompassed Me,*
And the floods of ungodliness made Me afraid.
The sorrows [cords] *of **Sheol** surrounded Me;*
The snares of death confronted Me.
In My distress I called upon the LORD,
And cried out to My God;
He heard My voice from His temple,
And My cry came before Him, even to His ears. (Ps. 18:4–6).

This is another Psalm which is reminiscent of the prayer of Jonah from the "belly of Sheol." As Jonah sought recovery to once again see God's temple (Jonah 2:4), so David in this prophetic Psalm impersonated Christ, and recognized God's response from "His temple."

Again, the words above describe the "three days and three nights" Christ spent in the state of death in Hell. "The pangs of death surrounding Him," "The sorrows of Sheol surrounded Him," and "The snares of death confronting Him" could never be reconciled with a place of bliss, comfort, or enjoyment, immediately following His "yielding up of His spirit" on the cross. On the contrary, this frightful condition was while Christ spent the three days and nights in Hell as our sin-bearer.

God did not *"loose the pains of death"* from Christ until He was raised from the dead—Acts 2:23, 24.

ACTS 2:23, 24 and ACTS 17:3

Any who would think that Jesus Christ's substitutionary death for our sins was limited to the cross should have Acts 2:23, 24 rearranged to read this way—

Him, being delivered by the determined purpose and foreknowledge of God, you have taken by lawless hands, have crucified, and put to death—thereby having loosed the pains of death.

When were the pains of death loosed? In this misrepresentation, "the pains of death" were loosed WHEN He was "crucified and put to death." However, as is obvious to an honest person, this is not a faithful rendering. Hear Acts 2:23, 24 as it really is—

. . . you have taken by lawless hands, have crucified, and put to death; **Whom God raised up, having loosed the pains of death,** *because it is not possible that He should be held by it.*

The NASB renders "pains" as *"agonies."* It is important to note, "having loosed the *agonies* of death" immediately follows Jesus Christ being *"raised up."* It does not immediately follow His being "crucified, and put to death." "Having loosed the *agonies* of death" is an adverbial clause which describes what took place at Jesus Christ's resurrection from the dead, not what took place at the time He physically died on the cross. The *"agonies* of death" obviously refers to sufferings, NOT to something enjoyed as a place of bliss in

Paradise. Since the "agonies of death" were not loosed until Christ's resurrection, and since the "*agonies* of death" refers to Christ's *sufferings*, we may, therefore, conclude that the termination of Christ's *sufferings* was not until he was raised from the dead—which was three days and three nights after His physical death on the cross.

In Acts 17:3, the next event after Jesus Christ's "sufferings" is His being raised from the dead. Again, the text does NOT say that after Christ's sufferings on the cross, He was then buried and finally, after being in a place of bliss and comfort for three days and three nights, He was raised from the dead. Please read the text as it really is, "*Christ had to suffer and rise again from the dead,* . . ." This then, is much like Acts 2:23, 24. Christ's suffering death was for three days and nights, after which He was resurrected from the dead.

The Baptism of Death

It would be appropriate at this time to emphasize the subject of Christ's suffering and death baptism which we mentioned briefly earlier.

Christ clearly spoke of His sufferings and death as being a "baptism" (Matt. 20:22, 23; Mk. 10:38, 39 and Luke 12:50). It was in this "baptism" of suffering and death that Christ was paying the penalty for the sins of the world. In both Matthew and Mark, Christ prefaced His statement about His coming "baptism" with careful explanation (Matt. 20:17–19 and verse 22):

> *Now Jesus, going up to Jerusalem, took the twelve disciples aside on the road and said to them, 'Behold, we are going up to Jerusalem, and the Son of Man will be betrayed to the chief priests and to the scribes; and they will condemn Him to death, and deliver Him to the Gentiles to mock and to scourge and to crucify. And the **third day** He will rise again.'. . . the **baptism** that I am about to be baptized with.*

318

In other words, Christ's "suffering and death baptism" was going to be a three day baptism. After being plunged into this suffering, mockery, scourging, crucifixion and death, Christ would not be "raised" from this baptism until the "third day." This means that the *time* of this death was a vital part of the "baptism," and did not merely cease the moment He expired physically on the cross.

The amazing thing is that in the reckoning of Almighty God, each one who places his faith in Jesus Christ is supernaturally identified with Christ in this baptism of suffering and death. The apostle Paul, by divine inspiration, says—

> *Or do you not know that as many of us as were baptized into Christ Jesus were **baptized into His death**? Therefore we were **buried with Him** through **baptism into death**, that just as Christ was **raised from the dead** by the glory of the Father, even so we also should walk in **newness of life**.* (Rom. 6:3, 4).

No one should contend that Christ's baptism into death was completed on the cross. Christ most certainly was not "buried" on the cross. The Scriptural texts make it plain that this death baptism was not completed until three days later at the resurrection of Christ from the dead. In Colossians 2:10–12 we are told,

> *. . . and you are complete in Him, Who is the head of all principality and power. In Him you were also circumcised with the circumcision made without hands, by putting off the body of sins of the flesh, by the circumcision of Christ, **buried with Him in baptism**, in which you also were raised with Him through the faith in the working of God, Who raised Him from the dead.*

Exactly when was Christ raised out of this horrible death baptism for our sins? The Scriptures are very clear. It was exactly three days and three nights after Jesus Christ died physically on the cross of Calvary. Humble students of the Bible will not conclude that this suffering and death baptism terminated when Christ was taken down off the cross. *Christ's sufferings did not begin on the cross, nor were they terminated on the cross.* These passages are another biblical reason why careful students of the Scriptures will know that the sufferings of Jesus Christ were not merely limited to, nor completed upon, the cross of Calvary.

"My Father! Behold, Here is the Fire, . . ."

I will never forget the time when we were having a private discussion of this subject with a father in leadership in an assembly. We were introducing this father to the subject in a more thorough way. I was reading this passage from Genesis 22, which was the famous story of Abraham's offering up of his own son, Isaac. When I was reading the passage and came to verse seven, I paused and emphasized the words of Isaac to his father, *"Behold, here is the fire, . . ."* We heard an audible groan from this father, as the full realization of what Abraham was going to do came to him. Abraham was not going to merely kill his son, but he was also going to totally burn his body upon this altar. The body of his son would, after several hours, be nothing but ashes!

Many fathers, no doubt, have often thought of this test being presented to them instead of to Abraham. What would they have done? It appears to be an unbelievable request! To kill your own son—how could any father bring himself to do such a thing? Of course, Abraham had received the promise that it would be through Isaac that all the world would be blessed (Gen. 12:3 and 17:19). Therefore, if Abraham were to kill this son of promise, God would have to raise him from the dead in order to fulfill His promise. And therefore, Abraham believed that God would raise up Isaac from the dead (Heb. 11:17–19 and Gen. 22:5—note Abraham's words, "we will come back"). So, therefore, it might seem easier to believe that Abraham was willing, by faith, to kill his son. After all, God would just raise him up right off that altar after he had been killed. However, when we add the ingredient of the total consumption of the son's body by the fire, it becomes, indeed, an almost impossible request.

Furthermore, we would naturally have to ask—why the fire?? Why would not the death alone be sufficient?? Why the necessity of totally burning the offering after it was dead?? What purpose would the fire serve? Should not the death be sufficient??

No, the mere death of the sacrifice was not sufficient in the sight of God! There would be no satisfaction of sins being covered or paid for until the sacrifice was totally consumed by fire! Obviously, the fire symbolizes what happens after the death of the substitute. The total purifying process involves the judgment of the guilt and penalty of sins through the process of burning. The burning process represents the wrath of God against sin. Until the wrath of God is satisfied, the penalty of sin is not paid. If there is no fire, there is no satisfaction against sin. If there is no fire, there is no cleansing and purification from sin. If there is no fire, we are still in our sins.

Yes—"BEHOLD, THE FIRE"

I had read the story (Gen. 22) of Abraham offering up his son, Isaac, many times. I never actually realized the implication of the "fire" until I read it again with this subject in view. Then, it "jumped out" at me!

What an amazing story this is. What exacting details are in the manner in which it prefigures the offering of God's dear Son some 1700 or 1800 years later, *on the very same spot.* But more than that—"behold, the fire" as it applies to the total consumption of the antitypical Lamb of God, the Lord Jesus Christ! Abraham was not merely told to sacrifice his only son, whom he loved so dearly, but he was told to offer him as a *"burnt offering."* Jesus Christ was our burnt offering—offered by His own heavenly Father. Abraham named that hilltop "Jehovah-Jireh [Jehovah will provide]; as it is said to this day, 'In the mount of the LORD HE shall be provided'" (verse 14, literal trans.).

As I previously said, I have sometimes asked fathers when we were studying this account, "Could you put the knife to your own son?" Any father would balk at that command, even if it was given by God. And yet further, "Could you put the fire to your son's body and see it consumed into ashes?" Incomprehensible, to say the least! And yet that is precisely what Abraham was told to do. And furthermore, that is exactly what God the Father did with His Son—on our behalf—so that the whole world might be blessed with the forgiveness and cleansing of sins.

Of course, as I stated before, everyone should ask, "Why the fire?" After the son is dead, what need was there to burn the body and consume it into ashes? What is God's purpose in this? Wasn't it enough to just kill the boy? The typology would still be satisfied; after all, Christ just died for our sins, and there was no fire—*or was there*? My dear friend, if the typology was fulfilled, then there was a "fire" after Christ's physical death, and the only fire it could be was—**Hellfire**!

There is no secret to the purpose of "fire" as it is used in the Scriptures. Everywhere it is used of wrath and judgment and purging by judgment. The real problem is the vain effort by some to try and find some other meaning for it—other than what is prescribed in the Scriptures, which is the divine judgment on sin.

The Type of the Sacrifices

As we have just seen, Isaac was to be offered as a "burnt sacrifice." In the book of Leviticus we are given the details about the "Law of the burnt sacrifices" (Lev. 1 and 6:8–13). Obviously the most important thing about the "burnt offerings" was the very fact that, after the animal was killed and placed upon the altar, it was to be totally consumed by fire. These animal sacrifices spoke of our redemption in the Lord Jesus Christ. If Christ's physical death on the cross completed our redemption, then the antitypical animal sacrifices should have ended with their physical death and nothing more. If this were true, then at the exact time of the slaying of the animal, the priest should have said something like, "The atonement for your sins is now complete." Of course, this is not what happened. Following the death of the animal, the fire was to be made on the altar and the body of the animal was to be placed upon the fire to be totally burned until there was nothing left but ashes, even if the burning lasted all day and night. Later the ashes were carried outside the camp.

Sometimes it is interesting to read certain classical statements by well-known theologians on issues like this. For instance, one of the old standard commentaries on Leviticus is by S.H. Kellogg. He certainly recognized the implications of the fire for the burnt offering, but at the very same time he was repulsed by the thought that it could be applied to Christ. Notice his words:

> And now a question comes before us, the answer to which is vital to the right understanding of the burnt-offering, whether in its original or typical import. What is the significance of the burning? It has been very often answered that the consumption of the victim by fire symbolized the consuming wrath of Jehovah, utterly destroying the victim which represents *the sinful person* of the offerer. And, observing that the burning followed the killing and shedding of blood, some have gone so far as to say that the burning typified the eternal fire of hell! But when we remember that, without doubt, the sacrificial victim in all Levitical offerings was a type of *our blessed Lord*, we may well agree with one who calls this interpretation 'hideous.' And yet many, who have shrunk from this, have yet in so far held to this conception of the symbolic meaning of the burning as to insist that it must at least have typified those fiery sufferings in which our Lord offered up His soul for sin. They remind us how often in the Scriptures, fire stands as the symbol of the consuming wrath of God against sin, and hence argue that this may justly be taken here as the symbolic meaning of the victim on the altar. (*The Book of Leviticus*, pages 51 and 52.)

Now this is a classical statement on the subject which would serve to represent the repulsion some have in rejecting the conclusion that Jesus Christ suffered for our sins in the fiery wrath of God as the antitypical burnt offering. Notice please, that the rejection of this conclusion is NOT based upon the fact that *sinners* will go to Hell and suffer the torments of the fiery wrath of God. All of us know that the Scripture gives us ample warning of the destination of the unrighteous. The rejection of the conclusion is based upon the obvious implication that "OUR BLESSED LORD" was suffering in Hellfire! And herein, he forgets all about the fact that "our blessed Lord" has taken the "SINNERS' place!" Everyone knows Christ did not deserve to die such a death—He was sinless! However, Kellogg forgets all about the fact that Christ died bearing the load of all the sins, of all the world, of all the ages—having been made "to be SIN" in our place! (2 Cor.5:21).

Kellogg continues to try and find some other explanation for the FIRE. The only thing he comes up with is a few statements concerning "purification" by fire. Even here he forgets that purification by fire is only because the fire consumes and burns away the impurities.

Another statement by a renowned teacher, Ridout, who wrote concerning the altar of burnt offering, will demonstrate the opposite conclusion. First of all, he establishes beyond any shadow of a doubt, from the vast occurrences in the Scriptures concerning the fire of God's wrath, that the symbolic meaning of fire is—judgment against sin and the sinner. And then he says—

> For our Lord did not bear the fire of divine judgment in any external, superficial way. It is but a feeble and partial view of those sufferings which would enlarge upon the persecution of ungodly men, or even the malice of Satan who urged them on. These might explain the bodily anguish to which our holy Lord permitted Himself to be subjected; but the fire of divine holiness, heart-searching judgment against sin went down into the utmost center of His being. Reverently may we tread such holy ground. Sin is not an external thing, though it mars the outward man. Its source is the heart, the center of man's being; and therefore in the sinless Substitute the flame searched down into His holy soul. Atoning suffering, like the sin of man, was in the heart. The piercing of the nails, the crown of thorns, the jeers of the people, the spear-thrust, did not set forth the deep essence of His sufferings. God only,

Who searcheth the heart, knows what it meant. The Son, Who bore this judgment, knows the intensity of that fire which burned down into His soul when 'made an offering for sin'. . .In view of all this, how low is the view that our Lord's sufferings were abated penalty, as some would have it—something less than what the sinner will have to endure. Scripture is perfectly plain, that our Lord bore the full penalty of sin—the wrath, the forsaking of God in the 'outer darkness' (God having withdrawn in forsaking judgment) and death. (*Lectures on the Tabernacle*, pages 433 and 434.)

The overwhelming number of times that fire is mentioned in the Scriptures is specifically concerned with judgment upon ungodly idols, people, or cities, or nations, or even the earth itself. The words commonly associated with "fire" are *"punishment, torment, fury, vengeance, anger, consuming, wrath, jealousy, judgment, destruction, rebuke, purification, etc., etc."*

In addition, let it be pointed out that the altar of burnt offering was to be built exactly "three cubits high" (Exo. 38:1–7), and the substitutionary, atoning death of our Substitute was for "three days and nights." This might be significant to one looking for meaning in measurement.

Could any honest person conclude from this God-given, inspired typology that Jesus Christ went to a place of bliss, comfort and enjoyment after His physical death on the cross? To make that conclusion is to fight against the clear revelation of God. Man's natural sentimentality, though it be ever so dignified, could and should never be accepted in the place of Divine revelation.

The Day of Atonement

"And the Goat Shall Bear upon Him all Their Iniquities Into a Land of Separation"

I realize that I have given this passage our attention earlier in this book in demonstration of the afterlife in Hell. However, I believe it is necessary to repeat it here with the emphasis upon the fact that it was our Savior, the Lord Jesus Christ, Who thus suffered in Hell, bearing our sins "into the land of separation."

When one explores the sacrificial system given to the nation of Israel through the prophet Moses, it is like walking into a great art museum, passing before numerous paintings displaying the struggles and passions of the nation as manifested in their sacrificial system of blood and death, yet resulting in forgiveness, life and redemption with victories and hopes of the future. As you walk along you finally come to stand before the last grand work, a massive panoramic painting named "The great Day of Atonement" (Lev. 23:26 and 27), on which you gaze as if mesmerized in an attempt to fully comprehend the details.

Here in the book of Leviticus we enter into the sacred halls of Divine revelation portraying before us the many sacrifices which speak of the story of sinful human beings on a sin-cursed earth being reconciled to the Creator of heaven and earth. Finally in chapter 16, we stand before the most important sacrifice of Israel's sacred year calendar. Here is the sacrifice of all sacrifices. There is none other like it and there is none other of equal importance. Amazingly, here is a sacrifice which is not sacrificed! Here is a living animal which does not die and yet represents a dead animal. Here portrayed before us will be the sacrificial afterlife existence of a substitute bearing away the sins of mankind into the horrible wilderness of the dead, where it is said by certain Jewish sages, "all life is in a state of death and only death is alive." Here is the story of the primary sacrifice which has come to be called "the Scapegoat." And here is where the total story of the price paid for our redemption is spelled out in unusual detail. Let us explore those details.

On the tenth day of the seventh month of Israel's sacred year calendar, a very special High Sabbath was held. It is literally called "the Sabbath of Sabbatism" (Lev. 16:31), more commonly known as the great "Day of Atonement" (*Yom-kipper*), or simply "The Day" (*Yoma*). See Lev. 23:26. This day represented the culmination of the Levitical sacrificial system. It is also referred to as the "climax" of all purificatory sacrifices and ordinances. On this day the sins of the nation of Israel will be "atoned" for another year. This day will actually bring to a close the special sacrificial calendar of Judaism which would not open again until the spring sacrifice of the Passover Lambs, representing the beginning of another year. Furthermore, it was only on the "Day of Atonement" that the fifty year cycle of the great "Jubilee" would be announced (Lev. 25:9).

This would be the one and only time of the year that the high priest had access to the holiest of all in the tabernacle, or later, the temple (Lev. 16:2). On this day the sins of Israel would be put away and "covered," or "atonement" made for them. It clearly represents the most mysterious and yet most significant of all Israel's sacrificial services. This sacrifice will explain—by an outward visual demonstration—the deep hidden spiritual reality of how God has put away, for all eternity, all our sins by the antitypical "Scapegoat," the Lord Jesus Christ. The inspired writer of the book of Hebrews would say, "but now, once at the *climax* of the ages, He [Christ] has appeared to put away sin by the sacrifice of Himself" (literal translation, Heb. 9:26). Most certainly at this particular sacrifice, strange and unusual things took place. Only by this putting away of sins could AT-ONE-MENT with God ever be achieved. Here we will see Christ die and shed His precious blood, and yet beyond His immediate death, we will see Christ bearing the horrible guilt of sins upon His soul into a wilderness of suffering and despair where the only inhabitants are the spirits of the wicked dead, demons of Hell and *Azazel*.

No ordinary priest could officiate at this service—only the high priest. In addition, the high priest must bathe his flesh in water before adorning himself in special priestly garments for this occasion (Lev. 16:3, 4). Outside the sanctuary and throughout the land of Israel, the people would afflict their souls all day long. Not only would they be humbling themselves (Lev. 16:29 and 31) but any Jew who would not be humbling himself would be "cut off and destroyed" from the nation (23:29). The major passages of Scripture to look at are Lev. 16:1–54; 23:26–32; Exo. 30:10; Num. 29:7–11; Hebrews 9:6–12 and 9:24–28.

The sequence of events is as follows:

First, the animals to be sacrificed are chosen. For the high priest and his family separately, there must be a bullock for a sin offering. This animal, the high priest was to provide. Then the congregation would provide for themselves two male goats, looking almost like twins, according to ancient tradition. They would be the same age and size and color. These would be presented to the high priest who would take them (Lev. 16:3 and 5, 6). In addition, they would produce a ram for a burnt offering.

Second, the focus will concern the two goats. They would be presented together before the Lord (Lev.16:7) at the doorway of the Tent of Meeting. These two goats will represent ONE sacrificial offering. This is important to remember. There is no disputing this by any commentator of whom I know, be he Jewish or Christian. Here an interesting event takes place. There are two lots to be cast on behalf of these goats. It will be the means by which each of the goats will be selected for its particular assignment in this sacrifice (Lev.16:8). Though this is regarded as just one sacrifice, yet two goats are needed in order to depict the whole picture of events which take place regarding the disposal of the nation's sins. We might remember that in the ritual service regarding the cleansing of the leper, two birds were selected for that sacrifice (Lev. 14:1–9). Only one bird is slain, and the second bird is then dipped into the blood of the first bird and set free to fly away. In a very simple and beautiful way, it is the picture of both the death of Christ for cleansing, and then the resurrection of the Lord Jesus Christ as the basis for giving new life. In the case of these two goats, one will die and the other will be taken away, but NOT into a blissful future of freedom. Therefore the second goat will not be depicting resurrection.

Third, let us take note of the lots that are cast. The text says that one lot is for "Jehovah" and the other lot is for "Azazel" (not 'scapegoat,' as later designated). The literal Hebrew is *AZ* (goat) and *AZEL* (departure). The meaning is—*the goat of departure*. However, most Lexical works point out that the Hebrew word *Azazel* stands in opposition to the name of Jehovah. That can only mean that the word is now personified and represents or stands for another person. Furthermore, since this goat will depart into "a land not inhabited," or "the wilderness desolation" from which they will make sure it will never return, *Azazel* came to represent a goat demon (Lev. 17:7) or evil spirit or Satan himself. Throughout the Scriptures, evil things (even demons) are said to occupy the desolate wilderness (Isa. 13:21; 34:14; Matt. 12:43; Lk. 8:27; 11:24; and Rev. 18:2). The wilderness itself represented all that is "great and terrible" (Deut. 1:19; 8:15 and Jer. 2:6). For this reason, to this very day, the goat head has come to represent a symbol of Satan. From one of the oldest books of the Pseudepigrapha (the book of Enoch), Azazel was a halfgoat and halfSatan. This ancient Jewish tradition was also found in the Dead Sea Scrolls. In the Pesher (commentary), Azazel was the goat-headed Satan. So we can see that the tradition of associating this goat as being designated for Satan existed even before the time of Christ. In the middle ages of the Christian era, up to and beyond the 15th century, Jewish commentary depicted this goat as being offered to Satan in the wilderness. Thus, from both a Biblical and traditional perspective, the understanding of this goat being assigned for Azazel meant it would be sent to the place where Satan or his demons were to reside, and that is Hell. The casting of lots is described in verses 8–10 of Lev. 16.

Fourth, The high priest would slaughter the bullock of the sin offering for himself and his own household (v. 11).

Fifth, the high priest would prepare a fire pan of hot coals from off the sacrificial altar and also finely ground incense. With these two items he would then make his first trip inside the holy place, and beyond the veil into the most holy place, where the ark of the covenant and the mercy seat were with the two cherubim over the top. There he would set the fire pan down before the ark and place the incense upon the hot coals to give off a fragrant odor, so that he would not die in that most holy place before God (vs. 12, 13).

Sixth, the priest would make a second trip inside the most holy place with the blood of the bullock for himself and his family and sprinkle it before the ark and on the mercy seat (v. 14).

<u>Seventh,</u> they would now slaughter the goat selected for Jehovah which represented the whole congregation of Israel. For the third time the high priest would enter the most holy place and sprinkle the blood of the goat upon the mercy seat on behalf of the people (vs. 15–17). No one else was allowed within the holy place while the high priest was doing this service.

<u>Eighth,</u> the high priest would then take both the blood of the bullock and that of the goat and sprinkle the altar for burnt offerings, and anoint the horns of the altar with the blood (vs. 18, 19).

<u>Ninth,</u> we come to the offering of the live goat set aside for Azazel (vs. 20–22). The text says Aaron *"shall offer the live goat"* (v. 20). However, the goat is not to be sacrificed. According to Jewish tradition when the lots were cast, a scarlet cord was tied upon the horn of the goat for Azazel and a scarlet cord was placed around the neck of the goat to actually be slaughtered, so that the function of each of the goats would be established. Now the high priest would go up to the goat with the scarlet cord upon his horn and place *"both his hands upon the head of the live goat, and confess over it all the iniquities of the children of Israel, and all their transgressions, concerning all their sins, putting them on the head of the goat"* (v. 21). Now normally this would have been done with the goat which was slaughtered. However, since there are two goats in this singular sacrificial offering, it is the second of the two which actually has the sins of the people placed upon it, for this will depict the actual transporting of the sins of the people into the final place of judgment. This goat will *"bear upon him all their iniquities to a solitary land"* (v. 22). And by divine application we can hear the words of Isaiah the prophet say, *"And the LORD has laid on Him* [Jesus Christ] *the iniquity of us all"* (Isa. 53:6).

<u>Tenth,</u> the trek of the second goat was most solemn. Bearing the condemnation of all the sins of Israel upon it, it was led by a strong man (vs. 21, 22) out into the wilderness where it would be abandoned to certain oblivion. In later years the goat was taken out of Jerusalem into the Judean wilderness, totally away from any

forms of life or food or water and into the heat and the desolation of canyons and cliffs. When the goat was thought to be thoroughly lost, the strong man would release the goat and slip away to abandon the goat to a certain, gradual death of thirst. Sometimes they would even push the goat over a cliff. Different authors have written of the sadness and desolation of this trek into this abysmal land.

However the most vivid example was made not too many years ago by the modernistic preacher, Bishop Pike, of the Episcopal Church. He thought he would try personally to find evidences of "the Historical Jesus," because he was not satisfied with the Christ of the Bible. Amazing as it may seem, he came to this same Judean wilderness to try to find some evidence the archaeologists might have overlooked. He became lost in that wilderness and could not find his way out. The search parties finally found his body below a precipice. He had died of thirst. It was reported that his tongue was said to have swollen to almost fill his whole mouth. How sad it is that he did not trust in the antitypical "scapegoat," the Lord Jesus Christ.

The first goat which was actually sacrificed represents the sub-stitutionary death of Jesus Christ as the world's sin offering. This is what was openly seen by the world looking on. The second goat, being a continuation of the sacrifice of the first goat, actually had all the sins placed upon it and bore this great burden into a hellish place of oblivion. This is the portrayal of what happened to Jesus Christ our substitute, after His physical death and during His three day sojourn in Hell. All the while this is happening, the congregation of Israel remained in mourning, afflicting their souls.

Finally, the "scapegoat" was so unclean that each who touched it, especially the man who took it into the wilderness, must totally bathe himself and his garments in water for purification before he could ever be received back into the camp of Israel (vs. 24, 26, 28). In finality, let us remember that both goats represent the divine plan whereby sin is put away. The one that dies does not suffice. There are two aspects of the atonement for sin—death, and the bearing away of sins in judgment. Christ died as the antitypical sin offering, and then He bore away our sins as the antitypical "scapegoat," bearing that awful load into Hell until the court of heaven was satisfied.

Thus, Almighty God has provided for us a visual representation of all that Christ has done in His substitutionary sacrifice for our sins. When Christ died some two thousand years ago, all that the people could see was His crucifixion on the cross. What happened afterwards as to the disposition of Christ's soul in Hell could not be seen by anyone except God. Here in this typology we have a visual manifestation of what happened.

The Type of Joseph

It has been well-known by Bible believing teachers that there were many details in the life of Joseph which prefigured the life of the Lord Jesus Christ. In fact, the Jewish people came to look forward to *Messiah ben Joseph* (Messiah, the son of Joseph). The Jewish sages taught Israel this because they, themselves, recognized that Joseph became a great ruler over his own people, and so it would be true of the Messiah. However, the significance of Joseph's life was that it really came in two stages. There was his first appearance before his brethren wherein he was rejected and then much later, his second appearance to his brethren in a time of great trial wherein he did rule over them and deliver them in a time of worldwide famine. Of interest to us here is his rejection at his first presentation before his brethren.

Joseph was the favored son of Jacob. His coat of many colors was indeed a princely garment. His brothers became envious of him. Joseph faithfully exposed the sins of his brethren which brought more animosity toward him. When he told his family his dreams of ruling over them, they briskly responded—"Shalt thou indeed rule over us?" (Gen. 37:8). Finally his brethren rejected him, even conspiring to kill him. They cast him into a pit, dipped his coat into the blood of a goat and returned this coat to Jacob as evidence of his death (37:20, 24, 27, 31). Secretly, they sold him to the Gentiles (37:36).

Of interest to us is this pit into which Joseph was cast. The text says, *"Then they took him and cast him into a pit. And the pit was empty: there was no water in it"* (37:24). In addition, when Jacob was shown the evidence that Joseph was dead, he *"refused to be comforted, and he said, 'For I shall go down into Sheol to my son in mourning.' Thus his father wept for him"* (37:35). So the "Pit," once again in Scripture, became a picture of the pit of Sheol, as with the Psalmist and with the prophet Jonah. Moreover, I believe that Joseph actually spent the equivalent of three days in that pit. Why do I believe that? Watch what Joseph did with his brethren when they first met him in Egypt, not recognizing him (Gen. 42:17–24)—

> *So he* [Joseph] *put them all together in prison for three days.* Then Joseph said to them [speaking through an interpreter] *the third day, 'Do this and live, for I fear God: . . .'* Then they [Joseph's brothers] *said to one another,* [not realizing that Joseph understood them] *'We are truly guilty concerning our brother, for we saw the **anguish of his soul*** [while he was in that **pit**] *when he pleaded with us, and we would not hear; therefore this distress* [their three days in prison] *has come upon us.' And Reuben answered them, saying, 'Did not I speak to you, saying, "Do not sin against the boy;" and you would not listen? Therefore behold, his blood is now required of us.' But they did not know that Joseph understood them, . . . And he* [Joseph] *turned himself away from them and wept. . . .*

So it is that their three days in a prison brought back to their minds what they had done to Joseph when they rejected him and cast him into the pit from which he had pled with them, but they would not hear. So I say again, Joseph, as a type of Christ, was cast into a pit, as if it were Sheol itself, possibly for three days and nights. *And most obvious of all—it was not pleasant in that pit!*

The Type of Jeremiah

When the Lord Jesus Christ asked His disciples the question "Who do people say that the Son of Man is?" (Matt. 16:13, 14), they responded that at least a segment of the people thought He was "Jeremiah." We might wonder why Jeremiah's name would come up in relation to the identity of Jesus Christ. The answer I believe is clear that the life of Jeremiah, who so severely rebuked the nation of Israel and in return was persecuted so harshly, prefigured that of the Messiah. In this regard there are many ways in which Jeremiah prefigured Christ.

Jeremiah was called "The Weeping Prophet" because of his weeping over the calamities which would befall Israel in light of their rejection of God's Word (Lam. 3:48); Jesus Christ, likewise "wept over Jerusalem" because of the calamities that would soon befall her in light of her rejection of the Word of God (Luke 19:41). Jeremiah had great "sorrow" because of Israel's rebellion and persecution towards him (Lam. 1:12); Jesus Christ, likewise, was spoken of as "A Man of Sorrows and acquainted with grief" (Isa. 53:3). Jeremiah spoke of himself "like a gentle lamb led to the slaughter" (Jer. 11:19); Jesus Christ was "like a lamb led to the slaughter" (Isa. 53:7). Jeremiah looked upon Israel as "the flock of the Lord which had been taken captive . . . and scattered into exile" (Jer. 13:17, 24); the Lord Jesus Christ also looked upon Israel as "scattered sheep" (Matt. 9:36 and Mark 14:27). The enemies of Jeremiah were constantly "watching for his fall . . . so that they could denounce him" (Jer. 20:10); so, likewise, the enemies of Jesus Christ were always "seeking to catch Him . . . so that they might accuse Him" (Luke 11:54). Jeremiah had the "sentence of death" placed upon him (Jer. 26:11 and 38:4); the Lord Jesus Christ had the sentence of "death" placed upon Him (Matt. 26:65, 66). Jeremiah assured the leaders of Israel that they would "bring innocent blood upon themselves" (Jer. 26:15); "His blood be upon us, . . ." was the haughty response of the leaders of Israel when they rejected the Lord Jesus Christ (Matt. 27:25). And in finality Jeremiah "cried out from the lowest pit . . . as a man who has seen affliction by the rod of His wrath" (Lam. 3:55 and 3:1); this typifies Christ in the Pit of Sheol.

The punishment that Jeremiah suffered was to be taken into the dungeon and lowered into a deep pit where there was only darkness and loneliness—no food, no water, only the mire into which he sank (Jer. 38:6). The horrors of that pit prompted the third chapter of Lamentations. The many times "the Pit" has been associated with Sheol or Hell in the Bible leaves no room to doubt its significance— Numbers 16:30, 33; Isa.14:15; 24:22; Ezek. 26:20; 31:14–18; 32:18–30; Rev. 9:1, 2, 11; 11:7; 17:8 and 20:1, 3. In addition, there are the many times we have already seen the Pit directly associated with the suffering of Christ after His death on the cross—Jonah 2:6; Psalm 40:2; 69:2, 15; 88:4, 6; Gen. 37:24 and now Lam. 3:55. All this leaves no room to doubt its significance once again. After His death, Christ descended into Hell, the lowest and most detestable pit of all. And He remained there for three days and nights.

SUMMARY —

The Total Story

As I said at the beginning of this particular study, there are many passages of Scripture which summarize the whole substitutionary, sacrificial work for our redemption in terms of what was obvious to man—the cross work of Jesus Christ. By no means whatsoever was this meant to be the whole story of our redemption. It served as the focal point of the gospel, but not the total story of the gospel. In light of all the various passages which we have been studying, no Bible believer who is endeavoring to please the Lord of his salvation will deny that there was much more done in God's plan of redeeming sinners than Christ's immediate death on the cross.

The total inspired story is also told by—

Jonah,
"Out of the belly of Sheol I cried"

The Psalmist,
"You have laid Me in the lowest pit"
"The sorrows [cords] of Sheol surrounded Me"
"He also brought Me up out of a horrible pit"

Christ,
"I have a baptism to be baptized with"

Isaac,
"My father . . . behold, here is the fire!"

The Sacrifices,
"The burnt sacrifice . . . upon the altar of burnt offerings"

The Scapegoat,
"And the goat shall bear upon him all their iniquities
into a land of separation"

Joseph,
"And they cast him into a pit . . .
we saw the anguish of his soul"

Jeremiah,
"Cried out from the lowest pit . . .
as a man who has seen affliction
by the rod of His wrath"

Peter,
"Whom God raised up, having loosed the agony of death"

Paul,
"If Christ be not raised, you are yet in your sins"

This last statement by the apostle Paul says in effect, *"until the resurrection of Christ we are still in our sins!"* And if I am "still in my sins" until the resurrection of Christ, then it follows that Christ is still in my sins as well! Yes, Christ was in my sins the remainder of the first day, all that night, all of the next day and night, and all of the third day and night—until He was gloriously raised from the *"agony of death"* (Acts 2:24 and 1 Cor. 15:17).

CHAPTER EIGHTEEN

OBJECTIONS ANSWERED

The following passages of Scripture have been put forward in opposition to the position presented in this Bible study that Christ's death continued in agony for three days and nights in Hell. In other words, the following arguments are designed to contend that the total payment for sins was obtained at the time Christ expired on the cross and there was no further suffering. We must give an honest examination of these arguments and Scriptures presented. First we will present the Scriptures used with the argument and then we will present the answer.

Objection No. 1

We am going to give all the passages used that fall into the same category of reference to the blood of Christ being spilt on the cross for our redemption.

Matt. 26:28 *"For this is my blood . . . shed for many for the remission of sins."*
Acts 20:28 *". . . purchased with His own blood."*
Rom. 3:25 *". . . propitiation through faith in His blood."*
Rom. 5:9 *". . . justified by His blood."*
Eph. 1:7 *". . . redemption through His blood."*
Eph. 2:13 *". . . made nigh by the blood of Christ."*

Col. 1:14 *". . . redemption through His blood."*
Col. 1:20 *". . . made peace through the blood of His cross."*
Heb. 9:12 *". . . by His own blood . . . obtained eternal redemption."*
Heb. 9:14 *". . . the blood of Christ . . . purge your conscience. . . ."*
Heb. 9:22 *". . . without the shedding of blood is no redemption."*
1 Pet. 1:18, 19 *". . . redeemed . . . with the precious blood of Christ."*
1 John 1:7 *". . . the blood of Christ cleanses us from all sins."*
Rev. 1:5 *". . . washed us from our sins in His own blood."*
Rev. 5:9 *". . . redeemed us to God by Thy blood."*
Rev. 7:14 *". . . washed robes . . . in the blood of the Lamb."*

> ➤ Now the argument goes like this: "Christ's blood was shed on the cross so that our sins were remitted and paid for in completion at that moment, and not with a three day installment needed to complete the payment."

ANSWER: On the one hand, we could answer this very quickly and say that the blood of Christ simply represents Christ's LIFE which was given as the substitute for our sins. Furthermore, it is an indisputable fact that this LIFE was not "taken up again" by Christ until after three days and nights had transpired. Consequently, the judgment against our sins could not have been paid until the restoration of that LIFE which guaranteed its payment. Therefore all these Scriptural statements should be recognized as speaking metaphorically of a spiritual transaction which demanded the payment of a LIFE—the only LIFE which could stand as a substitute for the sins of the whole world was the LIFE (blood) of the Divine Son of God, the Lord Jesus Christ. The giving of that LIFE lasted for three days and nights, until the court of heaven was satisfied!

For a more complete explanation, let us walk through this beautiful truth more slowly. The last few passages (Rev. 1:5 and 7:14) illustrate the fact that these passages of Scripture should not be taken in a literal, physical sense. No one is physically "washed in the blood of Christ." If this was all that these passages were talking about, then all you would have is a physical cleansing and a physical salvation. But no one in his right mind believes that there is a literal washing in the blood of Christ. So we understand that these passages about cleansing through the blood of Christ are metaphors. The physical blood of Jesus Christ which was spilt at Calvary represents the total LIFE which was given for the actual remission of sins. The separation of Jesus Christ from God the Father had already taken place before the literal blood of Jesus Christ was spilt. The soldier ran the spear into Christ's side to guarantee that Christ was dead. The blood and water came forth, therefore, as merely the *token* of the physical death of Christ—His LIFE had now been given. So our salvation is often spoken of in terms of the metaphor, "*Christ shed His blood for our sins.*" Our sins were imputed to Christ and now His LIFE, contaminated by our sins, was placed under condemnation and judgment so as to effect a cleansing of our souls. This is the sense in which we are "washed by the blood of Christ."

So Christ actually died as to His relationship with the Father when the sins of the world were placed upon Him. The sun was darkened at high noon and Christ cried out *"My God, My God, why hast Thou forsaken Me?"* This is the indicator that Christ had been "separated" (died spiritually) in His relationship to the Father. Christ's *spiritual LIFE* in relationship to the Father had terminated. The sins of the world had been placed upon Him and He had "become sin for us."

Christ's physical life was later terminated (probably two or three hours later) when he yielded up His spirit for God's disposition. That is when Christ's spirit separated from His body and He experienced physical death.

Christ's total separation (death), both spiritually and bodily, is the basis for our redemption. That redemption consists of two aspects. *First,* as a result of our substitute bearing our spiritual death, all those who believe in Him are counted as dead and condemned spiritually in Christ's death. The judgment against our sins was being paid for and we will not go to Hell in an eternal spiritual separation from God as a result. However, we only receive spiritual regeneration and life when Christ was raised from the dead. This is when we were raised spiritually "with Christ to walk in newness of life." This also means that Christ's spiritual life was not unburdened from our sins until the time of His ascension from Hell and His resurrection from the dead. *Secondly,* as a result of our substitute bearing our physical death and being raised from the dead, we are guaranteed a physical resurrection as a part of our redemption. That physical resurrection is yet to come.

The Scriptures which we have been studying abundantly testify to the fact that the spirit or soul of Jesus Christ was not delivered from the suffering of death (separation) until three days and nights had transpired in Sheol. In addition, for three days and nights the physical body of Christ lay inactive and silent in a borrowed tomb. There was no life in that body, and much of the blood was still in that body. Only a token part of Christ's blood had been spilt. So, we speak of Christ's spiritual death, or separation from the Father, at the time the sins of the world were laid upon Him. And then the physical death of Christ took place at the moment His spirit departed from His body. It was not until the resurrection of Christ that His total death for sins had terminated and the concluding payment for our sins was met! Otherwise, "If Christ be not raised, we are yet in our sins" (1 Cor. 15:17).

Please remember that if the physical shedding of blood is the real atonement, then that atonement is only physical. This can never be! Christ's spiritual death did not come as a result or consequence of His physical death. On the contrary, just the opposite is true. Christ's physical death came as a result of His earlier spiritual death and separation from God. And then Christ yielded up His spirit to God's disposition in Sheol. The real atonement is first of all spiritual, not physical. 2 Cor. 4:18 is a reminder to us—". . . we do not look at the things which are seen, but at the things which are not seen. For the things which are seen are temporary, but the things which are not seen are eternal."

Objection **No. 2**

Again, we are going to present a group of passages that speak of the crucifixion of Christ for our sins.

Rom. 6:6 ". . . *the old man is crucified with Him.*"
1 Cor. 1:17,18 ". . . *lest the cross of Christ should be made of no effect.*"

341

1 Cor. 15:3,4 *". . . Christ died for our sins. . . ."*
Gal. 3:13 *"Christ . . . was made a curse . . . hanged on a tree."*
Gal. 6:14 *". . . glory, save in the cross. . . ."*
Eph. 2:16 *". . . reconciled by the cross, . . ."*
Philip. 2:8 *". . . death on the cross."*
Col. 2:14 *". . . nailing it to the cross."*
Heb. 9:26 *". . . put away sin by the sacrifice of Himself."*
Heb. 10:10 *". . . sanctified through the offering of the body of Jesus Christ. . . ."*
Heb. 12:2 *". . . endured the cross, . . ."*
1 Pet. 2:24 *". . . Who bore our sins in His own body on the tree."*

> ➢ Now the argument is basically the same as before. "Christ's death on the cross paid for our sins and not His suffering for some three days and nights."

ANSWER: The answer is basically the same as before. No one disputes the fact that Christ died for our sins on the cross. The question is, HOW LONG DID THAT DEATH LAST? Was it a fraction of a second? Was if fifteen minutes or an hour? Or did it last, as the Scriptures clearly say, for three days and nights, until His resurrection from the dead? When did Christ revive from that death? And when was new LIFE granted to the repentant believer so identified with Christ? Notice, please, the following Scriptures:

Romans 5:10 *"We are saved **by His LIFE!**"*
Romans 6:4–13 *". . . that just as Christ was **raised from the dead** by the glory of the Father, even so we also should walk **in newness of LIFE**"* (v. 4).
"For if we have been united together in the likeness of His death [for 3 days], *certainly we also shall be **in the likeness of His resurrection**"* (v. 5).
"Knowing this, that our old man was crucified with Him, that the body of sin might be done away with, that we should no longer be slaves of sin" (v. 6).
"For he who has died [for three days] *has been freed from sin"* (v. 7).

"Now if we died [for three days] *with Christ, we believe that we shall also **LIVE with Him**"* (v. 8).

*" Knowing that Christ, **having been raised from the dead**, dies no more. Death no longer has dominion over Him"* (v. 9).

"For the death [three days] *that He died, He died to sin once for all; but the **LIFE** that He lives, He **LIVES** unto God"* (v. 10).

*"Likewise you also, reckon yourselves to be dead indeed to sin, **but ALIVE to God in Christ Jesus our Lord**"* (v. 11).

*"...present yourselves to God **as being ALIVE from the dead**"* (v. 13).

Now here are passages (Rom. 5:10 and 6:4–13) which many times stress the fact that we don't get our NEW LIFE in Christ until the resurrection of Christ from the DEAD! It was NOT at the moment Christ expired on the cross that either Christ got new life or that the believer gets new life. The imparting of our new spiritual life takes place in conjunction with the resurrection of Christ from the dead. Therefore, and consequently, the death of Jesus Christ for our sins was a *three day death*—till the court of heaven was satisfied!

Other passages will say the same thing, such as Colossians 2:12, ". . . raised with Him [Christ], through the faith in the working of God, Who raised Him from the dead." The Scripture says Christ was not "PERFECTED until the third day" (Luke 13:32).

The startling corollary emerges that, if after those three days and nights in Sheol Christ was not resurrected from the dead, Christ would still be in Sheol, *and we would still be in our sins*. We got out of our sins precisely when Christ got out of SHEOL! We are "perfected" in the sight of God WHEN Christ was perfected. Several times in the Hebrew Scriptures it is indicated that purification was not obtained until a "three day" time period had elapsed—Exo. 3:18; 5:3; 8:27; Exo. 19:10, 11 and 14, 15; Esther 4:16; Hos. 6:1, 2. Some of the sacrificial offerings were taken as food to be eaten the first and second day, but not on the third day, which was typical of resurrection (Lev. 7:17, 18; 19:6, 7). Therefore we must realize that the purging of our sins process was not completed until the third day in the reckoning of Almighty God.

Objection No. 3

The passage—Luke 23:43, "Today shalt thou be with Me in Paradise."

ANSWER: Earlier in this study we actually answered this objection (see again pages 188 and 189). This passage is most often given as the evidence that when Christ died He went into the Paradise section of Hell. No doubt the thief could rejoice in the reality of his safety and comfort in Christ in Paradise after his death. However, we cautioned the student of the Scriptures to not allow this truth to blot out the possibility of Christ also being in a place of suffering as manifested in such an abundance of other passages as has been demonstrated. We pointed out that Christ said similar things in other cases which we need to compare.

For instance, the fundamental truth which Christ gave to His own apostles that after His death and ascension into heaven He would yet "*manifest*" Himself to them, be "*in*" them and "*with*" them (John 14: 20–23) did not nullify the fact that as to His actual residence He would be in heaven at the "right hand" of His father. Both are obviously true. We should not select one truth to wipe out the other truth. We accept both as factual and we should accept the same on this subject. It is true that the thief was with Christ in Paradise, yet at the very same time Christ was actually suffering in Hell.

In a similar way, Christ assured believers that "where two are three are gathered together in His name, there *He would be in the midst of them*" (Matt. 18:20). Christ gave this as being true throughout this whole age. Do we quote this truth as meaning that Christ is not in heaven at the right hand of the Father as many other passages state? No, of course not! Neither does the passage in Luke contradict all the other truths given in this Biblical study as to the sufferings of Christ in Hell.

Objection No. 4

Matt. 27:51, "And, behold, the veil of the temple was torn in two from top to bottom; and the earth quaked, and the rocks were split."

➢ The argument is, "because of Christ's sacrifice on the cross, the temple veil was rent, indicating access to God was now (at the very time Christ died) available. Therefore, the believer can have 'boldness to enter into the holiest by the blood of Jesus' (Heb. 10:19, 20) right then."

ANSWER: Let us remember that no matter how beautiful this typology is, and there is no denying its implication regarding our salvation, nevertheless, in the actual fulfillment of the typology, Christ did not enter into the heavenly temple with His own blood (to fulfill the typology) until after His resurrection from the dead—Heb. 9:24. Many Bible teachers believe that this took place at an earlier ascension of Christ not long after His resurrection. Christ's final ascension into heaven was not for another 40 days.

Objection No. 5

Matt. 27:52 says that at the time Christ died, there was an earthquake—"And the graves were opened; and many bodies of the saints who slept arose."

➢ The argument is, "this would not have happened at the time Christ died on the cross if our sins had not been completely paid for."

ANSWER: It is true that at the time Christ died on the cross there was a great earthquake and the graves were opened. But the rest of the verse makes it clear that "many bodies of the saints who slept arose and came out of the graves—AFTER HIS RESURRECTION." This actually verifies the truth which we are stating in this study, that it was not until Christ was liberated from the sufferings of death that the atonement for our salvation was completed and guaranteed.

Objection No. 6

Luke 23:46 "Father, into Thy hands I commit My spirit."

> ➤ The argument is, "that at this moment of the actual point of Christ's physical death, the fellowship between the Father and the Son had been restored, and therefore, the payment for sins had been completed." It is also argued that "this is similar to Stephen in Acts 7:59 saying, 'Lord Jesus, receive my spirit.' Stephen went right into God's presence."

ANSWER: This does not at all mean that Christ's fellowship with the Father was restored and that He went right into the presence of God as had Stephen. This is a mere conjecture which cannot be established beyond someone's sentimental feelings. This passage in Luke tells us that at the point of death, Christ was simply releasing His spirit for the disposition by God the Father Who sent His (Christ's) spirit into Sheol as we all agree.

Furthermore, this is a similar statement as that which Christ made while He was suffering in the garden of Gethsemane when He prayed, "O My Father, if it be possible, let this cup pass from Me; nevertheless, not as I will, but as You will" (Matt. 26:39). This statement of Christ by no means meant that Christ was not going to suffer any longer, or that His suffering would be terminated shortly. It simply meant that Christ was resigned to do the will of God.

The case of Stephen was just the opposite. We know that his spirit went immediately into heaven at the point of his death.

Objection No. 7

John 12:32 "And I, if I be lifted up from the earth, will draw all men unto Me."

➢ The argument is simply made that Christ's dying on the cross would draw all men to Him only if the payment for sins was completed on the cross and not somewhere else.

ANSWER: This passage only indicates that Christ's cross work was to be used of God as the drawing factor for lost mankind. This is what mankind could visually see as the physical manifestation of Christ's substitutionary death for the sins of the world. It represents the gospel in a "nutshell," so as to speak. It tells us in capsule form the story of Christ's unique death. It points to the only way to heaven. It was not designed to tell us all the details of all Christ's suffering for sin.

Objection No. 8

John 19:28 Toward the end Jesus said ". . . all things were now accomplished."

➢ The argument is, "The most difficult part (Christ being God-forsaken) was now accomplished, and Christ was near to the point of physical death. At this point He could say the penalty paid for our sins was now accomplished."

ANSWER: Notice please that similar statements were made by Christ throughout the gospel of John account, which indicate something was accomplished, but actually not at the very instant Christ made the statement—

John 4:23 "The hour is coming AND NOW IS, when true worshipers will. . . ."
John 12:27 ". . . Father, SAVE ME FROM THIS HOUR?. . ."
John 12:31 "NOW IS THE JUDGMENT OF THIS WORLD; . . ."
John 16:32 "Indeed, the hour is coming, YES, HAS NOW COME, . . ."
John 17:11 "NOW I AM NO LONGER IN THE WORLD, . . ."

John 19:28 "Jesus, knowing that ALL THINGS WERE NOW ACCOMPLISHED, . . ."

When one looks at the context of each one of these statements he will recognize that they fall into the category of a figure of speech. A statement is made of an action, or a circumstance, which has the *potential of effecting a condition* as if that condition had happened right then. In reality, we are to understand that the *potential* was then present, but the actual event was only near at hand, and had not yet actually happened.

For instance, when Christ said "the hour . . . NOW IS when true worshipers will (do such and such)," did He mean it had actually happened at that precise moment? Of course not. He meant the time was imminent and very near!

When He said, "save me from this HOUR," did He mean the actual hour of His death was there? Of course not. He meant it was then imminent.

When He said, "Now is the judgment of this world" did He mean that at that very moment it had arrived? Of course not! It was several days yet before the cross.

When He said, "The HOUR is coming, yes, has NOW come . . . ." did He mean at that instant the apostles would be scattered (see the context)? No! It was close, yet several hours away.

When He said, "Now I am no longer in the world," was He, as of that very moment, no longer in the world? No! It would be the next day before He would die and forty days later before He would finally ascend into heaven.

And when He said ". . . ALL things were NOW accomplished," did He mean as of that moment there was *nothing else to be accomplished?* Of course not. The potential was accomplished, but the execution of that potential would take another three days and three nights, and the triumphant resurrection from the total state of death.

Objection No. 9

John 19:30 Jesus said "IT IS FINISHED."

➤ The argument goes like this, "In making this statement Christ signified that the payment for our sins was finished as He gave up the ghost. There was nothing more to do. It was all done. The Greek word signifies 'Paid in Full'; therefore, there was no more payment to be made."

ANSWER: The answer is similar to number **8** above. The *full potential* of Christ's sustitutionary death on our behalf is certainly summed up in the words "*it is finished.*" In addition to signifying 'paid in full,' the Greek word is in the perfect tense and could be literally translated "It has been finished." This has long been a beautiful truth about the substitutionary death of Christ for our sins. His death for us fully satisfies the judgment of the court in heaven against us. It is as if at that moment Christ appeared before the judgment bar of God, with His body torn and bleeding, and said, "I pay in full the penalty for sins by My substitutionary DEATH." Christ uttered this truth just before He yielded up His spirit in death.

However, as we all should know, the execution of that *potential* was a long way from being fulfilled. "IT IS FINISHED" has a three day duration to it because the *DEATH* that "finished" and "paid in full" all that was against us **lasted that long**! Therefore, the apostle Peter was inspired to say, "And God raised Him up again, putting an end to the AGONY OF DEATH, . . ." (Acts. 2:24, NASB). And furthermore, as many other Scriptures illustrate, "If Christ be not raised, *you are yet in your sins.*" In the early Sunday morning hours, after being in Sheol for three days and nights, if Christ's spirit had not been reunited with His body and come out of that tomb—we would all still be "in our sins" and Christ would still be in Hell.

The substitutionary DEATH that Jesus Christ died in our place was not "finished," in the sense of *total execution*, until His **glorious resurrection**.

IN CONCLUSION

⚜

At the beginning of this book, in the INTRODUCTION, and in response to the uncertainty expressed by the poem, *Hymns for Infant Minds*, that ". . . none was e'er sent back to tell the joys of heaven, or pains of hell," I stated that contrary to infidel assertions there was such a man—none other than Jesus Christ the Lord!

This was the Man Who at His birth was "wrapped in swaddling clothes, and laid in a manger" (Luke 2:7). Yes, this was the Man Who in humbleness and simplicity came to identify Himself with all humanity. As we saw in this study, this was also the Man Who explained to us the spiritual physiology of man. In addition, for the sake of all those who stubbornly deny the essential spiritual nature of man, He took us right inside the heart and soul of man to see the real moral sickness and diseases under which mankind labors. Furthermore, He also exposed the religious hypocrisies of men, often held in high esteem, as no one else in all of history, whether the infidel critic, the agnostic or prophet. Yet, at the very same time, as the "*good* Physician" (Luke 4:23), He thoroughly explained the remedy for all man's ills. He further laid before all the blessings of *immortality*, both spiritual life now, and physical life at the resurrection of the bodies. Yes, this is the Man Who walked the dusty trails in the heartland of this earth, calling upon all mankind with words which have never lost their meaning and comfort—

Come unto Me, all you who labor and are heavy laden,
and I will give you rest. Take My yoke upon you
and learn of Me, for I am gentle and lowly in heart,

and you will find rest for your souls. For My yoke
is easy and My burden is light (Matt. 11:28–30).

To all those who have responded with a genuine and submissive
"yes" to this call, He instantly would say, "Go in peace, thy faith has
saved you" (Luke 7:50).

Finally, at that climactic moment of His earthly sojourn, He
allowed Himself to be silhouetted against the skyline of history—
crucified—bearing in His own sinless person the horrible stain of
the guilt and penalty for all the sins of all the world of all the ages.

And then, as we learned in the last chapter of this book, by
gathering from a vast assortment of Scriptural evidences, Christ's
spirit was released into the hands of God and He was disposed into
that deepest of all subterranean chambers, called *Hades* in the Greek
or *Sheol* in the Hebrew. He "descended" not, as is often stated by
shortsighted and soulish teachers, into the temporary residence of
"Paradise" for the righteous, but rather to that chamber of "destruction" originally designed for the master deceiver, himself—Satan
(Matt. 25:41). There, as the antitypical "scapegoat" which was
designated "for Azazel" (the Devil, Lev. 16:8 and 21), He endured
three days and three nights in the wilderness and anguish of Hell
until, as is expressed in Isaiah 53, the court of Heaven was satisfied
with His personal payment for sins—

> . . . *Yet it pleased the LORD to bruise Him;*
> *He has put Him to grief, when You make His soul*
>   *an offering for sin,*
> *He shall see His seed, He shall prolong His days,*
> *and the pleasure of the LORD shall prosper in His hand,*
> **HE** [God the Father] **SHALL SEE THE LABOR**
>   **OF HIS SOUL, AND BE SATISFIED.** . . .
> (Isaiah 53:10, 11).

That Jesus Christ went into Hell is historically believed by
most all Christendom because of clearly specified and undeniable
statements—

Matthew 12:40; 16:4 and Luke 11:30—Jonah 2:2
Acts 2:31—Psalm 16:10
Ephesians 4:8–10—Psalm 68:18
Romans 10:6, 7—Deuteronomy 30:12–14

That this Hell into which Christ descended was specified, as well as prefigured, in the Hebrew Scriptures as a place of suffering and pain, is likewise very plainly and consistently given. Here are the primary examples I have given—

by Isaac, (Genesis 22:7)
"My Father . . . behold, here is the fire! . . ."

by Joseph, (Genesis 37:24 and 42:17–24)
"And they cast him into a pit . . . we saw the anguish of his soul."

by the Scapegoat, (Leviticus 16:22)
"And the goat shall bear upon him all their iniquities into a land of separation."

by the Psalmist, (Psalm 88:6, 7)
"You have laid Me in the lowest Pit, . . .
Your wrath lies heavy upon me,
You have afflicted me with all Your waves."

by Jonah,(Jonah 2:2)
". . . Out of the belly of Sheol I cried."

By Jeremiah, (Jeremiah 38:6–13, Lamentations 3:1 and 55)
"I am a man who has seen affliction by the rod of His wrath.
I called upon Your Name, O LORD, from the Lowest Pit."

—And then there was the glorious Resurrection—

when Peter says (Acts 2:23, 24 and 31, 32),

... Him, being delivered by the determined purpose and foreknowledge of God, you have taken by lawless hands, have crucified, and put to death; Whom God raised up,

having loosed the agony of death, ...

he, foreseeing this, spoke concerning the resurrection of Christ,

that His soul was not left in Hades,

nor did His flesh see corruption. This Jesus God has raised up, of Whom we are all witnesses.

On the top of Mars Hill in Athens, Greece, and before the Gentile world of wise philosophers, the apostle Paul would *IN CONCLUSION* warn —

*Truly, these times of ignorance God has overlooked, but now commands all men everywhere to repent, because He has appointed **a Day** on which He will judge the world in righteousness by the Man Whom He has ordained. He has given assurance of this to all by raising Him* [Jesus Christ] *from the dead.*
(Acts 17: 30, 31.)

—THE END—

SCRIPTURE INDEX

HEBREW SCRIPTURES

Genesis
Gen. 2:7, *74, 76*
Gen. 2:17, *xx, 34, 269*
Gen. 2:27, *78*
Gen. 3:1–7, *xix*
Gen. 3:3, *34*
Gen. 3:15, *289*
Gen. 3:19, *59, 263*
Gen. 6:1–5, *121, 234*
Gen. 9:22, *120*
Gen. 11:10–32, *120*
Gen. 12:3, *320*
Gen. 15:5, *136*
Gen. 18:15, *257*
Gen. 18:25, *113*
Gen. 19:19, *320*
Gen. 19:24, *138*
Gen. 19:28, *258*
Gen. 22, *320, 321*
Gen. 22:5, *320*
Gen. 22:7, *353*
Gen. 22:7, 8, *138,*
Gen. 25:8, *135*
Gen. 25:17, *136*

Gen. 35:29, *136*
Gen. 37:8, *332*
Gen. 37:20, 24, 27, 31, *332*
Gen. 37:24, *335, 353*
Gen. 37:35, *137, 333*
Gen. 37:36, *332*
Gen. 42:12–24, *353*
Gen. 42:17–24, *333*
Gen. 42:38, *137*
Gen. 44:29, *137*
Gen. 44:31, *137*
Gen. 49:29, *136*
Gen. 49:33, *136*

Exodus
Exo. 3:18, *343*
Exo. 4:22, 23, *262*
Exo. 5:3, *343*
Exo. 8:27, *343*
Exo. 12:2, *302*
Exo. 19:10,11, *343*
Exo. 19:14,15, *343*
Exo. 20:18–21, *258*
Exo. 24:9, 10, *159*
Exo. 30:10, *142, 327*
Exo. 24:17, 18, *258*

Leviticus
Lev. 1, *139, 322*
Lev. 6:8–13, *139, 322*
Lev. 7:17, 18, *343*
Lev. 10:1–7, *259*
Lev. 14:1–9, *143, 328*
Lev. 16:1–54, *142, 327*
Lev. 16:2, *142, 327*
Lev. 16:3, 4, *142, 327*
Lev. 16:3–7, *143, 328*
Lev. 16:8–9, *143*
Lev. 16:8, 21, *352*
Lev. 16:15–17, *145*
Lev. 16:20–22, *145*
Lev. 16:21, 22, *145, 146*
Lev. 16:22, *140, 353*
Lev. 16:29, 31, *142, 327*
Lev. 16:31, *141, 326*
Lev. 17:7, *329*
Lev. 19:6, 7, *343*
Lev. 20:27, *151*
Lev. 23:26, 27, *140, 141*, 326
Lev. 23:26–32, *142, 327*
Lev. 23:29, *142*
Lev. 25:9, *141, 327*

Numbers
Num. 16:22, *60, 69, 113*
Num. 16:30, *148, 335*
Num. 16:33, *148, 335*
Num. 21:4–9, *298*
Num. 23:21, *262*
Num. 27:16, *60, 69, 113*
Num. 29:7–11, *142, 327*

Deuteronomy
Deut. 1:19, *144, 329*

Deut. 4:24, *258*
Deut. 5:22–26, *258*
Deut. 8:15, *144, 329*
Deut. 9:3, *258*
Deut. 18:9–12, *151*
Deut. 21:22, 23, *296*
Deut. 21:23, *304*
Deut. 30:12, 13, *244*
Deut. 30:12–14, *353*
Deut. 32:22, *149, 199*
Deut. 32:50, *136*
Deut. 34:6, *136*

Joshua
Josh. 15:8, *225*
Josh. 18:6, *225*

1 Samuel
1 Sam. 2:6, *150*
1 Sam. 28:1–24, *150*
1 Sam. 28:3, *152, 194*
1 Sam. 28:3, 14–19, *90*
1 Sam. 28:12, *152*
1 Sam. 28:13, *153*
1 Sam. 28:13–19, *65*
1 Sam. 28:14, *153*
1 Sam. 28:17–20, *154*
1 Sam. 30:3, *222*
1 Sam. 30:18–20, *168*
1 Sam. 30:26–31, *222*

2 Samuel
2 Sam. 11:5, *155*
2 Sam. 12:22–23, *155*
2 Sam. 22:6, *156*

1 Kings
1 Kings 2:6, *156*
1 Kings 2:9, *156*

2 Kings
2 Kings 18:1–4, *300*
2 Kings 21:6, *225*
2 Kings 23:10, *225*

1 Chronicles
1 Chron. 10:13, *151*
1 Chron. 28:9, *77*

2 Chronicles
2 Chron. 16:9, *77*
2 Chron. 28:3, *225*

Ezra
Ezra 6:11, *296*

Nehemiah
Neh. 11:30, 225

Esther
Est. 4:16, *343*

Job
Job 1:6, *121*
Job 1:6–12, *98*
Job 1:6,7, *234*
Job 2:1, *121*
Job 4:12–17, *122*
Job 4:18,19, *49, 57, 123*
Job 7:9, *127*
Job 10:21,22, *131, 168*
Job 12:15, *120*

Job 14:13, *125, 127, 128*
Job 14:22, *123*
Job 17:13, *125, 127, 174*
Job 17:15, 16, *124, 127, 136*
Job 19:23–27, *126*
Job 21:13, *129*
Job 21:30, *129*
Job 22:15–17, *120*
Job 24:19, *129*
Job 26:5–6, *64, 126, 127, 129,*
    130, 158, 168,
188, 229, 315
Job 26:6, *245*
Job 27:3–4, *76*
Job 28:22, *64, 130*
Job 31:12, *130,131,149,168,199*
Job 32:8, *xviii, 49, 75, 101, 123*
Job 32:18, *123*
Job 33:4, *75*
Job 33:17, *168*
Job 33:18, *167, 174*
Job 33:22, *174*
Job 33:24, *174*
Job 33:28, 175
Job 33:30, *175*
Job 38:4, 7, *124*
Job 38:17, *96, 97, 124, 136, 168*
Job 42:16, *119*

Psalms
Psalm 2:7, *70*
Psalm 2:12, *70*
Psalm 6:5, *163, 214*
Psalm 9:17, *163*
Psalm 16:8–11, *67, 217*
Psalm 16:10, *139, 163, 187, 353*
Psalm 18:4–6, *316*

Psalm 18:5, *164*
Psalm 19:1–4, *108*
Psalm 22:1, 14–17, *308*
Psalm 28:1, *169*
Psalm 30:3, *164, 169, 188*
Psalm 30:9, *170*
Psalm 31:17, *164*
Psalm 40:2, *313, 314, 335*
Psalm 42:1–3, 7, *312*
Psalm 42:7, *107*
Psalm 45:1–17, *241*
Psalm 49:14, *164*
Psalm 49:15, *164, 188*
Psalm 51:6, *26, 60, 113*
Psalm 51:6, 10, *49*
Psalm 55:15, *164*
Psalm 55:23, *169*
Psalm 68:18, *168, 221, 353,*
Psalm 69:1–4, *313*
Psalm 69:2, 15, *335*
Psalm 69:14, 15, *313*
Psalm 69:15, *169*
Psalm 71:20, *164*
Psalm 82:6, *153*
Psalm 86:13, *165, 188, 314*
Psalm 88:1–5, *314*
Psalm 88:3, *165*
Psalm 88:3–4, *170*
Psalm 88:4, 6, *335*
Psalm 88:6, *107, 170*
Psalm 88:6, 7, *353*
Psalm 88:6–9, *314*
Psalm 88:9–12, *315*
Psalm 88:10, *315*
Psalm 88:10–11, *64, 130, 158,*
    229
Psalm 88:13–18, *315*

Psalm 89:14, *278*
Psalm 89:48, *165*
Psalm 103:4, *175*
Psalm 115:17, *214, 266*
Psalm 116:3, *165, 314*
Psalm 116:15, *305*
Psalm 119:18, *xviii*
Psalm 139:8, *96, 99, 128, 165*
Psalm 141:7, *165*
Psalm 143:7, *170*
Psalm 146:4, *214, 266*

Proverbs
Prov. 1:2, *170*
Prov. 1:12, *165*
Prov. 2:18, *130, 229, 315*
Prov. 5:5, *166*
Prov. 7:27, *125, 166, 168*
Prov. 9:18, *130, 158, 166, 188,*
    229, 315
Prov. 15:11, *64, 96, 98, 126,*
    130, 166, 168
Prov. 15:24, *166*
Prov. 20:27, *77, 101*
Prov. 21:16, *130, 188, 315*
Prov. 23:14, *166*
Prov.27:20, *64, 118, 130 166, 168*
Prov. 30:4, *71*
Prov. 30:15–16, *118, 167*

Ecclesiastes
Ecc. 1:2, *264*
Ecc. 1:3, *264*
Ecc. 3:7, *178*
Ecc. 3:18, 19, *264*
Ecc. 3:20, *264*
Ecc. 5:15, *265*

Ecc. 9:5, 10, *214, 265*
Ecc. 9:10, *167, 266*
Ecc. 11:9, *264*
Ecc. 12:7, *77, 123*
Ecc. 12:13, *264*
Ecc. 12:13, 14, *179, 195*

Song of Solomon
Song 8:6, *167, 199*

Isaiah
Isa. 2:10, 11, *201*
Isa. 5:14–16, *156*
Isa. 9:6, *71*
Isa. 11:6–8, *201*
Isa. 13:21, *144*
Isa. 14:9, *64, 130, 157, 158, 188, 229*
Isa. 14:9, *315*
Isa. 14:9–20, *157*
Isa. 14:9–21, *65*
Isa. 14:11, *158*
Isa. 14:12, *159*
Isa. 14:15, *158, 159, 170, 335*
Isa. 14:17, *168*
Isa. 14:19, *170*
Isa. 24:1–6, *201*
Isa. 24:21–23, *170*
Isa. 24:22, *168, 375*
Isa. 26:14, *315*
Isa. 26:14, 19, *130, 229*
Isa. 26:19, *315*
Isa. 28:15, *160*
Isa. 28:18, *160*
Isa. 30:33, *225*
Isa. 32:15–18, *201*
Isa. 33:10–14, *201*

Isa. 33:14, *177, 199, 259*
Isa. 34:8–10, *201*
Isa. 34;14, *144*
Isa. 38:10, *160*
Isa. 38:17–18, *175*
Isa. 38:18, *160, 171*
Isa. 40:3, *198*
Isa. 52:14, *303*
Isa. 53:2, 3, *303*
Isa. 53:4, *313*
Isa. 53:5, 7, *303*
Isa. 53:6, *106, 145, 330*
Isa. 53:10, 11, *352*
Isa. 57:9, *161*
Isa. 61:1, *168*
Isa. 66:15, 16, *201*
Isa. 66:24, *177*

Jeremiah
Jer. 2:6, *144, 329*
Jer. 7:31–33, *225*
Jer. 11:19, *334*
Jer. 13:17, 24, *334*
Jer. 19:1–13, *225*
Jer. 20:10, *334*
Jer. 23:35, *225*
Jer. 26:11, *334*
Jer. 26:15, *334*
Jer. 38:4, *334*
Jer. 38:6–13, *353*

Lamentations
Lam. 1:12, *334*
Lam. 3:1, *334, 353*
Lam. 3:48, *334*
Lam. 3:55, *334, 335, 353*

Ezekiel
Ezek. 2:12–15, *237*
Ezek. 8:3, *237*
Ezek. 11:1, 24, 25, *237*
Ezek. 11:17–20, *201*
Ezek. 16:49, *109*
Ezek. 18:4, *36*
Ezek. 26:20, *335*
Ezek. 28:14, *159, 171*
Ezek. 31:14–18, *335*
Ezek. 31:15, *161*
Ezek. 31:16, *161, 168, 171*
Ezek. 31:17, *161*
Ezek. 31:17, 18, *172*
Ezek. 32:17–31, *173*
Ezek. 32:18, *172*
Ezek. 32:18–30, *335*
Ezek. 32:20, *168, 171, 172*
Ezek. 32:21, *65, 161, 193*
Ezek. 32:23, *172*
Ezek. 32:24, *168, 172*
Ezek. 32:25, *172*
Ezek. 32:27, *161*
Ezek. 32:29, *172*
Ezek. 32:30, *173*
Ezek. 32:32, *174*
Ezek. 36:24–30, *201*
Ezek. 37:1, *237*
Ezek. 39:25–29, *201*
Ezek. 40:2, 3, *237*
Ezek. 43:5, *237*

Daniel
Dan. 3:25, *71*
Dan. 7:8, 9, *175*
Dan. 7:9, 10, *259*
Dan. 7:11, *175, 195*

Dan. 12:2, *39, 64, 176, 179, 249, 268, 273*

Hosea
Hos. 6:1, 2, *343*
Hos. 13;14, *162, 217*

Joel
Joel 2:28, 29, *201*
Joel 2:30, 31, *201*

Amos
Amos 9:2, *96, 99, 129, 162*

Jonah
Jonah 1:17, *307*
Jonah 2:2, *139, 162, 353*
Jonah 2:2–6, *307*
Jonah 2:4, *316*
Jonah 2:6, *168, 175, 335*

Zephaniah
Zeph. 1:14–18, *201*

Habakkuk
Hab. 2:5, *162*

Zechariah
Zech. 12:1, *22, 73, 76, 123*

Malachi
Mal. 3:1, 2, 5, *200*
Mal. 4:1, *200*

GREEK SCRIPTURES

Matthew

Matt. 1:18, *71*
Matt. 1:20, *71*
Matt. 1:23, *71*
Matt. 3:3, *198*
Matt. 3:7, *198*
Matt. 3:11, *199*
Matt. 3:12, *199*
Matt. 5:22, *226*
Matt. 5:29, 30, *226*
Matt. 7:19, *199*
Matt. 8:10–12, *202*
Matt. 8:12, *269*
Matt. 8:28–32, *46*
Matt. 8:29, *230*
Matt. 8:31, *51*
Matt. 9:36, *334*
Matt. 10:15, *230*
Matt. 10:14, 15, *275*
Matt. 10:28, *38, 63, 123, 228, 306*
Matt. 11:21–22, *276*
Matt. 11:22, 24, *230*
Matt. 11:23, *202*
Matt. 11:23, 24, *275*
Matt. 11:28–30, *352*
Matt. 12:40, *100, 139, 203, 244,*
    308, 353
Matt. 12:41, 42, *230*
Matt. 12:43, *144, 324*
Matt. 12:45, *46*
Matt. 13:30, *203*
Matt. 13:40–42, *203, 269*
Matt. 13:48–50, *204, 269*
Matt. 16:4, *353*
Matt. 16:13, 14, *334*

Matt. 16:18, *206*
Matt. 16:21–23, *304*
Matt. 16:22, 23, *247*
Matt. 17:3, *90*
Matt. 18:8, *65*
Matt. 18:8, 9, *228*
Matt. 18:20, *286, 344*
Matt. 20:17–19, 22, *318*
Matt. 20:22, *316*
Matt. 20:22, 23, *318*
Matt. 22:1–14, *241,*
Matt. 22:13, *204, 269*
Matt. 22:29–32, *91*
Matt. 22:32, *90*
Matt. 23:15, 33, *229*
Matt. 23:33, *304*
Matt. 24:51, *204*
Matt. 24:51, 52, *269*
Matt. 25:1–13, *241*
Matt. 25:30, *205*
Matt. 25:31, *170*
Matt. 25:32, 46, *171*
Matt. 25:41, *146, 148, 243*
Matt. 25:41, 46, *205, 352*
Matt. 25:46, *269, 270*
Matt. 26:28, *338*
Matt. 26:63–65, *92*
Matt. 26:65, 66, *334*
Matt. 26:67, *303*
Matt. 27:25, *334*
Matt. 27:26–31, *303*
Matt. 27:34, *313*
Matt. 27:43, *312*
Matt. 27:46, *107, 305*
Matt. 27:48, *313*
Matt. 27:50, *291*
Matt. 27:51, *345*

Matt. 27:52, *345*
Matt. 27:60, *314*

Mark
Mark 1:23–26, *46*
Mark 6:11, *230*
Mark 8:36, 37, *219*
Mark 9:4, *90*
Mark 9:43–48, *227*
Mark 9:44, 46, 48, *159*
Mark 10:38, 39, *318*
Mark 12:26, 27, *90*
Mark 14:27, *334*
Mark 14:61–63, *92*
Mark 14:62, *93*
Mark 15:23, 36, *313*
Mark 15:43–45, *291*
Mark 16:16, *219*

Luke
Luke 2:7, *351*
Luke 3:7, *198*
Luke 3:9, *199*
Luke 3:16, *199*
Luke 3:17, *199*
Luke 3:31, 34, 38, *71*
Luke 4:23, *351*
Luke 7:29, *108*
Luke 7:36–50, *127*
Luke 7:50, *352*
Luke 8:26–30, *46*
Luke 8:27, *144, 329*
Luke 8:31, *243*
Luke 9:6, *34*
Luke 9:23, 24, *39*
Luke 9:29–31, *90*
Luke 10:15, *202*

Luke 10:18, *159*
Luke 10:38, *316*
Luke 11:14, *45*
Luke 11:16–20, *46*
Luke 11:17–20, *57*
Luke 11:24, *144, 329*
Luke 11:24–26, *46, 57, 123*
Luke 11:30, *353*
Luke 11:37–40, *48, 57, 59, 123*
Luke 11:40, *26, 73*
Luke 11:54, *334*
Luke 12:4, 5,
Luke 12:42–48, *276*
Luke 12:50, *316, 318*
Luke 13:5, *204*
Luke 13:27, 28, *204*
Luke 14:15–24, *241*
Luke 15:3–7, *207*
Luke 15:8–10, *207*
Luke 15:11–32, *207*
Luke 15:20, *39*
Luke 15:24, 32, *34*
Luke 16:1–9, *207*
Luke 16:19, *208*
Luke 16:19–31, *207*
Luke 16:20, 21, *208*
Luke 16:22, *209*
Luke 16:22, 23, *136, 146*
Luke 16:23, 24, *210, 199*
Luke 16:24, *210*
Luke 16:25, 26, *211*
Luke 16:27–29, *211*
Luke 16:30, 31, *211*
Luke 18:3–8, *290*
Luke 19:41, *334*
Luke 20:34–38, *91*
Luke 20:37, *90*

Luke 20:45–47, *277*
Luke 22:3, *389*
Luke 22:44, *302*
Luke 22:53, *289*
Luke 22:63–65, *303*
Luke 23:11, *303*
Luke 23:36, *313*
Luke 23:43, *146, 285, 344*
Luke 23:46, *146, 346*

John
John 1:1, *70*
John 1:1, 4, *28*
John 1:3, *74*
John 1:9, *74, 101, 107, 108*
John 1:12, 13, *81*
John 1:14, *72*
John 1:29, *106, 107, 147,*
    263
John 2:17, *313*
John 3:3, 6, 8, *79*
John 3:14, 15, *290, 298*
John 3:16, *28, 218*
John 3:16–17, *107*
John 3:17, *71*
John 3:19, *108*
John 3:36, *28, 37*
John 4:14, *28*
John 4:23, *347*
John 4:24, *80*
John 5:24, *28, 30, 32, 38, 107,*
    231, 304
John 5:28, 29, *64, 250*
John 6:42, *71*
John 6:47, *28*
John 7:5, *313*
John 8:14, *72*

John 8:23, *72, 218*
John 8:24, *37*
John 8:42, *72*
John 8:58, *70*
John 9:34, *36*
John 10:12–15, *230*
John 10:18, *291*
John 10:27, 28, *29*
John 10:28, *219*
John 10:34, 35, *153*
John 11:25, 26, *29, 33*
John 11:28–44, *212*
John 11:46–53, *212*
John 12:27, *294, 347*
John 12:27, 32, *302*
John 12:31, *247*
John 12:32, *287, 346*
John 13:3, *72*
John 13:27, *289*
John 13:32, *343*
John 14:18, *285*
John 14:20, *285*
John 14:20–23, *344*
John 14:21, *285*
John 14:23, *285*
John 14:30, *289*
John 16:28, *72*
John 16:32, *347*
John 17:5, *70*
John 17:11, *347*
John 19:28, *347*
John 19:29, *313*
John 19:30, *349*
John 19:33, *291*
John 20:22, *74*

Acts
Acts 1:2, *75*
Acts 2:23, 24, *317, 353*
Acts 2:24, *306, 337, 349*
Acts 2:25–27, *66, 146*
Acts 2:27, *163, 187, 217, 294, 306*
Acts 2:27, 31, *284*
Acts 2:31, *66, 139, 146, 187, 217,*
 244, 353
Acts 2:31, 32, *353*
Acts 5:1–11, *39*
Acts 5:30, *297*
Acts 10:39, *297*
Acts 13:29, *297*
Acts 14:15–17, *100*
Acts 17:3, *317*
Acts 17:11, *282*
Acts 17:23–31, *100*
Acts 17:30, 31, *354*
Acts 17:31, *220, 231*
Acts 20:28, *338*
Acts 23:8, *61*
Acts 24:15, *64, 250*
Acts 26:18, *284*

Romans
Rom. 1:16, *108*
Rom. 1:19–22, *108*
Rom. 1:21, 22, *109*
Rom. 1:32, *37, 101*
Rom. 2:2, 3, *231*
Rom. 2:5, 6, *277*
Rom. 2:5–8, *220*
Rom. 2:6, 8, *231*
Rom. 2:14, *101*
Rom. 2:14, 15, *108*
Rom. 2:16, *xvii*

Rom. 3:4, *108, 204*
Rom. 3:5, *206*
Rom. 3:19, *36*
Rom. 3:23, *36*
Rom. 3:25, *313*
Rom. 3:26, *107*
Rom. 5:9, *338*
Rom. 5:10, *342*
Rom. 5:12, 15, 17, 21, *35, 36*
Rom. 6:3, *316*
Rom. 6:3, 4, *319*
Rom. 6:3–8, *38*
Rom. 6:4, *81*
Rom. 6:4–13, *342*
Rom. 6:6, *299, 341*
Rom. 6:11, *38, 81*
Rom. 6:11–12, *38*
Rom. 6:16, *36, 39*
Rom. 6:21, *36*
Rom. 6:23, *36*
Rom. 7:2, *59*
Rom. 7:5, *36*
Rom. 7:9, *38*
Rom. 7:9–13, *36*
Rom. 7:17, 18, 20, *299*
Rom. 7:22, *49*
Rom. 8:3, *72, 299*
Rom. 8:6, *39*
Rom. 8:13, *38*
Rom. 8:30, *88*
Rom. 10:6, 7, *139, 353*
Rom. 10:7, *244*
Rom. 10:18, *108*
Rom. 13:1–7, *101*
Rom. 15:3, *313*

1 Corinthians

1 Cor. 1:17, 18, *341*
1 Cor. 1:23, *288*
1 Cor. 2:2, *288*
1 Cor. 2:6–8, *45*
1 Cor. 2:10, 11, 12, *77, 123*
1 Cor. 2:12–14, *78*
1 Cor. 2:13, *267*
1 Cor. 3:10–15, *278*
1 Cor. 4:3, *237*
1 Cor. 4:9, *39*
1 Cor. 5:4, 5, *61*
1 Cor. 5:5, *39*
1 Cor. 5:9–13, *39*
1 Cor. 6:19, *49, 57*
1 Cor. 6:19–20, *62*
1 Cor. 7:34, *62*
1 Cor. 11:30–32, *39*
1 Cor. 15:1–4, *288*
1 Cor. 15:2–4, 14, *288*
1 Cor. 15:3, 4, *342*
1 Cor. 15:6, 18, *39*
1 Cor. 15:17, *288, 337, 341*
1 Cor. 15:22, *36*
1 Cor. 15:29–31, *39*
1 Cor. 15:45–47, *36*
1 Cor. 15:47, *72*
1 Cor. 15:50–54, *30*
1 Cor. 15:54, *31*
1 Cor. 15:55, *217*
1 Cor. 15:55–56, *299*
1 Cor. 15:56, *289*

2 Corinthians

2 Cor. 1:5, *39*
2 Cor. 2:15, 16, *40*
2 Cor. 4:4, *289*

2 Cor. 4:8–12, *39*
2 Cor. 4:16, *26, 50, 51, 55, 59, 87*
2 Cor. 4:18, *45, 341*
2 Cor. 5:1, 2, *49*
2 Cor. 5:1–8, *39, 123*
2 Cor. 5:1–9, *52, 55, 57, 124*
2 Cor. 5:14, *35, 36*
2 Cor. 5:14–21, *106*
2 Cor. 5:15, *37*
2 Cor. 5:17, *50, 79*
2 Cor. 5:17, 18, *82*
2 Cor. 5:21, *37, 295, 298, 305, 324*
2 Cor. 7:1, *63*
2 Cor. 11:4, *208, 257*
2 Cor. 12:1–4, *237*
2 Cor. 12:2–5, *55, 57, 124*

Galatians

Gal. 1:4, *291*
Gal. 1:6–7, *xx*
Gal. 2:19, *38*
Gal. 2:20, *83*
Gal. 3:1, *288*
Gal. 3:13, *107, 296, 297, 304, 342*
Gal. 5:24, *38*
Gal. 6:7, *109*
Gal. 6:14, *342*
Gal. 6:15, *82*
Gal. 6:17, *39*
Gal. 6:18, *63*

Ephesians

Eph. 1:7, *338*
Eph. 1:22, 23, *206*
Eph. 2:1, *81*
Eph. 2:1, 5, *35*
Eph. 2:6, *286*

Eph. 2:8, 9, *84*
Eph. 2:10, *84*
Eph. 2:13, *338*
Eph. 2:16, *342*
Eph. 3:16, *87*
Eph. 7–10, *65, 139*
Eph. 4:8, *168*
Eph. 4:8–10, *353*
Eph. 4:8–11, *221*
Eph. 4:9, *169*
Eph. 4:9, 10, *244*
Eph. 4:13, 14, *88*
Eph. 4:19, *37*
Eph. 4:22–24, *84*
Eph. 4:24, *50, 85*
Eph. 5:8–14, *39*
Eph. 6:12, *45*

Philippians
Phil. 1:21–25, *54, 55, 124*
Phil. 2:6, *70*
Phil. 2:8, *37, 342*
Phil. 2:9, 10, *222*
Phil. 2:17, *39*
Phil. 3:10, 11, *39*

Colossians
Col. 1:14, *339*
Col. 1:16, *74*
Col. 1:20, 339
Col. 1:24, *39*
Col. 1:27, *88*
Col. 2:9, *72*
Col. 2:10–12, *319*
Col. 2:12, *343*
Col. 2:13, *35*
Col. 2:14, *342*

Col. 3:1–11, *38*
Col. 3:5, *38*
Col. 3:9, 10, *82*

1 Thessalonians
1 Thess. 1:10, *221*
1 Thess. 4:14, *39*
1 Thess. 5:9, *221*
1 Thess. 5:21, *101, 282*
1 Thess. 5:23, *67*

2 Thessalonians
2 Thess. 1:7, 8, *259*
2 Thess. 1:7–9, *221*
2 Thess. 2:10, *108*
2 Thess. 3:6, *39*

1 Timothy
1 Tim. 2:4–6, *37*
1 Tim. 3:16, *72*
1 Tim. 4:1, *245*
1 Tim. 4:2, *37*
1 Tim. 4:7–8, *87*
1 Tim. 5:6, *33*
1 Tim. 6:9, *222*
1 Tim. 6:15, 16, *27*
1 Tim. 6:16, *31*

2 Timothy
2 Tim. 1:10, *27, 299*
2 Tim. 3:1, 2, 5, *261*
2 Tim. 3:16, *78*
2 Tim. 4:3, *261*

Hebrews
Heb. 1:6, *72*
Heb. 1:14, *209, 216*

Heb. 2:9, *xxii*
Heb. 2:9, 14, *37*
Heb. 2:14, *72, 289*
Heb. 3:17, *262*
Heb. 4:12, *68*
Heb. 6:1, 2, *xvii, 222*
Heb. 6:2, *235, 267*
Heb. 6:2, 8, *231*
Heb. 6:4, *37*
Heb. 7:26, *299*
Heb. 9:6–12, *142, 327*
Heb. 9:12, *339*
Heb. 9:14, *339*
Heb. 9:22, *339*
Heb. 9:24, *345*
Heb. 9:24–28, *142, 327*
Heb. 9:26, *107, 142, 327, 342*
Heb. 9:27, *41*
Heb. 9:29, *231*
Heb. 10:5–7, *312*
Heb. 10:10, *342*
Heb. 10:26–29, *260*
Heb. 10:26–31, *37*
Heb. 10:27, 29, *231*
Heb. 10:39, *231*
Heb. 11:17–19, *320*
Heb. 12:2, *342*
Heb. 12:5–11, *262*
Heb. 12:22–23, *69*
Heb. 12:25, 26, *258*
Heb. 12:29, *256*

James
James 2:26, *34, 124*
James 5:20, *39*

1 Peter
1 Peter 1:11, *309*
1 Peter 1:18, 19, *339*
1 Peter 1:23, *85, 86*
1 Peter 2:2, 3, *83*
1 Peter 2:24, *297, 342*
1 Peter 3:18–20, *219, 220*
1 Peter 3:18–22, *286*
1 Peter 3:19, *168*
1 Peter 3:19, 20, *121, 129*
1 Peter 4:1, *39*

2 Peter
2 Peter 1:4, *85, 153*
2 Peter 1:14, *39*
2 Peter 1:13, 14, *49, 56, 57, 123, 124*
2 Peter 1:21, *309*
2 Peter 2:1–4, *234*
2 Peter 2:4, *121, 232, 234*
2 Peter 2:5, *220*
2 Peter 2:6, *233*
2 Peter 2:9, *232*
2 Peter 2:17, *124, 232, 274*
2 Peter 3:5–7, *257*
2 Peter 3:7, *232*
2 Peter 3:9, *108*

1 John
1 John 1:7, *339*
1 John 2:2, *37, 106*
1 John 3:9, *85*
1 John 3:14, *29, 38*
1 John 4:8, *256*
1 John 4:9, *72*
1 John 5:11–13, *29*
1 John 5:12, *34*

1 John 5:16, 17, *39*

Jude
Jude 6, *121, 232*
Jude 7, *65, 232*
Jude 12, *35, 37*
Jude 13, *233, 274*
Jude 23, *233*

Revelation
Rev. 1:5, *339*
Rev. 1:9, *236*
Rev. 1:10, *56, 236*
Rev. 1:18, *217*
Rev. 2:11, *250*
Rev. 4:8–9, *66*
Rev. 5:4, *237*
Rev. 5:9, *339*
Rev. 5:13, *238*
Rev. 6:8, *218*
Rev. 6:9–11, *238*
Rev. 7:1–8, *239*
Rev. 7:9–17, *239*
Rev. 7:14, *339*
Rev. 9:1, 2, 11, *242*
Rev. 9:1–12, *130, 229*
Rev. 9:11, *168, 229, 245*
Rev. 10:9, 10, *237*
Rev. 11:1, *237*
Rev. 11:7, *242, 245*
Rev. 12:7–9, *98*
Rev. 12:7–12, *159*
Rev. 12:9, *298*
Rev. 13:1, *237*
Rev. 13:7, *245*
Rev. 14:9–11, *246*
Rev. 14:11, *274*

Rev. 14:13, *237, 239*
Rev. 15:2–4, *240*
Rev. 17:3, *237*
Rev. 17:6, 7, *237*
Rev. 17:8, *242, 145*
Rev. 18:2, *144, 329*
Rev. 19:3, *274*
Rev. 19:7–9, *240*
Rev. 19:10, *237*
Rev. 19:20, *175, 195, 245, 247, 248*
Rev. 20:1, *93*
Rev. 20:1–3, *159, 170, 242*
Rev. 20:1–10, *218*
Rev. 20:4, *241*
Rev. 20:4–6, *250*
Rev. 20:5, *37*
Rev. 20:6, *251*
Rev. 20:6, 10, *38*
Rev. 20:7, *242*
Rev. 20:10, *65, 200, 215, 233, 247, 268, 274*
Rev. 20:11, *37*
Rev. 20:11–15, *38, 112, 179, 195, 247*
Rev. 20:12, 13, *277*
Rev. 20:13, *37*
Rev. 20:13, 14, *64, 93*
Rev. 20:13, 14, 15, *218, 224, 247, 248*
Rev. 20:14, *251*
Rev. 20:14, 15, *200, 233*
Rev. 20:20, *64*
Rev. 21:8, *38, 247, 249*
Rev. 22:11, 15, *249*

CPSIA information can be obtained
at www.ICGtesting.com
Printed in the USA
FSOW02n1731230616
21935FS

9 781628 712216